Palgrave Studies in Creativity and Culture

Both creativity and culture are areas that have experienced a rapid growth in interest in recent years. Moreover, there is a growing interest today in understanding creativity as a socio-cultural phenomenon and culture as a transformative, dynamic process. Creativity has traditionally been considered an exceptional quality that only a few people (truly) possess, a cognitive or personality trait 'residing' inside the mind of the creative individual. Conversely, culture has often been seen as 'outside' the person and described as a set of 'things' such as norms, beliefs, values, objects, and so on. The current literature shows a trend towards a different understanding, which recognises the psycho-socio-cultural nature of creative expression and the creative quality of appropriating and participating in culture. Our new, interdisciplinary series Palgrave Studies in Creativity and Culture intends to advance our knowledge of both creativity and cultural studies from the forefront of theory and research within the emerging cultural psychology of creativity, and the intersection between psychology, anthropology, sociology, education, business, and cultural studies. Palgrave Studies in Creativity and Culture is accepting proposals for monographs, Palgrave Pivots and edited collections that bring together creativity and culture. The series has a broader focus than simply the cultural approach to creativity, and is unified by a basic set of premises about creativity and cultural phenomena.

More information about this series at
http://www.palgrave.com/gp/series/14640

Bruce Kirkcaldy
Editor

Psychotherapy, Literature and the Visual and Performing Arts

palgrave
macmillan

Editor
Bruce Kirkcaldy
International Centre for the Study
of Occupational and Mental Health
Düsseldorf, Germany

Palgrave Studies in Creativity and Culture
ISBN 978-3-030-09226-9 ISBN 978-3-319-75423-9 (eBook)
https://doi.org/10.1007/978-3-319-75423-9

Cover credit: Tom Van Heel @ Sapphire&Steel/gettyimages

Printed on acid-free paper

This Palgrave Macmillan imprint is published by the registered company Springer International Publishing AG part of Springer Nature.
The registered company address is: Gewerbestrasse 11, 6330 Cham, Switzerland

Contents

Notes on Contributors

Alexander-Stamatios Antoniou is a lecturer in psychology at the University of Athens, Greece. He holds a PhD in Occupational Health from UMIST and a PhD in Organisational Psychology and Behaviour from the University of Manchester. His publications include research papers and chapters in refereed academic journals, books and edited volumes. His main research interests include occupational stress, work values and attitudes, transformational and charismatic leadership, and individual power and organisational politics and communication networks in organisations. He teaches occupational health and organisational behaviour in undergraduate and postgraduate programmes and delivers seminars to staff in public and private organisations on relevant issues. He has served as a human resource consultant in a number of HRM projects. He is the coordinator of the Division of Organisational Psychology of the Hellenic Psychological Association.

Anthony R. Beech is Chair of Criminological Psychology and a fellow of the British Psychological Society. He is currently the Director of the Centre for Forensic and Criminological Psychology at the University of Birmingham. Anthony has published over 125 peer reviewed articles and over 30 book chapters, and has written/edited four books mainly in the area of sexual offending. Moreover, he recently received the Senior Award for a significant lifetime contribution to Forensic Psychology in the UK from the Division of Forensic Psychology, BPS. He also received the significant achievement award from the Association for the Treatment of Sexual Abusers (ATSA) in Dallas, Texas, October 2009.

Dinesh Bhugra is Professor of Mental Health and Cultural Diversity at the Institute of Psychiatry, King's College London. He is also an Honorary Consultant at the Maudsley Hospital, where he runs the sexual and couple therapy clinic. Professor Bhugra's research interests are in cultural psychiatry, sexual dysfunction and service development. He has authored/co-authored over 300 scientific papers and chapters and 20 books. His recent volumes include *Principles of Social Psychiatry*, *Textbook of Cultural Psychiatry* (awarded a recommendation in the BMA Book Awards in 2008), and *Culture and Mental Health and Management for Psychiatrists*. His most recent monograph, *Mad Tales from Bollywood: Portrayal of Madness in Conventional Hindi Cinema*, was published in 2006. He is the Editor of the *International Journal of Social Psychiatry*, *International Review of Psychiatry*, and *International Journal of Culture and Mental Health*. Professor Bhugra has been instrumental in developing various training packages for health service professionals and developing strategies for psychiatric education. In conjunction with this, in 2007 the Royal College of Psychiatrists published *Workplace-Based Assessments in Psychiatry*, of which he was one of the editors. He has developed teaching modules and short courses for medical students and psychiatric trainees on Cultural Psychiatry and on Cinema and Psychiatry. In 2008 he was elected President of the Royal College of Psychiatrists.

Laurence Burrow is Nurse Team Leader in a psychogeriatric care setting. He studied Art Psychotherapy at Goldsmiths College, London, Related Arts at West Sussex Institute of Higher Education, Psychiatric Nursing at Chichester & Greylingwell School of Nursing, and Art at Eastbourne College of Art and Design. As Monty Oxymoron (http://www.montyoxymoron.com/), he has had an active professional musician's life, working with Punk Floyd and the Dr. Spacetoad Experience. Most notably, Laurence joined venerable garage-punk-psychedelic goth band The Damned in early 1996 and continues to tour and record with them. Monty also works as keyboardist and percussionist with the Sumerian Kyngs, and with a number of improvisational groups. He is also interested in art, history, philosophy, spirituality, and, as all know, is an all-round good egg.

Marina Dalla has a doctorate in social psychology from the Psychology Department, Faculty of Philosophy, Education and Psychology at the University of Athens. She graduated with honours. She has published widely in scientific journals and in book series both in English and Greek. Her current research interests centre on acculturation and adaptation of immigrants, resilience and vulnerability of immigrant children and adolescents, social stigma and mental health of immigrants, and immigration and drug abuse. Marina is a member of the International Association of Cross Cultural Psychology of the Hellenic Psychology Society and the Greek Society for Social Psychology.

Vincent Egan obtained a B.Sc. (Honours) in psychology from Goldsmith's College (University of London) in 1984, a Ph.D. in Psychology from the University of Edinburgh in 1991, and a Doctorate in Clinical Psychology from the University of Leicester in 1996, when he became a Chartered Clinical Psychologist. In 2000 he was made a Chartered Forensic Psychologist. Between 1987 and 1993 he was a research associate with the Department of Psychiatry at the University of Edinburgh. He has over 110 academic publications (on topics including mental speed, brain evoked potentials, personality, intelligence, HIV and AIDS, shoplifting, sex offending, violence, and many other subjects). He is an associate fellow of the British Psychological Society and a director of the International Society for the Study of Individual Differences. The Central Nottinghamshire Health Service NHS Trust at the East Midlands Centre for Forensic Mental Health previously employed him as a clinical psychologist. He remains fully licensed as a clinical and forensic psychologist through the Health and Care Professions Council. He has written over 360 court reports. He was Professor and course director of the MSc Forensic Psychology at Glasgow Caledonian University for 6 years. In September 2007 he became Director of the MSc in the Assessment and Treatment of Sexual Offenders, and then the full Forensic Psychology MSc at the University of Leicester. He is now Associate Professor in Forensic Psychology Practice at the University of Nottingham and Programme Director for the Forensic Psychology doctorate at that institution. He continues to work with offenders through his work with independent solicitors.

Sayyed Mohsen Fatemi (University of British Columbia, 2003, Post Doctorate, Harvard University, 2009–2013) is a psychologist and a fellow in the department of psychology at Harvard University and works on mindfulness and its psychological implications for cross cultural, clinical and social psychology. He is a frequently published author and has been the keynote speaker at numerous international conferences. He brings mindfulness in his psychological and therapeutic interventions and has run training and coaching programs for clinicians, practitioners and corporate people in North America, Europe and overseas. His works have been published by Springer, Wiley, Cambridge University Press and Oxford University Press and in journals such as APA's *Journal of Theoretical and*

Philosophical Psychology. In addition to teaching at Harvard, he has also taught in the psychology departments at the University of British Columbia, Western Washington University, the University of Massachusetts in Boston and the University of Toronto. He is working on the clinical implications of mindfulness for anxiety and stress management.

He has consulted and coached corporate managers and executives on the application of mindfulness in enhancing a broad array of vital business skills. His work includes the development of mindful intercultural understanding, negotiation, communication, conflict resolution, influencing, team building, presentation skills, creative decision-making and crisis management. His areas of research focus on the psychological implications of mindfulness for negotiations, media, cultural understanding and communication, creativity and leadership, persuasive and influencing skills, and clinical and counseling psychology. His latest books will soon be published by Routledge, Lexington, and Palgrave Macmillan.

Adrian Furnham was educated at the London School of Economics where he obtained a distinction in an MSc Econ., and at Oxford University where he completed a doctorate (D.Phil) in 1981. He has subsequently earned a D.Sc (1991) and D.Litt (1995). Previously a lecturer in psychology at Pembroke College, Oxford, he is now Professor of Psychology at University College London. Adrian has lectured widely abroad and held scholarships and visiting professorships at, amongst others, the University of New South Wales, the University of the West Indies and the University of Hong Kong. He has written over 1250 scientific papers and 85 books. He is on the editorial board of a number of international journals, as well as being past elected president of the *International Society for the Study of Individual Differences*. Adrian writes regularly for the *Sunday Times* and the *Daily Telegraph* and is a regular contributor to BBC radio and television.

Ahmed Hankir is Associate Professor of Psychiatry with the Carrick Institute for Graduate Studies (USA) and Research Fellow with the Bedfordshire Centre for Mental Health Research in association with Cambridge University (UK). He left his family in war-torn Lebanon when he was 17 years old and subsequently worked as a janitor in Leeds, England. He continued to work full-time hours to sustain himself throughout college and medical school. Whilst in medical school he experienced an episode of mental distress during the 2006 Lebanon War and this had a profound effect on his values. Ahmed consequently developed an interest in broadening participation into medical school for people from lower socioeconomic backgrounds, the mental health of healthcare professionals and students, Muslim mental health, the policy and provision of mental health services in conflict zones, the power of art and faith in curing mental health conditions and mental health stigma. He has published extensively in these areas, co-authoring book chapters with the President of the World Psychiatry Association Professor Dinesh Bhugra. Together with scholars from Cambridge University, Ahmed conceived the anti-stigma, contact-based Wounded Healer programme, which has been described as an innovative method of pedagogy that blends art with science. He has delivered the Wounded Healer to over 50,000 people in 9 countries across 5 continents worldwide, and has given Keynote Lectures alongside Nobel Prize Laureates in international conferences. Ahmed is the recipient of the 2013 Royal College of Psychiatrists Foundation Doctor of the Year Award, which marks the highest level of achievement in psychiatry in the UK. He was also a finalist for the 2015 Royal College of Psychiatrists Communicator of the Year Award.

Gurvinder Kalra is currently working as a psychiatrist at the High Dependency Unit of the Adult Inpatient Unit at La Trobe Regional Hospital in Victoria, Australia. He completed his specialist training in psychiatry in India, where his area of work was focused on culture, migration, and sexualities including alternate sexualities and transgenderism. He has also worked extensively in the area of psychiatry education with innovative methods such as Psychiatry Movie Clubs. His further interests include cross cultural aspects of sexualities, evolving sexualities, paraphilias, and acute psychiatry.

Bruce Kirkcaldy has academic degrees in psychology from the Universities of Dundee and Giessen, as well as postgraduate professional training as a behavioural therapist and clinical psychologist. He is Director of the International Centre for the Study of Occupational and Mental Health, and runs his own psychotherapy practice specializing in the treatment of anxiety, compulsive and depressive disorders. Since 1995, he has been Visiting Lecturer at the University of Jena, Germany, and was Affiliate Professor at the EuroCentre for Educational Resilience and Socio-Emotional Health, University of Malta. In addition, he has been Visiting Professor of Psychology at Jagiellonian University, Cracow, Poland and is a fellow of the British Psychological Society. He has published over 220 articles including 30 book chapters and 11 authored/edited books, more recently *Psychotherapy in Parenthood and Beyond: Personal Enrichment in Our Lives* (Minerva Medical Publ., Torino); *Promoting Psychological Wellbeing in Children* *and Families* (Palgrave Macmillan, London and New York), *Chimes of Time: Wounded Health Professionals. Essays on Recovery* (Sidestone, Leiden, Netherlands) and *The Art and Science of Health Care: Psychology and Human Factors for Practitioners* (Hogrefe, Boston, Göttingen, Toronto). His research and writing interests are directed towards clinical and health issues and organizational and leisure psychology. He is/was on the Editorial Board of 6 international journals in the area of organisational and health care, and has served as reviewer for some 30 peer-reviewed scientific journals.

Christine Korol is an adjunct professor in the Department of Psychology at UBC and a psychologist at BC Children's Hospital. She is currently creating therapeutic courses for an online therapy platform that will be used by therapists throughout Vancouver. She is also a cartoonist and columnist for *TILT Magazine*, a publication focused on integrating technology into therapy practice, and is host of a series of online self-help podcasts on wiredtoworry.com. She holds a PhD in Clinical Psychology from the University of Ottawa, and was a postdoctoral fellow in the Department of Psychology, University of British Columbia. Dr. Korol is particularly interested in mindfulness, cognitive therapy, contemplative art, and, most recently, the development and evaluation of online psychoeducational content emphasizing knowledge translation and good user experience design. In her spare time, Dr. Korol draws cartoons, creates online content and trains other therapists.

Ellen Langer Harvard Professor of Psychology, artist, and recipient of a Guggenheim Fellowship, three Distinguished Scientist Awards, the APA Staats award for unifying psychology, among a host of other awards, has authored 11 books and over 200 research articles on topics such as perceived control, ageing, learning, and decision-making. Each of these is examined through the lens of her theory of mindfulness. Her research has demonstrated that by actively noticing new things – the essence of mindfulness – health, well-being, and competence will follow. Her best-selling books include *Mindfulness*; *The Power of Mindful Learning*; *On Becoming an Artist: Reinventing Yourself Through Mindful Creativity*; and her most recent book, *Counterclockwise: Mindful Health and the Power of Possibility*. Her recently published book, the *Wiley Mindfulness Handbook*, is an anthology on mindfulness in which leading researchers integrate work derived from her western scientific theoretical base of mindfulness with research on eastern derived forms of meditation. Ellen has been described as the "mother of mindfulness" and has written extensively on the illusion of control, mindful aging, stress, decision-making, and health.

Shauna Shapiro is a professor at Santa Clara University, a clinical psychologist, and an internationally recognized expert in mindfulness. Dr. Shapiro is the recipient of the American Council of Learned Societies teaching award, acknowledging her outstanding contributions to education, and is a fellow of the Mind and Life Institute co-founded by the Dalai Lama. Dr. Shapiro lectures and leads mindfulness programs internationally and has been invited to present for the King of Thailand, the Danish Government, and the World Council for Psychotherapy, Beijing, China. Dr. Shapiro serves on the Advisory Board of Axialent, a leader in Conscious Business, and has brought mindfulness to pioneering companies including Genentech, Cisco Systems, and Google. She has published over 150 articles and book chapters and is co-author of the critically acclaimed texts *The Art and Science of Mindfulness* and *Mindful Discipline: A loving approach to raising an emotionally intelligent child.* Dr. Shapiro's work has been featured in *Wired* magazine, *USA Today*, the *Huffington Post*, *Yoga Journal*, and *American Psychologist.*

Kimberley Sogge is a Canadian registered clinical health psychologist who has worked in academia (Texas A&M College of Medicine, Trent University), hospital leadership (Alberta Children's Hospital, Peterborough Regional Health Center, Royal Ottawa Hospital) and at Sogge & Associates Practice in Psychology in Ottawa, Canada. Kimberly and her colleagues focus on third wave, mindfulness, and compassion-based interventions for mind/ body health and performance challenges. Kimberly has researched and published work on simulation in medical education, physician patient communication and the therapeutic working alliance, mindful medical practice, and compassion and burnout in mental health professionals. She has been practicing insight meditation for 12 years since meeting Jon Kabat Zinn and completing professional mindfulness training during her doctoral residency at the University of Texas at Austin. More recently, she has been engaged in explorations of mindfulness in nature and has received accreditation to teach Awake in the Wild under the guidance of her teacher Mark Coleman (Spirit Rock senior teacher and author).

Kimberly spends her time engaging in psychotherapy, teaching and practicing mindfulness, and rowing or trail running in the beautiful Outaouais region of Canada's capital. She became interested in the conditions that influence the development of the mind as a child, observing the lives of the animals who were part of her family's farming life in rural Saskatchewan.

Sarah de Sousa holds a first degree in modern thought and literature from Stanford University and an MA in counseling psychology from Santa Clara University. She has contributed to a number of publications addressing the relationship between mindfulness and psychological well-being, including the *Oxford Handbook of Positive Psychology* (3rd. Ed.). Sarah works as an educational consultant for adolescents in Cupertino, Ca, where she is also the founder and lead instructor for LifePrep, a course designed to help teens cultivate emotional intelligence. Sarah and her husband, Miguel de Sousa, are competitive dancers, travelling nationally and internationally to teach and perform. Together, they teach workshops on mindfulness in dance to help dancers and non-dancers cultivate greater presence in their bodies. Beyond academia and dance, Sarah's true love is poetry and her work has most recently appeared in the journals *2RiverView*, *Written River*, and *MothersAlwaysWrite*.

Antonio Ventriglio currently works at the Institute of Clinical and Experimental Medicine University of Foggia, Foggia, Italy. Until August 2011, he worked as a psychiatrist and psychotherapist at ASL Provinciale di Foggia, Dipartimento di Salute Mentale, Centro di Salute Mentale di Cerignola, sede di Orta Nova (FG) and thereafter as a psychiatrist and psychotherapist at ASL Provinciale di Foggia, Servizio Psichiatrico di Diagnosi e Cura di Foggia. In Autumn last year he took on the dual role of psychiatrist and psychotherapist at ASUR, Regione Marche, Area Vasta 2, Centro di Salute Mentale di Jesi. He was awarded a research fellowship at Harvard University, Massachusetts (USA) – McLean Hospital, Harvard Medical School- Schizophrenia and Bipolar Disorder Clinic-Belmont, MA (USA). Antonio is a member of the executive committee of Società Italiana di Psichiatria Sociale (SIPS), Triennium 2015–2017 Member of the Ethics and Review committee of World Psychiatric Association (WPA), Editorial Board (Letters to Editor) for the International Journal of Social Psychiatry. His main fields of research interest are social psychiatry, psychopharmacology, schizophrenia, bipolar disorders, and metabolic issues among psychiatry patients.

Arnold Weinstein earned a PhD in Comparative Literature from Harvard University in 1968. He is currently Edna and Richard Salomon Distinguished Professor of Comparative Literature at Brown University, USA. His books include *Vision and Response in Modern Fiction* (1974), *Fictions of the Self: 1550–1800* (1981), *The Fiction of Relationship* (1988), *Nobody's Home: Speech, Self and Place in American Fiction from Hawthorne to DeLillo* (1993), *A Scream Goes Through the House: What Literature Tells Us About Life* (2003), *Recovering Your Story: Proust, Joyce, Woolf, Faulkner, Morrison* (2006), *Northern Arts: The Breakthrough of Scandinavian Literature from Ibsen to Bergman* (2008), and *Morning, Noon and Night: Finding the Meaning of Life's Stages Through Books*

(2011). *Northern Arts: The Breakthrough of Scandinavian Literature from Ibsen to Bergman* was runner-up for best book of 2009 for the *Atlantic,* and his most recent book, *Morning, Noon and Night,* was nominated for a Pulitzer Prize in nonfiction. He has lectured regularly to medical students and audiences on the topic of literature's relevance for the practice and understanding of medicine. He was an associate editor of the journal *Literature and Medicine* from 1998 to 2003, and edited its Special Volume on *Infection and Contagion* (2003).

Daniel J. Wiener is a professor of counseling and family therapy at Central Connecticut State University and in private practice, in Northampton, MA, as a licensed psychologist. He is an APA Diplomate in Family Psychology, a licensed MFT in Connecticut, an AAMFT Approved Supervisor and a Registered Drama Therapist/Board Certified Trainer. Having founded Rehearsals! for Growth™ (RfG) in 1985, he has presented over 220 workshops, nationally and internationally, at agencies, training institutes, professional conferences and as part of the RfG Certificate Program. In addition to authoring numerous professional articles and book chapters, Dr. Wiener has published *Rehearsals for Growth: Theater Improvisation for Psychotherapists* and two volumes of his Collected Papers *(Vol. I, 1991–2004 and Vol. II, 2005–2016).* He has edited or co-edited several other books (*Beyond Talk Therapy: Using Movement and Expressive Techniques in Clinical Practice; Action Therapy with Families and Groups*: *Using Creative Arts Improvisation in Clinical Practice;* and *Interactive and improvisational drama: Varieties of applied theatre and performance).* His DVD *Experiential Methods in Couple Therapy: Rehearsals for Growth* was recently distributed by Psychotherapy.net. He is the recipient of a number of teaching awards: the 1997 Zerka T. Moreno Award (by the American Society for Group Psychotherapy and Psychodrama) and both the Research Award in 2006 and the Gertrud Schattner Award in 2010 by the National Association for Drama Therapy (now the North American Drama Therapy Association).

Glenn Wilson served as Visiting Professor of Psychology at Gresham College, London, from 2009 to 2014. He had previously been Reader in Personality at the Institute of Psychiatry, King's College, University of London, and Adjunct Professor with the University of Nevada, Reno. Glenn has published widely and his publications exceed 100 scientific articles and some 33 books, encompassing topics ranging from personality and attitude measurement to psychophysiology, sexual behaviour and psychology as applied to performing arts. He has been a pioneer in the field of evolutionary theories of sex differences, attraction and love; in 2001 he was ranked among the 10 most cited British psychologists.

Glenn is a fellow of the British Psychological Society and appears regularly on TV and radio, particularly in news and documentary programmes. His major books include *Psychology for Performing Artists* (Second Edition), (Wiley, 2002). *The Science of Love* (with C. McLaughlin, Fusion Books 2001), *CQ: The Secret of Lasting Love* (with J. Cousins, Fusion, 2003), *and Born Gay: The Psychobiology of Sex Orientation* (with Q. Rahman, Peter Owen, 2005).

Jeff Zinn has been active in the performing arts as musician, actor, director and producer for over forty years. A graduate of Franconia College in New Hampshire where he majored in theatre and dance, he also received an MA from New York University. Postgraduate studies include the American Repertory Theatre Institute for Advanced Theatre Training at Harvard University as well as the Kennedy School of Government. He made his off-Broadway debut as Danny in David Mamet's *Sexual Perversity in Chicago*; performed as a member of the Boston-based improvisational troupe The Proposition; and appeared on Broadway with Derek Jacobi in *The Suicide*. Jeff was the artistic director of Wellfleet Harbor Actors Theater (W.H.A.T.) from 1988 to 2011, and is now the Managing Director of Gloucester Stage Company in Gloucester Massachusetts. His most recent work is the major publication The Existential Actor: Life and Death, Onstage and Off, Smith and Kraus Publishers, 2015.

List of Figures

List of Tables

1

Introduction: Psychotherapy and the Arts—A Practitioner's Guide

Bruce Kirkcaldy

There are many books focusing on the arts and therapy. A Google search on the number of titles of books with "art (and) therapy" numbered 1.7 million, with three-quarters of a million titles on "film therapy", followed by 229,000 titles on "drama therapy" and 226,000 titles on "dance and therapy". Indeed, Malchiodi (2005, 2013) traces a long history of using arts in healthcare. Less common are texts written by clinicians and academics from faculties of medicine and psychology who themselves express an additional, personal passion for the visual and/or performing arts. Many of the contributors in this book are professionals working in both domains. Every contributor to this book was invited to begin their chapter by describing their personal motivation for participating and, more specifically, what inspired them to pursue their interest in visual and/or performing arts alongside their primary professional commitments as clinicians or academics. Each author was asked to conclude their reflections and their reviews of

B. Kirkcaldy (✉)
International Centre for the Study of Occupational and Mental Health, Düsseldorf, Germany

B. Kirkcaldy (ed.), *Psychotherapy, Literature and the Visual and Performing Arts*, Palgrave Studies in Creativity and Culture, https://doi.org/10.1007/978-3-319-75423-9_1

relevant literature with some key points relevant to clinical practice. I will begin by outlining my personal reasons for deciding to edit this book.

At the age of about 15 years, my English grammar school education required me to direct my learning towards either the natural sciences (biology, chemistry and physics) or the arts and languages. This was the passive acceptance of a dichotomy which would have a significant influence upon my educational and occupational pursuits over my lifetime. My ambition was to enter medical circles, so I felt committed to select the sciences. As a consequence, from the age of 16, I felt compelled to forgo all pursuits related to my interest in the arts, for example, no more handicrafts, paintings, literature or foreign languages. Looking back, this represented a form of "alienation" or "emotional distancing" from my more creative side, which to some extent I now sincerely regret. Over the following years, from entering university and pursuing undergraduate learning, I focused on biology, chemistry, physics and physiology. However, after my second year of university studies, I gained exposure to the arts and social sciences through psychology and philosophy. Fortunately, I had been able to transfer faculties from the pure sciences to the social sciences (psychology was not then recognised as a pure science discipline). I possessed a strong proclivity for the arts and the subject of human movement after graduating with a master's thesis on "Expressive movements as a psychodiagnostic technique". After graduating, I received the offer of a scholarship to attend as a graduate and researcher at the Laban Art of Movement Centre in London. I declined, opting instead for a research associate position at the University of Birmingham carrying out animal research into stress and allowing me to increase my expertise in biometrical statistics. Even then, what interested me more in stress research were those aspects of qualitative movement, such as ambulatory responses and the grooming behaviour of animals. My decision to leave the United Kingdom in 1977 and begin work at the Psychology Institute of the German University of Sport Sciences was also a shift towards an interest in human movement and sport and leisure pursuits.

Almost 20 years after graduation and having worked in diverse fields in academic research in various institutes (Medical Research Council project at the University of Birmingham, German University of Sport Sciences, Rehabilitation Clinic of the Medical School at the University of Cologne,

Psychosomatic and Psychotherapy Institute of Cologne University Clinic, Westphalia Clinic for Child and Adolescent Psychiatry and Psychotherapy, Marl-Sinsen), I decided to move into clinical practice.

Whilst in Germany, I had trained as a clinical psychologist and also completed professional training as a behavioural therapist whilst completing my doctorate in psychology at the University of Giessen. However, my refocus into clinical work was delayed in part through concerns about my German language abilities coupled with an enduring anxiety about public speaking. Nevertheless, with a young family to think of and the need for financial security, I was motivated to make the move into clinical practice, and "then" (1994) some 17 years had elapsed since I came to Germany, during which my language skills had significantly improved. The experiential learning through my clients over the years has given me an increased insight into the fragility and anguish of the human condition, and I have been able to incorporate ideas from the visual arts, photography and film therapy, dance and movement therapy, music and drama therapy, and the creative arts, including literary and narrative therapy. I have found value in asking my clients to bring photographs of themselves as children, adolescents, young adults and in successive phases of their life, including from major events such as weddings, birthdays and graduation days. I also encourage clients to complete a genogram wherever possible to gain insight into their ancestral history, including dates of births and deaths, marriages and divorce. This work includes, where possible, clients providing three adjectives to describe extended family members and indications of alcohol or substance misuse and/or mental illness in family members.

Wherever patients felt a need to paint or express their difficulties in pictorial form, this would be encouraged, as well as in narrative texts, for example, writing four consecutive days for approximately 15 minutes about their problem and self-character sketches and so on. In addition, I try to gather information about the leisure and sporting pursuits and interests of my patients, and encourage them wherever possible to engage in social activities, including drama and theatre. I have also compiled an array of books which could best be described as "biblio-therapeutic": giving clients homework assignments which involve reading books such as biographies or self-help manuals supportive of facilitating personal development. In contrast to my earlier work in the domain of empirical research and the use of psychometric questionnaires, the second half of my career has almost gone full circle, with a return to my earlier interest in the arts, including integrating this into my therapeutic work with clients.

Whilst reflecting upon the four decades of my career to date, I could not summarise my feelings better than McNiff (1981), examining the arbitrary distinction between sciences and arts: "The separation of the arts in therapy is rooted in the product orientation of technological culture.... The artistic mode of perception keeps the mind in touch with a world possessing both archaic continuity and infinite novelty. The arts offer a valuable operational polarity to the use of discursive language in psychotherapy, and they allow us to communicate with the emotions in their own language. Their multi-sensory rhythms must be kept intact rather than be absorbed within the more conventional verbal exchange of psychotherapy" (pp. xii–xiii).

Although not dismissive of the first half of my career and the focus on publishing empirical research papers, I have become witness to a growing critical stance towards the biomedical model of physical and psychological health—including the perceived overreliance on evidence-based medicine (EBM). Poignantly expressed in an article in the *Lancet*, Charon and Wyer (2008) observe that

> EBM has earned the reputation of dismissing the importance of the singular predicament of the patient and the individual judgment of the doctor. EBM has inflamed clinicians who feel belittled by it, calling it elitist, authoritarian, imperialising, and even fascist... the fields of narrative medicine and literature and medicine have reminded doctors that illness unfolds in stories, that clinical practice transpires in the intimacy between teller and listener, and that physicians are as much witnesses to patients' suffering as they are fixers of their broken parts. More and more clinicians and trainees are being encouraged to write about their clinical practices so as to develop the capacity for reflection. New clinical routines that provide patients with copies of what their doctors write about them or that encourage patients to contribute directly to their medical records are challenging traditional notions of authorship of the clinical record.

Clinical practice has taught me the value of narrative texts and the benefits of "story-telling", so benevolently expressed by Meza and Passerman (2011): "Although telling stories is a normal part of our culture, medical practitioners are trained to think predominantly with the biomedical disease-oriented story. Doctors seem to have lost their ability to listen to illness stories. Learning how stories are constructed and the internal relationships within the story to discover the meaning is referred to as narrative competence" (p. xix).

Extending this further to the arts in general, the Australian Centre for Arts and Health (2017, www.artsandhealth.org) cites the research literature shedding light on the impact of the arts and humanities on enhancing staff morale and work satisfaction in the healthcare sector, promoting skills among health professionals (e.g. nurses and physicians), achieving clinical outcomes for the patient's benefits, improving quality of life of mental health users and enriching the quality of healthcare. The survey further reviews literature showing the value of the arts in cancer care, cardiovascular and intensive care units, medical screening and diagnoses, and pain management and surgery (Staricoff 2004). Moreover, Staricoff explores the different art forms, for example, creative writing, poetry and literature, resulting in significant benefits for patients and mental healthcare providers.

The focus in this book was to consider the domains of visual and performing arts as an "alternative point of entry" in uncovering potentially useful and powerful forms of therapeutic intervention. Completing this ambitious project within a single volume was made possible only through the participants who agreed to share their visions of psychotherapy; this included pioneering clinicians and research academics. Their task was to provide insightful overviews of the contemporary literature in their respective disciplines and to translate their reflections and discoveries into useful guidelines for clinical practice. The intention was to provide a space where the authors could fuse together their clinical and research pursuits with their more creative and artistic interests, enabling them to share their ideas for innovative yet practical therapeutic interventions in their own clinical domains.

Film Media

One domain of recreational life which impacts our well-being is television and film media. It can be labelled "cinema therapy" and refers to using movies to help address issues of psychological and mental wellbeing. Mental health practitioners underline the value of using film media as a supplementary therapy to influence emotions, cognitions and behavioural responses to potential stressors. Kalra et al. (2016, p. 67) reflect upon the influence of films in the area of mental health: "From a psychiatric and psychological perspective, it is important to understand the impact of films for two reasons. Firstly, that they *reflect the society* in that films show what is going on in the society and secondly, they *influence behaviours and attitudes* in the society as characters may act as role models. For psychiatrists and psychologists films also serve a useful function in that they can be used to learn about reflections of the relationships in the society but also how mental illness is seen and portrayed."

Stutz (2015, p. 53) framed the benefits of films in the therapeutic context by drawing on his own personal preferences for films in which "people are liberated from themselves, and especially those in which people grow and mature in the face of traumatisation and injustice. Abyssal, painful childhood experiences are also essential to my way of life…. A sentence from the Jewish Talmud condenses this trail of hope, which finds itself, interreligious in all earthed spiritual paths: *Only a broken body is a whole body*" (translated).

Another use of film in clinical contexts is video-based therapy (http://www.filmandvideobasedtherapy.com/). The introduction and development of the film recorder offers significant instructional and educational benefits in the form of video feedback.

Visual Arts

Art therapy is perceived as "a mental health profession in which clients, facilitated by the art therapist, use art media, the creative process, and the resulting artwork to explore their feelings, reconcile emotional conflicts, foster self-awareness, manage behaviour and addictions, develop social skills, improve reality orientation, reduce anxiety, and increase self-esteem … (aiming) to improve or restore a client's functioning and his or her sense of personal well-being" (http://www.americanarttherapyassociation.org/upload/aatafactsheet.pdf).

Staricoff (2004) promotes the importance of visiting art galleries among healthcare professionals, with the idea that by attempting assessments of the mental, physical and environmental characteristics of the subjects in painting, trainees may enhance observation skills and augment their awareness of health issues across cultures, thus strengthening confidence in their own clinical skills. "The idea of using fine arts in medical undergraduate courses has been discussed for many decades. Research carried out in this field has shown that first year medical students taking part in art appreciation classes, which involved describing photographs of dermatological lesions, significantly improved their observational skills (Dolev 2001). The development of this crucial skill in medical practice has also been achieved by using different techniques, including learning to look at artefacts in an art museum (Belkin 1992; Bardes 2001)" (Staricoff 2004, p. 21).

Narrative Writing and Theatre

The medical curriculum often includes courses in narrative writing. Skelton (2011) claims, "The aim of narrative therapy is to separate the 'problem' from the 'person'. As and when this is done, presents the opportunity for new stories to emerge... 'the social construction of preferred realities' (Freedman and Combs 1996). In particular, narrative therapy aims to see problems as being individual – of course. But also existing in a particular society, a particular framework, which consists of a socioeconomic context, a set of cultural preconceptions, for example, about sexuality, or the expectations of social class and so on" (p. 321).

Others have argued that drama therapy entails drama with a healing objective, in which changes are facilitated through the drama process. Jones (1996, p. 8) talks about how drama therapy

> uses the potential of drama to reflect and transform life experiences to enable clients to express and work through problems they are encountering or to maintain a client's well-being and health. Clients make use of the *content* of drama activities, the *process* of creating enactments, and the *relationships* formed between those taking part in the work within a *therapeutic* framework. A connection is created between the client's inner world, problematic situation or life experience and the activity in the dramatherapy session... to achieve a new relationship towards the problems of life or life experiences they bring to therapy.

Bertolt Brecht, one of the most influential German playwrights, devised methods which could be deemed potentially valuable in therapeutic settings. It could be argued that specific tools which he applied in drama could equally well be transferred to therapeutic contexts. Brecht constructed dramas which expressed unresolved conflicts (rather than augmenting catharsis and empathy) with the goal of generating social political action on the part of the audience. It could be argued that Brecht's method of "estrangement" (Wikipedia 2017) is akin to contemporary concepts in therapy such as mindfulness, intended to reduce the importance of verbal content and evaluative processes. Acceptance and commitment theory uses "defusion" as a technique to minimise the influence of maladaptive thought processes. Brecht's notion of "Spass" or a fun factor was intended to pierce tensions escalating from the audience's identification with the emotional aspects of a character. To this extent it could be argued that Brecht acknowledged the therapeutic potential of "humour". Finally, the aspect of "Gestus" was central to his work, referring to the different facets of non-verbal communication, for example, body posture, intonation of voice and facial expression, as well as attitudes. It could be argued that this was a predecessor for modern-day social skills training. Others have contended for a different but equally "therapeutic" model of acting. Bradford (2017) summarises the key features of Stanislavski's system of acting in relation to therapeutic interventions Stanislavski advised performers to reach into their *personal memories* and draw upon a comparable life experience. Another is the implementation of a "magic if" (not unlike the therapeutic concept "als ob [as if]") introduced by Paul Watzlawick (1977). The idea is that trying to generate feelings associated with imagining oneself in that predicament may help by phrasing the question "what would one do in that situation?" He encouraged his students to astutely observe people in diverse life situations, monitoring their physical attributes as well as psychological personality traits. By disguising oneself in the clothing/appearance of another and socially interacting with unfamiliar persons in a novel environment, the individual could gain insights and be inspired by such observations.

The psychologist George Kelly (1955) also showed a strong interest in role play in psychotherapeutic settings. After the first session, clients were encouraged to create a self-characterisation of him or herself, usually in the third person (from the perspective of a reliable, sympathetic and close friend). This would be read by the client in the following session and would form the basis of the therapist structuring a fixed-role text: selecting construct dimensions orthogonal to the client's original constructs. My own preferred perspective on this is a joint venture, with client and therapist working collaboratively in the composition of a second narrative which would constitute an "ideal" sketch of who the person would desire to become after successful therapy. This characterisation would *not* be opposite to the current self-concept. In an enactment phase lasting about a week or two, the person is encouraged to become that new character, and during the few sessions thereafter both therapist and client can role play these novel options. The intention is not to convert the individual into a new character but to allow flexibility in taking on new costumes to experiment with. Once realising that the potential for change is possible, individuals can generate alternative models of behaving and responding.

The content of this book is divided into three sections: literature and narrative therapy, theatre and dance, and visual arts, music and the drama. Each section contains three to five chapters in which contributors reflect upon their personal interests for writing, provide a review of the contemporary literature and conclude by offering relevant clinical guidelines.

The first section of the book focuses on **Literature and Narrative Therapy**. Arnold Weinstein's opening chapter begins with his analysis of Edvard Munch as a psychotherapist. In initially examining three of Munch's canonical works—"The Scream", "Jealousy" and "Melancholy", Weinstein highlights that we are struck not only by the power of these psychic representations but also by their remarkable economy. They make use of a visual language that has uncommon suggestive force, and offer us a special "reading" of how the mind under stress works and also how the crucial relation between subject and setting is perfectly captured in visual representation. Weinstein describes how "The Scream" is the most notorious of Munch's pieces, and it expresses a spellbinding awareness not only that our inner anxiety and pain spill out into the world but that the roiled-up elements (sky, water) themselves penetrate the porous subject, leaving us to wonder whether the "scream" comes from within or without. "Jealousy" is a diptych of sorts, where each half of the painting comments on the other half; we see, on the left, the woman offering her body to her lover (done specifically with overtones of Adam and Eve) and then, on the right, the frontal agonised face of the "lover" who is doubtless "imagining" this betrayal scenario; the very traffic of jealousy is expressed here, with its endless creative/masochistic energy. "Melancholy" is a less well-known piece, and it depicts Munch's sister Laura—disturbed since childhood, diagnosed as mad later and institutionalised—sitting at a table; Munch has created a portrait of multiple imprisonments: the winter sun casts a prison-bar shadow on the wall, and the face of Laura is one of complete lostness, trapped within her own psychic disorder and demonstrably unable to escape.

The chapter that follows by Sayyed Mohsen Fatemi and Ellen Langer focuses on distinct features of Langerian mindfulness and its clinical implications. The authors explore stories, parables and metaphors. By drawing on the latest scholarly findings of Langerian mindfulness, the chapter examines the benefits of mindfulness in dealing with anxiety, stress management and depression. The chapter examines how mindfulness and mindlessness would lead to different compositions of our life and its directions. By virtue of an emphasis on the role of narratives and its therapeutic implications, they discuss how an increase of mindfulness would give rise to empowerment in creating more powerful and opulently rich stories. Through a demonstration of the creative role of language in shaping our life, this chapter delineates how mindful deconstruction of our stories would remove limitations and open up possibilities for recomposing our life.

Film and mental health is the focus of the contribution of Dinesh Bhugra, Antonio Ventriglio and Gurvinder Kalra. Through film much can be learnt about cultural norms and cultural differences, increasing our understanding and awareness of cultural influences, cultural sensitivities and commonalities. The authors discuss how films which depict personal and family dynamics, social norms and mental illness can shape the public's attitudes to mental illness and that it is important to note that the portrayal of mental disorders often reinforces stereotypes and may not have a positive effect on destigmatising mental illness. However, according to the authors, when films portray mental illness in a humane empathetic manner, it can help to foster better understanding of many conditions and disorders, including dementia, depression, bipolar disorders and so on. Teaching with film can also be incorporated into medical studies to have a positive impact on medical students and other health professionals.

The final of the four chapters that are included in the Narrative and Literature section is by Bruce Kirkcaldy and Ahmed Hankir. The main aims of this contribution are to discuss and describe the role that the performing dramatic arts plays in the treatment of mental health problems and its utility as a teaching tool in undergraduate and postgraduate health education.

Biographical narratives offer a precious qualitative insight into the minds of people who have first-hand experience of mental distress. It is argued that expressing oneself whilst under mental distress through the mediums of narrative and the performing arts (theatre) can be a deeply therapeutic and even cathartic process.

In this chapter Ahmed and myself describe our personal experiences as mental healthcare providers by offering our own candid narratives. Ahmed not only is a physician specializing in mental health but also has first-hand experience of mental distress. In the chapter he chronicles his personal journey of utilising the power of poetry, prose, drama and film to facilitate his recovery.

In the second section, **Theatre and Dance Perspectives**, the chapter begins with a contribution from Jeff Zinn, a director and playwright, who provides a new theory of emotions and moods in the theatre. He argues that when we visit the theatre, we want what happens onstage to be an issue of "life and death". Others may dispute this as being wrong: that what we want most of all is to be entertained and distracted—"taken out" of the realm of our day-to-day existences and transported to an alternative, better, or at least, more aesthetically pleasing place. However, Jeff contends that, despite what we may think we want from our entertainments, what we genuinely desire is the "theatrical experience" that best entertains us—one in which the stakes are tremendously high, a matter literally of life and death. When those stakes are not sufficiently high, we often lose interest and, subsequently, alter the channel, switching off our attention. Theatre makers recognise this intuitively. As directors we implore actors to augment the stakes. As actors there is a search for deep connections to our characters, making their concerns *our* concerns, trying hard to generate a sense of heightened importance. Frequently, Jeff argues, we find ourselves employing the language of analogy and metaphor. He suggests we employ the technique of *substitution*, swapping out the actor standing right in front of us for an imaginary other—a parent, a lover—so that we might believe more fully in what we're doing. We employ the *magic if* made famous by Stanislavski: *What if* I was the prince of Denmark? *What if* I were a high school science teacher dying of cancer who goes into the meth trade? Jeff further explores the psychological dynamics behind and in front of the theatre, inviting us as the audience into understanding the psychodynamics of acting and theatre production. In this chapter he suggests how psychotherapists can profit from an "involvement" with concepts from the acting profession.

Shauna Shapiro and Sarah de Sousa examine the relationship between dance and mindfulness. It is tempting to conceive of mindfulness as a practice that takes place in the mind, but as yoga, Qi Gong and many other similar wisdom-based traditions teach, mindfulness is both a state of mind and an embodied way of being in the world. Though much of the literature evaluating the effects of mindfulness training focuses on formal mindfulness practice, as integrated into mindfulness-based interventions, preliminary research evidence offers insight into the benefits of mindful movement as informal mindfulness practice. This chapter seeks to explore these benefits with particular attention to the physiological and interpersonal dimensions of mindfulness that are enhanced by mindful movement. Research from multiple social science disciplines is beginning to show that dance training, for example, holds the potential to encourage prosocial behaviour and improve emotional coherence. In a way that physical exercise alone does not, dance offers the opportunity to experience the embodied harmony of physical and emotional expression. The authors offer this exploration of mindful movement both as a nonclinical intervention for clients to increase mindfulness, positive affect and social connectedness and as a tool for therapists to develop deeper levels of presence and awareness in their "dance" with clients. As dancers must, both therapist and client are compelled to be equal partners in building the trust, intimacy and connection that foster healing and create the art of a life well lived. It is the coming together with each other, but also with ourselves, that mindful movement offers, an opportunity to merge our inner and outer worlds—nurture the container and its contents to achieve the integration that underlies an authentic and fulfilling life.

The final contribution by Daniel J. Wiener is directed towards his work on providing a therapeutic environment using theatrical improvisation in the training of psychotherapists. Following his introduction to theatrical improvisation in 1984, the author performed team improvisational comedy for six years as a hobby, enjoying the role expansion of playing diverse characters unconstrained by social norms. After applying some of these theatre games both to assessment and intervention in his therapy practice, he began in 1991 to teach these methods to other therapists whom he supervised, finding that they accelerated the learning of skills important to effective clinical practice.

This chapter presents both anecdotal and empirical support for the beneficial effects of theatrical improvisation training on both beginning and experienced therapists. These effects include risk-taking, therapeutic presence, mindfulness, appropriate self-disclosure, access to intuition, therapeutic charisma, attention to power/status cues and manoeuvres, and present-centred awareness. Specific methods are described and pragmatic guidelines are offered for effective improvisational training of therapists. Also featured is an examination of the ethical implications both of improvisation training and its application to working with clients.

The third section is on **Visual Arts, Music and Drama**, and begins with a contribution by Christine Korol, herself a clinical psychologist and gifted artist, and her close colleague Kimberley Sogge, examining the value of increasing mental health information through art and good design and mindfulness practice. She reflects how for those new to meditation the practice of sitting, focusing and attempting to quiet their minds can be daunting. This chapter describes the experiences of the authors as they developed a new programme Contemplative Art for the Reduction of Stress (CAReS) in response to the challenges of teaching mindfulness to adolescents with a variety of chronic health conditions. There is a long history of using art as a mindfulness practice in a number of spiritual traditions. Art making can be an effective vehicle into the present moment, with the added benefits of being able to actively practice quieting your inner critic. The teenagers in the original development series also reported that they found the practice of contemplative art more accessible and enjoyable than the traditional mindfulness programme they had participated in previously. The chapter further describes the challenges of developing a new curriculum, change management concerns with administrators and colleagues and some unexpected benefits for the authors as a result of developing the programme.

Then follows the chapter by the British psychologists Vincent Egan and Anthony Beech, together with the musician Laurence Burrow, who discuss in their chapter the manifest psychopathology of musical performing artists, in particular those who emerged from the middle of the 1960s to the 1980s. They argue that these artists sometimes explored their difficulties through their creative work and performance, obtaining appreciation, remuneration, and some validation of their different experience. This creative career is conceptualised as having been constructive for modelling a means of therapeutic expression in persons who in other contexts may have been isolated and more dysfunctional due to psychological illness or at least conceptual oddity. Vincent, Anthony and Laurence discuss these ideas with reference to individuals with documented mental illness who thrived due to their inherent vulnerabilities, as well as the snares and tangles of the creative lifestyle such as substance abuse and professional stress. The authors discuss this with reference to known artists such as Lou Reed, Brian Wilson, Syd Barrett, GG Allin, Nick Drake, Sinéad O'Connor and Ian Curtis.

The chapter also develops ideas about the stable schizotypy as a creative trigger for protean work that may take an artist in a number of directions, potentially taking them away from the finite career that normally accompanies a "pop" or "rock" artist into new creative directions. It is concluded that whilst the creative environment can be a therapeutic milieu for some individuals, the arbitrary nature of commercial "success" versus "failure" (as compared to objective artistic work judged on inherent merits and the appreciation of the viewer), along with the professional pressures to conform to an increasingly structured artistic career, may reduce the possibility of popular performing arts being a feasible environment for an individual with psychological "issues" to constructively express themselves and so receive validation of their difference. This loss detracts from the increased empathy the audience once had for unusual or mentally unwell persons through their creative work.

The third chapter in this section, by Glenn Wilson, a recognised psychologist, author and professional opera singer, explores music and its value in therapy. He talks about how despite some reservations and limitations music is demonstrated to be potentially beneficial in medical context. It has been shown to directly enhance mood, bolster immunity, motivate people, reawaken pleasant memories or distract from unpleasant realities. Moreover, music can contribute to health and well-being by offering alternative/complementary, non-verbal channels of communication. Glenn writes that as verbal skills are most frequently used to assess mental competence—for example, in assigning children to special homes and/or older people to certain geriatric wards—there is a risk that people who are musically competent are submerged in what, for them, is an impoverished or unfamiliar environment. The author reflects upon how implementation of music in the treatment of various groups of individuals would seem particularly beneficial in our current culture which is too frequently characterised by stimulus overload.

The next chapter in this section is offered by Alexander-Stamatios Antoniou and Marina Dalla, who focus on the therapeutic implications of expressive art, particularly drama. They cite Aristotle, suggesting, "The aim of art is to represent not the outward appearance of things, but their inward significance". The psychotherapeutic process of substance abuse treatment requires restoring the ability of the addict to function without drugs. This process not only is limited to abstinence from drug abuse but most importantly builds on the lasting changes of personality, attitudes, behaviour and affect, acquiring a smooth adjustment and reintegration into the society. The field of psychology offers many forms of therapy that aid in substance abuse treatment, spanning from psychodynamic theories to cognitive, behavioural and motivational therapies.

Research over past decades has demonstrated that art therapy is effective in working and expressing uncomfortable experiences freely with image (Skeffington and Browne 2014). Art and drama therapy provides a safe space for certain clients, for example, drug abusers, who have lost the ability to verbalise their conscious and unconscious problems because of their trauma history (Hongo et al. 2015). Alexander's chapter explores theoretical and applied strategies used in the Drug Dependence Unit at the State Hospital of Attica: attempting to connect psychological models of drug treatment with art therapy, music therapy, drama therapy and dance therapy.

The final chapter of this volume is Adrian Furnham's contribution on emotional intelligence, personality disorders and the performing arts. This chapter, which addresses the aptitude and temperament of the performing artist, is divided into two sections. In the first section the concept of emotional intelligence replacing older ideas of interpersonal and social skills is discussed. The ideas that all performing artists need exemplary emotional awareness and management in their craft are discussed. The second section deals with the relationship between the subclinical personality disorders, in particular histrionic, narcissistic and schizotypal disorders, and success, particularly in acting. The chapter concentrates on how emotional awareness is taught. Consistent with the previous chapters, Adrian offers concrete advice on the clinical implications of his work for mental health practitioners.

Finally, it remains for me to express my deep appreciation for the support of Joanna O'Neill, editorial assistant at Palgrave Macmillan in London, the UK, and to Grace Jackson, commissioning editor; Hemalatha Arumugam, project manager at SPi; Lisa, who offered me emotional and psychological support during a difficult phase of my clinical career and was always reassuring in maintaining a hopeful attitude throughout my publishing ventures; and my daughters, Lisenka and Eliana, who continue to be a source of inspiration, hoping that they too will find their personal creative niches in their future careers and personal lives. Finally, my thanks are extended to my close friend and long-term colleague, Adrian Furnham, UCL, for his continued cooperation during the years and in commenting on the introduction of this book.

References

Australian Centre for Arts and Health. (2017). www.artsandhealth.org

Bradford, W. (2017, March 8). *The Stanislavski System. Elements of the Russian Method*. https://www.thoughtco.com/stanislavsky-system-acting-method-2712987.

Charon, R., & Wyer, P. (2008). Narrative Evidence Based Medicine. *The Lancet, 371*(9609), 296–297. https://doi.org/10.1016/S0140-6736(08)60156-7.

Hongo, A., Katz, A., & Valenti, K. (2015). Art: Trauma to Therapy for Aging Female Prisoners. *American Psychology Association, 21*(3), 201–207.

Jones, P. (1996). *Drama as Therapy Volume 1: Theory, Practice*. Abingdon/Oxford: Routledge.

Kalra, G., Bhugra, D., & Ventriglio, A. (2016). Film, Family and Changing Context. In Bruce Kirkcaldy (Ed.) *Psychotherapy in Parenthood and Beyond. Personal Enrichment in Our Lives*. Turin: Edizioni Minerva Medica.

Kelly, G. A. (1955). *The Psychology of Personal Constructs*. New York: Norton.

Malchiodi, C. M. (2005). Expressive Therapies: History, Theory and Practice. In C. M. Malchiodi (Ed.), *Expressive Therapies*. New York: Guildford Press.

Malchiodi, C. M. (2013, September 9). *Creative Arts Therapy and Attachment Work*. https://www.psychologytoday.com/blog/arts-and-health/201309/creative-art-therapy-and-attachment-work

McNiff, S. (1981). *The Arts and Psychotherapy*. Springfield: C.C. Thomas.

Meza, J. P., & Passerman, D. S. (2011). *Integrating Narrative Medicine and Evidence Based Medicine. The Everyday Social Practice of Healing*. London/New York: Radcliff Publ.

Skelton, J. (2011). Narrative Medicine. Stories to Some Purpose. In B. D. Kirkcaldy (Ed.), *The Art and Science of Health Care. Psychology and Human Factors for Practitioners*. Göttingen/Bern/Toronto: Hogrefe.

Skeffington, P., & Browne, M. (2014). Art Therapy, Trauma and Substance Misuse: Using Imagery to Explore a Difficult Past with a Complex Client. *International Journal of Art Therapy, 19*(3), 114–121.

Staricoff, R. L. (2004). *Arts in Health: A Review of the Medical Literature*. Research Report 36. Arts Council England.

Stutz, P. (2015). *Geh hinein in deine Kraft* [Go Inwardly Towards Your Inner Strength]. Freiberg/Basel/Vienna: Herder.

Watzlawick, P. (1977). *How Real Is Real? Confusion, Discomfort Communication*. New York: Vintage.

Wikipedia. (2017, August 17). *Distancing Effect*. https://en.wikipedia.org/wiki/Distancing_effect

Part I

Literature and Narrative Therapy

2

Edvard Munch as Psychotherapist: "The Horse Cure"

Arnold Weinstein

As a humanities professor with interests in painting as well as literature, I have always felt that the arts in general have an enormous role to play in the arena of medicine at large. Some in the field of "literature and medicine" have made the key distinction between "disease" and "sickness," pointing out (perhaps reductively) that "disease" is the bioscience disorder that medicine and its practitioners are geared to treat, whereas "sickness" is the human experience of disease: what it feels like to have it. From the Bible to Greek tragedy, through Shakespeare and the Moderns, writers and artists have focused on the key issues of medicine: pain, sickness, death-and-dying, madness, neurosis, psychological disorders of every stripe. They speak to us of the *subjective* dimensions of illness. Each year I teach a large course entitled "Literature and Medicine" at my university, and the great majority of these students are premedical students, poised to enter medical school (and then a career) in the years ahead. I believe that the visual arts have as much to teach us on this broad front as

A. Weinstein (✉)
Brown University, Providence, RI, USA
e-mail: arnold_weinstein@brown.edu

B. Kirkcaldy (ed.), *Psychotherapy, Literature and the Visual and Performing Arts*, Palgrave Studies in Creativity and Culture, https://doi.org/10.1007/978-3-319-75423-9_2

literature does: both offer an invaluable complement to the work of science. And psychotherapists may well find much to draw on, in those precincts.

The notion of the artist as someone emotionally wounded has been with us for eons, acquiring particular currency in nineteenth-century Romanticism, with its focus on imagination and affect, as well as its view of the artist as misunderstood but sensitive soul. Yet, as far back as Sophocles's late play, *Philoctetes*, we encounter the theme of a person at once damaged and gifted, turning out to be essential for the well-being of the larger community.[1] It is an intriguing thesis: private injury-as-social benefit. How, one wonders, does this work?

We recognize the sick artist: but what about the doctor-artist? There are splendid examples of doctor-*writers*—Rabelais, Chekhov, W.C. Williams and moderns such as Richard Selzer and Oliver Sacks—but I know of few world-class *painters* who practiced medicine. Edvard Munch most certainly did not. On the other hand—and the rationale for this essay—Munch is a fascinating case study for the *value* of art as window onto psychic disarray and injury, as social good. We know that Munch saw himself in quasi-pathological terms: "Disease, insanity and death were the angels which attended my cradle, and have since followed me throughout my life," he sovereignly pronounced. And one of his most bizarre later paintings actually depicts him being given shock treatment, with the lovely title, "Dr. Jacobsen is electrofying the famous painter, Munch." (There is also a fine Munch portrait of Jacobsen [who ran a Copenhagen clinic for the moneyed ailing]: thrusting his girth out at the viewer, he himself virtually radiates a smug sense of power and authority.) So, Munch, afflicted from childhood on with bouts of influenza, bronchitis, followed by chronic alcohol abuse and serial breakdowns, certainly had contact with doctors and clinics.

[1] See Edmund Wilson's pathbreaking essay on *Philoctetes* in his superb book, *The Wound and the Bow* (New York: Oxford UP, 1965), a suite of essays on the relation between psychic damage and the creation of art; Wilson's title stems from the paradox of the Greek play: the man with an incurable wound also possesses a magic bow, but the community cannot have the bow without the wound. It is worth bearing in mind that this view of wound-as-useful goes strictly *counter* to the Greek concern with contamination and defilement, often leading to scapegoating measures in the old plays.

And he wrote copiously about these intimate psychological/somatic matters. Munch's diaries are crammed with accounts of the voices and visions he frequently experienced. He often thought himself pursued by "fiends," felt that people he saw were in disguise and in pursuit of him, recorded even one conversation with an interlocutor who spoke Esperanto to him, in order to get him into his nets. Consider, as masterpiece of the genre, the following passage from the diaries, and decide for yourself what kind of man we are dealing with:

> A strange man with a bird's head, spindly bird-legs, wings and a cloak flew into the railway carriage. Detective.
>
> We chatted.
>
> "What is your métier?" I asked.
>
> "I am a psychiatrist from Vienna."
>
> "You can advise me then," I said. "I'm afflicted by nerves and drink. Shall I admit myself to a clinic?" "Better say you're a drunkard," he said. "Tell them it's nerves and you'll go from institution to institution," – like Laura [Munch's demented, institutionalized sister] – "God knows when you'll come out."
>
> I shivered.
>
> The rages were coming more and more often now. The drink was meant to calm them, especially in the morning but as the day wore on I became nervy, angry … I noted small paralyses particularly at night. Arms and legs went to sleep. In the daytime I noticed heaviness in my right leg. It dragged a little, and then there were the strange voices and visions. I asked the doctor for advice. He looked it up in a book.
>
> "In the end it will go to your head. You will have a stroke."
>
> I had these tearing pains under my heart, terror in the morning, giddy when I stood up. Quick, need a drink, I thought. Ring the bell. Port wine, half a bottle. It helped. Coffee, a little bread. Another panic attack. Go outside. To the first restaurant. A glass. Get out into the street. It will get better.[2]

---

[2] Quoted in Sue Prideaux's fine *Behind the Scream* (New Haven: Yale UP, 2005), pp. 245–246. An invaluable resource here is Poul Erik Tøjner's *Munch: In His Own Words* (Munich/London/New York), 2001; even if one knows that Munch kept a running account of his life and feelings, this book yields a portrait of Munch as quasi-novelist.

This long passage is both hysterical and about hysteria. Idea for a film: Dr. Sigmund Freud meets, on a train in 1895 (the year of Freud's first major paper, the "Etiology of Hysteria"), the painter Edvard Munch (the year of Munch's greatest masterpieces); it seems that Munch knew what that scenario would yield. It is easy enough to see that this man is disturbed. The counterintuitive point that I want to insist on here is that Munch did *not* seek to get well (*pace* the stint at Jacobsen's clinic in 1915). He had a profound intuition that his psychic disarray (referred to, in his diaries, as both "sickness" and "terror") was his lodestar, that it was inseparable from his art. Not merely as subject matter, but impetus, as fuel, as generative source.

And all viewers have felt that his work itself is disturbed and has a deeply repetitive character. One way of seeing this is to note how compulsively overdetermined his choice of subject matter is. The great traumas of his life—the death of his mother and his beloved sister Sophie by tuberculosis, the tumultuous love affairs, the gunshot wound he received from his lover Tulla Larsen—were *fertile* to his art, and he returned faithfully, almost despotically, to them, "to the scene of the crime," at regular intervals, to see if they could be represented anew, unpacked further. He did not want to be free of them. (When asked, suspiciously, about this fetish, he angrily replied: look at all the artists who paint haystacks obsessively, and no one asks why.)

Where is the psychotherapy here? It lies in the unique payload of the paintings themselves. They, the paintings, bequeath to us a vision of psychic energy and pathways—whether we categorize it as wound, or personality, or, more simply, life—that is wonderfully *immediate*, that possesses a power and economy that language itself cannot truly rival. To grasp Munch's breakthrough, it is essential to recognize language's own insufficiencies in representing the pulsions of both body and mind. All of us can articulate in words the direction to the bank; we can indicate whether the traffic light is red or green; we can verbalize our weight in pounds or our income in dollars. But can we find words to signify what chocolate ice cream tastes like? Or what orgasm feels like? Or what our deepest and most abiding emotions actually are like? Is it possible that pictorial art can serve us as a visual language for what we can neither see, unaided, nor put into words? Could art have an economy, pith and immediacy that words cannot rival? Could there be—for us, the non-artists—a takeaway from this?

To begin answering these queries, it's worth considering the odd titles that Munch often assigned to his greatest paintings (and the ones under examination here): *anxiety, jealousy, the scream, melancholy*. Odd names for paintings, wouldn't you say? We are a far cry from the normal mimetic representations of painting—landscapes, humans, things, buildings, scenes from history or legend or Scripture—because Munch was persuaded that the roiling life of the psyche itself is *graphic*. This is an astonishing notion. He could *see*—and then make us see—feelings. This artist was drawn—as moths are to the light—to scenes of affective overload, of moments and crises when rationality is cashiered, due to the intensity of either spirit's or flesh's fierce demands. He saw these irruptions and take-overs as scenic, as representable. He was bent on helping us deepen our grasp of our own strange equipment, our own sentience: how it works, when it breaks down, how it spells wreckage for many of our fondest beliefs and assumptions. He is a cartographer of the soul.

We begin with "Anxiety," painted first in 1894, redone repeatedly, not only as painting but also as lithograph and woodcut, as if the artist were fixated on finding new ways to deliver, indeed to exhaust, his quarry, to create and recreate its contours and valence (Figs. 2.1 and 2.2).

Munch had earlier represented, in fully "realist" manner, the bourgeois denizens of Christiania (today's Oslo) taking their Sunday promenade, with military band and all, and one needs to bear in mind just what a class and social ritual such events were. People put on their fine clothes, took to the grand boulevards (in Christiania: the Karl Johan), in order to see and to be seen. In some sense, it is a painter's dream: to see and to be seen. But for the prosperous *burghers* themselves, this was a ritual about self-worth, about displaying one's rank and place within the social system and about the crucial recognitions and validations that came from such displays. One was confirmed not only in one's rank, but in one's solidity. They were to be shored up in their sense of gravity and purpose.

Now, take another look at "Anxiety": we recognize, in these faces, what is to become Munch's trademark style of vacancy and blankness, consisting of white, featureless, hollowed-out visages, spectral countenances with gaping, staring pinpoint eyes, frozen and hieratic in their ghostly

Fig. 2.1 Munch, "Anxiety" [painting]

parade. There is no effort whatsoever to give us nuance or any rudiment of psychological features (smiles, frowns, grimaces) as such. These denizens appear, instead, to be ghouls, the walking dead. One might recall Thoreau's contemptuous reference to "the mass of men who lead lives of quiet desperation," but this mass seems surreal, ghastly. These spectral citizens seem risen from the dead, to resurface (as surface), outfitted with frock coats, top hats and fine gowns, while yet remaining dazed

Fig. 2.2 Munch, "Anxiety" [woodcut]

mannequins, as if will-less, soulless. A more modern literary reference would be T.S. Eliot's "Hollow Men" or—still earlier—William Blake's grisly characterization of Londoners as displaying "signs of weakness, signs of woe," shackled by "mind forg'd manacles."

No matter what interpretation we assign to this group, we sense their emptiness, as if they had been "scalped" of any individuality, inwardness or even intensity. They look alike, they form a tribe, indeed a tribe on the march, like zombies on parade, crossing a bridge en route to us, but with more to come, in line behind them, infinitely more to come, as if the mouth of hell had opened to expel this itinerant troupe. Yet they also appear horribly islanded, unconnected, alone in their vacancy. We are squarely in Munch country here: the Norrbro bridge, the striated heavens and the sinister aura of final things are to reappear, for a still stronger curtain call, in "The Scream."

Why on earth does Munch title this painting "Anxiety"? Many of us think of anxiety as a busy term, as a feeling of roiling undoing, allied to panic, beating heart, breathlessness and loss of control, allied to going under or being eclipsed. Not so, Munch. He is out to show us that what links us together, what we have in common, underneath all the noise, is blankness, nothingness. It's an unnerving perception: go deep enough inside, and you find a vacuum, not a plenitude. We're accustomed to thinking that our inner core of humanity, our authenticity, is what lies behind our exterior. An entire discourse of surface/depth has worked this concept forever. Munch feels otherwise; he also wants us to see just how generic this condition is, how *all* of us are cursed with this fraudulence, this loss (theft?) of soul or heart or individual conscience. There is something outright system-wide in this painting: an entire culture is on the chopping block. All its fantasies and illusions (such as soul, purpose, stability, sanity and the like) have been surgically removed, cashiered.

I have included the woodcut of "Anxiety," so that you can see just how cunning Munch is, when he changes his medium and reprises his motif. We see the same errant specters as before, but the artist has diabolically enlisted the very grain of the wood this time as expressive surface, so that it displays the very sores and scars of the soul, as it were, the inner wounds that are customarily hidden from view (to others, to ourselves). We see, in this pair of works, a collective portrait of slipped gears, of hypnotic trance. Kafka was later to write that art is the ax that chops through the frozen sea within us (as rebuke to our fond notions of empathy and responsiveness to others); Munch shows us the frozen sea. And we are meant to rethink what anxiety actually might entail: our exile from feeling, our dance of sleepwalkers. Anxiety relates to our dawning awareness of fraud and deception, of the lie built into the system.

The most distinguished doctor I ever had—a former Harvard junior fellow, well respected in Providence, known as a brilliant clinician—told me categorically, when I mentioned Munch to him, that the guy was clearly a "depressed neurotic." I've never forgotten that dismissive put-down, delivered by someone who appreciated the arts, and I have to believe that any reader of this essay is—at this juncture—likely considering the same verdict. Munch is hopelessly damaged, the claim would go; how can we possibly *use* him? And what type of psychotherapy could conceivably be imagined and put into operation here? It's a fair question.

I've already referenced Kafka's view of art as the ax that chops into our frozen sea; let me now propose a less edgy definition: art allows us to imagine a future we cannot afford to experience. On this head, we get a clearer insight into all the bleaker arts, including tragedy itself: our *vicarious* commerce with death-and-dying, as well as with pain and psychic distress on the order of madness, jealousy, or the like, *serves us*. It's a test run, a freebie. We will die only once, and none of us is likely to write about it; with good luck, moreover, we will not encounter "in the flesh" all those other nasties: insanity, murder and/or the dreadful trials found in Greek and Shakespearean tragedies. But Munch gifts us something: we are enlarged by our conversance with these ultimacies. And the greatest art enables us to dive—briefly via the encounter, again later via memory and reflection—into the wreck, *and then to return*.

This is not some form of neural slumming or adventure-seeking. It's about our own turf, for it is worth bearing in mind that the full record of our lives (if there ever could be one) utterly dwarfs the absurdly meager recorded data that each of us leaves, for it includes our imagined vistas and horizons, all that immense virtual territory that will never be stamped on a passport or mentioned in an obituary. On this front, Munch expands, immeasurably, our database. How can this not interest medical folks, especially psychotherapists?

We will now examine a different Munch painting, "Jealousy," also painted during the "masterpiece years" of the mid-1890s, now illuminating a radically different kind of "anxiety" [Fig. 2.3, "Jealousy"]. No crowd of ghouls this time, just a painting that looks for all the world like a strange diptych: a human figure whose mournful face stares at us occupies half the painting, and the other half depicts an iconic scene of sexual betrayal, with the woman opening her red gown to offer her body *and an apple* to the full clothed man who stands next to her. One can scarcely miss the classic Adam/Eve/serpent story here, enlisted by Munch to show

Fig. 2.3 Munch, "Jealousy" [painting]

that the oldest canonical motifs still carry out the work they were designed for, whatever the century, whoever the protagonists are. Upon inspection, we easily grasp the relation between the two halves of the painting: the fellow who seems to be looking at us is actually looking inward, to *imagine* the betrayal scene in play. We also grasp that this type of imaginative activity can take place over and over, and that it is a supremely creative act. Jealousy is bottomless; it is about spawning—"the green-eyed monster" is how Iago put it to Othello, and he was something of a specialist on this issue—and it is therefore a wildly, uncontrollably creative fiction. We create, in the theater of our mind, the betrayals we suffer. Our freedom to do so is terrifying. Every erotic adornment we can fantasize, every element of pleasure that we endow these acts with, functions as a boomerang. Half the painting is a hurting face, and the other half is what hurts it, with the added spice that the head is producing its hurt.

It turns out that the face Munch "uses" in this painting is a well-known one: it belongs to one Stanislaw Przybyszewski, Polish "Satanist" comrade of Munch's during his most creative period in Berlin, and a sexual rival.

(The lady in question is Dagny Juel, femme fatale who exerted great power over the males in her entourage, introduced to the group by Munch but who ended up as Przybyszewski's partner; it is thought that the well-dressed male is Munch, posing as the rival seducer/seduced.) Munch frequently enlisted the Pole's visage when he wanted to paint distress and misery. On the other hand, the real-life Przybyszewski (who wrote the first important study of Munch's work) insisted that it was Munch, not he, who was the odd man out when it came to Dagny. And, to move from triangles to more complex forms, the brilliant Swedish writer August Strindberg, also a member of this extravagantly talented group of artists in Berlin, insistently claimed that he—not Munch, not Przybyszewski—was the regnant male of the mix, the one who enjoyed Dagny's favors.

What makes this painting still more piquant is the remarkable commentary it received in the Parisian press when it was exhibited there in 1896, a commentary written (in French) by no less than Strindberg, who had his own theories of jealousy and felt that the French public needed his insights if they were to understand Munch's strange art. This is worth quoting:

> *Jealousy* – Jealousy, holy feeling of purity of soul which despises being conjoined with another of the same sex by the mediation of another person. Jealousy, legitimate egoism, stemming from the preservation instinct of both self and race. The jealous one says to his rival: leave, deficient one; you will warm yourself in the flames I have ignited; you will breathe my breath from her mouth; you will imbibe my blood and you will remain my slave since it is my spirit that will control you through this woman, now become your master.[3]

The displacements and conjunctions on show here are dizzying. Jealousy is not just a creative fiction but also a triangulated (and sublimated) sexual congress. Strindberg subscribed passionately to the Spiritist tenets of fin-de-siècle, whereby astral waves and libidinal cur-

[3] Quoted by Göran Söderström in his magisterial *Strindberg och Bildkonsten* (Stockholm: Forum, 1990), p. 304. Strindberg, largely known in the Western world as *writer*, was a remarkable painter in his own right (as well as being a shrewd art critic), and his pieces probably command the highest prices of any paintings found in Sweden today.

rents reach far and wide, leading him to claim he could feel others' hatred from afar, just as he could also feel the sexual betrayals committed by his former wife with her later lovers. He also expressed his conviction, citing Buffon, that fructified eggs have been found in men's penises, arguing that a man can get another man's semen inside him when he mounts a woman "over-filled with semen," concluding that "wombs are only birds' nests in which the cock lays his eggs."[4] This essay is about Munch, not Strindberg, but they each believed in a world of pulsating forces that traversed time and space, so that when a sharp gust of wind blew his easel and canvas onto the sand in Warnemünde, decades later, Munch had a clear explanation for the event: "That wind is Strindberg, trying to disrupt my work."[5]

This belief in undying forces and currents that roam the earth and shock us with tidings can be applied to "Jealousy," for it installs a regime that seems closer to Einstein than Newton, where mass and energy do not behave as we expect, yielding a world impregnated with spirit and spirits. In that light, Munch's painting teaches us something about the dynamics of *looking*: the jealous man stares at us while imagining betrayal, and *we* look at the entire painting, registering its crossed wires and flowing currents, linking its two halves, learning something about neural circuits that regulate memory, psychosis and much else. The ophthalmologists and optometrists can tell us a great deal about the intricate biology of the eye, but who can instruct us about the existential, sentient stakes of vision, both outer and inner? With Munch—with art in general—we sign on for a unique form not only of travel but also of *traffic*. The company we keep becomes visible. Munch initiates us into a world with senders and receivers, and in my view that world is possessed of a majesty and terror that have been utterly lost in today's digitally wired culture, whereby we log on and "choose" to receive whatever inputs we desire. No such freedom of choice for Munch and Strindberg: your life buzzes at all times, you can be invaded, you have no control.

[4] Quoted in Michael Meyer, *Strindberg: A Biography* (New York: Random House, 1985), pp. 288–289.

[5] Cited by Prideaux, p. 175.

Take a final look at "Jealousy." Today we can sign on for brain scans and MRIs that will disclose all our passages and conduits, to let us know if unwanted blockages or flows are there. Jealousy is also about unwanted blockages and flows, as well as surprising hookups. Przybyszewski offers us, in Munch's rendition, a mindscreen, a media representation of his thoughts and fears. Further, he is not simply registering this seduction scene: he is producing it. We possess no medical imaging device that could remotely match such traffic. And if we factor in Strindberg's more exponential view of such triangles, we end up with the suggestion that the key players in this steamy scenario are the jealous man and his rival, locked in their own *mano a mano*; the woman is merely the go-between. None of what I've advanced is remotely provable, but then, to cite *Othello* yet again, when ever do we have "ocular proof" for the data that means most to our heart and soul? There is no testable metric or proof for love or betrayal, even if we gobble up detective stories or employ "private eyes" to get a fix on our arrangements. Munch's painting should be studied in creative writing classes, as well as therapists' offices, for it presents a field picture of human connection and a generative theory of libido that art alone can produce (Fig. 2.4).

We now come to the archetypal Munch representation of psychic slippage in his most famous painting, "The Scream."

This radical, insolent painting may today have lost some of its punch, given its commercialization in popular culture and its presence in graffiti everywhere. With this work we are told, definitively, that we have no homeland, that the stability we take for granted—a stability required for the maintenance of sanity—is illusory. Here, particularly, my view of art as the imagined encounter of a future we cannot afford to experience needs to be kept in mind. No one could inhabit the world of "The Scream," yet this hallucinatory painting is crammed full of tidings about our human situation (exile?) in a body we did not make and in a world we do not control. Wallace Stevens, the great American Modernist poet, was later to celebrate just this exile as the very source of poetry: "From this the poem springs, that we live in a place that is not our own, and much more, nor ourselves, and hard it is, in spite of blazoned days." Munch is very much the geographer of these precincts.

Fig. 2.4 Munch, "The Scream" [painting]

We know that Munch was seeking, in this painting, to do justice to a memory he had had, earlier, of crossing the Norrbro bridge with two companions, and suddenly seeing a blood-red sky—"flaming clouds like blood and a sword" as he put it—causing him to feel "as though Nature were convulsed by a great unending scream."[6] We also know that this site was close to both an asylum and a slaughterhouse, so "real" screams might

[6] Quoted in Arne Eggum, *Edvard Munch: Paintings, Sketches, and Studies* (New York: Clarkson N. Potter, 1984), p. 81.

have been audible; some scholars have even suggested that the sky's coloration was the result of unique atmospheric conditions; it has even been posited that Munch's inspiration came from having seen, earlier in Paris, a recovered Peruvian mummy. Whatever its antecedents, Munch struggled with this painting, for he sensed that his resources were inadequate to his vision: how, he wondered, can paint itself not just approximate but "become," for the viewer, *blood*, for that was his aim.

Proust once described a dying character in terms of someone who suddenly felt the monstrous force of gravity itself pulling the body into the earth, and something similar is happening here: the fundamental contract that preserves human equilibrium—I am I, and the world is the world—has been scandalously breached. The world is hemorrhaging, the dike has collapsed, the flood rushes in. My terms may seem hyperbolic, but I write these lines on September 1, 2017, as the city of Houston, a full week after being hit by Hurricane Harvey, is still *under water* in many quarters, and I review these lines on September 11, 2017, when the entire state of Florida has suffered cataclysmic damage of both flood and wind by Hurricane Irma; and one is entitled to think about earlier catastrophes: tsunamis, volcanic eruptions, earthquakes, events that changed the shape of reality to stunned people who had believed that reality's shapes remained firm. History is dotted with moments when "Nature is convulsed by a great unending scream," and they remind us that the stability we take for granted is a fair-weather conviction, doomed to volatize when the horror comes. I also think it is utterly logical to recast this notion in strictly human somatic terms: seizure, stroke, infarctus designate a bodily collapse—a cashiering of the body's defenses, a moment of corporeal anarchy—that is rigorously parallel to the riotous power of this painting. The frame no longer holds.

Munch's central figure stands—barely stands—on a bridge that is meant to protect him from the swollen waters. Yet the feeling generated by this diagonal form is one of precariousness: you could fall off it. Edvard later wrote that his life was a narrow path next to a great precipice, that he knew himself destined to fall into the pit. Are all of us perched on bridges, doomed to fall off, all the while thinking we're on solid ground? Meteorologists use the term "fully risen sea" to indicate huge waves, but Munch's rendition literalizes the metaphor and seems quasi-biblical, offering, instead of God's divinely parted waters, a sheer mountain of water, likely akin to what the people bordering the Indian Ocean saw coming at them during the tsunami of 2004, or the one in Japan in 2011. One looks at the ever rising waters in this painting, and one sees more than flood: the sinuous flow is outright vertical, reaches into and alters both the land and the sky, yoking everything into its fiery arabesque.

The human figure in "The Scream" is the most denuded figure in all of Munch; he never again painted a human being this stripped and generic, where even the markers of gender are gone. The wavering figure stares out at us with its immense hollowed eyes and with its hands covering its ears. What is it seeing and hearing? The evident psychological reading is: the distress, the tempest, the scream, are all *inside*, are the affective miasma that can no longer be kept in tow and must now out, as the subject vomits its anguish. But a glance at the paroxystic setting of the piece—the charged vertical waters, the blood-red sky, the swirling lines of a natural setting gone berserk—tells us, just as the hands over the ears tell us, that the scream is (also) *outside*, environmental, coming from the upended material world itself. Food for thought here: *we cannot know whether the scream is inside or outside.* Arguably this constitutes the painting's true horror: inside and outside are in dreadful collusion. Nothing can be kept "in" or "out."

"Keeping" is a cultural myth, derived from fond notions of stability that make sense, when things seem to stand still, to *those who are well.* Pain, fever, sickness and terror initiate us routinely into the maelstrom Munch has painted, even if we do not care to see our entry in such garish terms. Even drunkenness and orgasm move in this direction. In sickness, in old age, the body's circuits and channels play us false: obstructions can block pathways, fluids move where they shouldn't, the entire hydraulic, plumbing and electrical arrangements go amok, the thermostat is off, the organs mutiny, viruses and bacteria invade, the immune system fails. This central drama of the human subject under siege, attacked from within and without, characterizes our somatic fate. I'd like to cap this line of thinking by referencing one more astonishing feature of this painting: Munch himself scribbled, on the back of one of the four versions he did,

"Could only have been painted by a madman."[7] With this announcement, we see the conjunction of soma and psyche. The artist tells us that his apocalyptic view of the human condition—one of takeover and capsizing—is inseparable from a mental state he himself regards as "insane." I'm reminded of R.D. Laing's thesis that sanity itself mandates our being blinded to our actual arrangements. Edvard Munch ascribed the driving vision of this terrifying painting to his unbalanced mental state, telling us that he must, indeed, have fallen out of the world, to be able to see it in these awful terms. Was he right? And, if so, what is in this, for us, the (putatively) sane?

One reply is: you don't need to be crazy to get Munch. Let me rephrase this: it has been pointed out that something as innocuous as a blood-pressure reading by a doctor generates an unwelcome sense of mortality and malaise in the mind of many patients. And of course it goes up from there, when the serious ailments and tests arrive. What Munch termed "anxiety" and "scream" are felt, at lower intensity (thankfully), by all of us as we ponder the vulnerabilities of our mental and physical condition. The sheer discipline that keeps most of us cogent and rational may well be a thin membrane, underneath which something more roiling and turbulent resides. It does not take much, to see it, hear it, spring it loose, trigger it into action. The appearance of normalcy that we take for granted—after all, I never see people shrieking and collapsing on the streets of the city where I live—may well be exposed as a beautiful charade when major trouble comes. Doctors and therapists have always known this. At some hard-to-accept level, the "scream" is but one catastrophe away.

The last Munch painting I want to discuss, "Melancholy," is less known than the others mentioned, but is arguably among the most poignant works he ever did (Fig. 2.5).

---

[7] Not surprisingly, there are some modern scholars, such as Patricia Berman (in *Edvard Munch: The Modern Life of the Soul* [ed. Kynaston McShine, New York: Museum of Modern Art, 2006], pp. 35–51), who are deeply suspicious of Munch's grandiose pronouncements about madness and the like; they contend that he was a canny figure bent on producing and managing his image, and that we need to be alert to the posturing and stratagems associated with his persona. I find this position intelligent but wrong-headed; it seems to me that its distrust of the artist—turning him into something of a performance artist—yields dubious results while locking us out of what is epochal in his work.

Fig. 2.5 Munch, "Melancholy: Laura" [painting]

The title is one Munch had used earlier, to depict his friend Jappe Nilsson in a state of jealousy, but this version depicts Laura Munch, the painter's younger sister, who had been "strange" from childhood on—in adolescence she was said to have a "schizoaffective illness"—and who ended up having intermittent hospitalizations for mental illness during her entire life. This portrait of a young woman "inside" on a frigid but sunny day, hunched over in her chair, done in 1899, has a haunting power. Munch, with all the sympathy and love he can muster, cannot find his way into Laura's mind. What he can do, however, is to represent her imprisonment in multiple fashion: she sits dead still; her eyes seem vacant and inner directed; the reflection of the wall repeats her incarceration; the vivid coloration of the tablecloth (compared by some critics to raw meat) contrasts gruesomely with the deadness of the captive. The entire painting is a symphony of lostness, entrapment, hopelessness.

Munch also did other studies of Laura, but I feel that this one stands as a kind of warning: this is what I could be. Or, later in life, this is what I might have become. Those angels of "disease, insanity and death" that "attended his cradle" obviously attended hers as well, but there is nothing angelic in what they wrought. Laura is a quantum step beyond the horde of zombies in "Anxiety," for she participates in no promenades, has no like-minded (like-afflicted) peers; Laura is perhaps the truest and saddest expression of what it can mean to inhabit the Munch-world, for she has no defenses, and is hence utterly undone.

What defenses did Edvard have? Why did he not become his mother or Sophie who each died of their tuberculosis? Or Laura who was institutionalized for madness? The answer to that question is close to hand, for it governs the logic of this entire essay: he has his art. He acquired the unique, peculiar mastery that art alone confers: to represent, via painting, what otherwise might have killed him. He is scarcely our only mad painter—Van Gogh comes obviously to mind, but one can go back to Dürer's "Melancholia" and Hogarth's "Rake's Progress" for earlier depictions of mania, and a number of modern figures also fit the bill, such as the Japanese artist Yayoi Kusama, who takes up residence in a psychiatric ward when she is not painting—but he occupies a special place in this list of the damned, because so many of his paintings lay the very groundwork for such outcomes. Lionel Trilling wrote, years ago, a brilliant essay on "Art and Neurosis," in which he argued that the sheer amount of discipline and control that are indispensable to the *making of art* are signs of sanity, no matter what the artist's vision might be.[8] When Edvard Munch elects to do "Anxiety" in painting, then in lithograph, then in wood cut, he is not merely furthering his exploration of the topic, he is also furthering his mastery of it, his artisanal capacity to give it expression.

Munch knew himself to be sick. Perhaps we all are. But he knew that his somatic vulnerability and psychic distress would serve his art. And he has to have known that the art would, in turn, serve him, save him. There is nothing easy here. I suspect that large numbers of my university students

[8] Lionel Trilling, *The Liberal Imagination* (New York: Doubleday, 1953), pp. 155–175.

have an inner conviction they could become the great American artist or novelist for tomorrow, but few if any of them will have the talent or—especially—put in the hard labor required to make this happen. Munch did. And, given what we know about him, what his paintings tell us about him, we have to realize that his efforts were enormous. He, more than most, knew the imperious power of mania. One of his intriguing later paintings is titled "Galloping Horse," and it shows a huge horse rampaging directly towards us, the viewers, and we have to look carefully to see that this horse is pulling a wagon with a driver, both almost in miniature, given the sheer energy and scale and foreshortening of the animal rushing towards us. (So many of his paintings rush headlong at us: look again at "Anxiety" and "The Scream.") But, in this instance, it is hard not to think mythically, not to see in this horse the raw power of the animal (in nature, in us) vs. the puny scale of human reason that is supposed to be in charge.

That galloping horse never quite disappears from Munch's life and work, even though the motif itself does not return. I want to back up that claim in a circuitous fashion. Munch coined an odd phrase for the way he treated his finished paintings: "Hestekur" or the "Horse Cure." He was referring to his strange habit of abusing his work: he not only walked among his paintings, but he manhandled them, kicked at them when angry, tossed them about, spilled on them, punched them, and above all left them outside, exposed, in the elements, shat upon by birds, tossed into trees. Visitors would ask in disbelief, why? And he would answer: it is good for them; they improve with age, they weather with the elements. It is well known that Munch disliked varnish, glossy finishes and gold frames; he thought they suffocated his work. It is also well known that Munch was quasi anal-retentive when it came to his paintings; he found it hard to be separated from them and frequently begged his patrons to lend back to him works they had earlier bought. Further, he, who never married, who thought himself unfit for siring children, called his paintings his children. And in shockingly many of the photographs we have of Munch, we will see his paintings, his children, in the background. They are his family.

Why do I tell this story? I want to make the point that Munch's art was his creation, his progeny, his grounding, his outlet for love, his sanity, his lifeline (in every sense of the term). Is it too much to claim that these paintings can also be that for us? Our Hestekur? These extremist works testify to fates that could be ours, and they broadcast the lineaments of a Power System that is entirely inhospitable to human comfort and well-being. The world unveiled in "Anxiety," "Jealousy," "The Scream" and "Melancholy" is not one that any of us could fashion into a home or place of safety. The creature who lives there is without shelter, without blinders, without any of the essential protections and fictions that make life possible. We depend on the belief that we have will power. We believe that our own anxiety can be understood by a licensed specialist, and that a regime of therapy and/or pills will help us find our way. We feel that our imagination enhances our world, gives vibrancy and point to our existence, deepens our feelings, and hence the toxic, corrosive portrait of "looking" that we find in "Jealousy" is unpalatable, to say the least. We also tend to believe that things stay inside their defining contours, that the surfaces we encounter every minute of life remain what they are, retain their shape, so that nothing ever jumps out of its definitional skin; "The Scream" brings us news of a regime where that belief is scuttled, where—as in Picasso's "Guernica"—shapes tumble, metamorphosis rules, nothing remains itself, except perhaps the "great unending scream" that convulses nature. We subscribe, finally, to a measure of freedom and self-determination. We can exit at least some of the prison houses we are thrust in: doctors can aid us in ministering to our bodies and minds; rationality assists us in managing our libidinal and other unwanted wants; education teaches us to see through some of the fog of convention, propaganda and the sad historical record so that progress might actually be achievable. Laura Munch of "Melancholy" has no such maneuvering room or agency. She is stuck for good, with a sentence of life imprisonment: imprisoned in her own life.

Munch as psychotherapist? No, he has no diploma, no office hours, no pills to dispense and not really any wisdom as such to impart. But his paintings are his gift to us. Their dark picture of our arrangements does not lessen us; it *lessons* us. These pieces perform something of the role that the Greeks found in tragedy, and which they called *catharsis*, by which they meant: the spectator experiences something purgative and life-enhancing, even through the pain and waste of these grim stories. Munch's works are rough going. They remove a good bit of the scaffolding and supports that make life bearable. They remove the varnish, polish and gold frames from the picture we have of our situation. They expose us to the elements, to the forces that inhabit bodies, earth, sea and sky. They bid us to make knowledge of their tidings. They are a kind of Hestekur.

There is no magic formula for the psychotherapist in putting the Hestekur into practice, in deriving a measurable benefit from the study of Edvard Munch. But a case can be made that these paintings—"Anxiety," "Jealousy," "The Scream" and "Melancholy"—add something unique to our "database" in understanding the workings of the human mind under stress, as well as in widening our own optic about the relation between subject and world. The startling *economy* of Munch's paintings brings to visibility certain lines of force that can be found nowhere else: not in photographs or in even the most sophisticated modern imaging. Munch instructs us about the company we keep, and the setting where we live: his vision of each of these arrangements differs radically from the views put forth by traditional daytime logic, because he not only honors the affective and libidinal forces that course through us—that can sometimes erupt and destroy us—but proffers a new kind of map, a cartography if you will, of our psychic whereabouts and behavior. He may never find his way into the medical books as such, but he can contribute something unique to the entire psychotherapy project.

References

Berman, P. (2006). In K. McShine (Ed.), *Edvard Munch: The Modern Life of the Soul* (pp. 35–51). New York: Museum of Modern Art.

Eggum, A. (1984). *Edvard Munch: Paintings, Sketches, and Studies* (p. 81). New York: Clarkson N. Potter.

Meyer, M. (1985). *Strindberg: A Biography* (pp. 288–289). New York: Random House.

Prideaux, S. (2005). *Behind the Scream* (pp. 245–246). New Haven: Yale University Press.

Söderström, G. (1990). *Strindberg och Bildkonsten* (p. 304). Stockholm: Forum.

Trilling, L. (1953). *The Liberal Imagination* (pp. 155–175). New York: Doubleday.

Wilson, E. (1965). *Philoctetes*. In *The Wound and the Bow. Seven Studies in Literature*. New York: Oxford University Press.

3

Langerian Mindfulness and Its Psychotherapeutic Implications: Recomposing/Decomposing Mindlessly Constructed Life Stories

Sayyed Mohsen Fatemi and Ellen J. Langer

Personal Motivation for Interest in the Arts and Psychotherapy

Besides our scholarly and academic interest in writing this chapter, we also have in mind our personal experiences and engagement in living through art. Understanding the exquisite power of aesthetics may reveal the transformative role of art in giving rise to mindfulness. Artistic works, albeit in different manifestations, may point to the lively presence as the essential component of mindfulness.

Through painting and poetry, we have lived through art and have understood its ontologically solid power in developing radical transformation of consciousness. They both can revitalize people's liveliness and help them be in touch with their lived experiences more mindfully.

A wide variety of psychotherapeutic techniques and conceptualizations have addressed clients' problem situations, with each prescribing or

S. M. Fatemi (✉) • E. J. Langer
Department of Psychology, Harvard University, Cambridge, MA, USA
e-mail: smfatemi@wjh.harvard.edu; langer@wjh.harvard.edu

B. Kirkcaldy (ed.), *Psychotherapy, Literature and the Visual and Performing Arts*, Palgrave Studies in Creativity and Culture, https://doi.org/10.1007/978-3-319-75423-9_3

recommending sundry ways of helping the clients to manage or solve their so-called problem situations, including depression and anxiety.

Among the widely used techniques and perspectives, one may see the word "mindfulness" in plenty of psychotherapeutic contexts (see, for instance, Langer (1975, 2005, 2009), Fatemi (2016a, b, c), Hayes et al. (2004), Kabat-Zinn (2003, 2005), Linehan et al. (2002), Segal et al. (2002)).

On the other hand, narrative therapy posits that people are *embedded* within their stories and stories they tell themselves will have an impact on their responses. Stories, in this sense, are created and creational as they construct realities for clients (Lieblich et al. 1998).

White and Epston (1990) and White (2007) have argued that in helping the clients, psychotherapists need to help them understand that their problems should not be confused with their identity: the problems need to be separated from people. This *externalization* would help the clients explore the possibility of being in charge for revisiting or recreating their stories.

Both narrative therapy and mindfulness-based psychotherapies have in common a view that *language can create realities*. Understanding a client's world requires understanding his/her use of language. A world shaped by negative language including self-doubts, despondency, despair, insecurity, anxiety and negativity would espouse a negative world view followed by negative behaviors and feelings.

In different forms of mindfulness, including mediation-based mindfulness and Langerian *critical mindfulness*, the goal is to develop an intentional, flexible, open and presence-oriented attention that can act proactively.

Meditation-based mindfulness, which is mainly characterized through the works of Jon Kabat-Zinn and is also associated with mindfulness-based stress reduction (MBSR), would highlight the role of meditation in achieving mindfulness.

Langerian mindfulness, rooted in terms of empirically validated experiments, argues that mindfulness can also be obtainable through non-meditation-based components (see Langer 1989, 2000, 2005, 2009).

Perspective is of great significance in understanding Langerian mindfulness as it may be the underlying element of one's indulgence in a repetitive course of living interwoven with helplessness, anxiety, fear, isolation and negativity. A change of perspective, however, can create a new course of action where responsibility, responsiveness, proactivity, choice and empowerment can give rise to a novel mode of being.

The proactive nature of mindfulness may begin with reexamining the mind-sets. Plenty of empirically based experiments indicate that when placed in a state of *mindlessness*, people lose their creativity and agency and merely succumb to a passive mode of reactivity (see Langer 1989, 2000, 2005, 2009). Mindfulness enhancement would help people notice their power of creativity, their choices in making a decision, their efficacy in dealing with challenges and their novelty in improving their performance (see Fatemi et al. (2016).

In other words, mindlessness would deprive people of questioning the dominant discourses of their lives whether these discourses have been brought to them through their upbringing, schooling, culture, environment or even therapeutic discourses. So people can be mindlessly following the patterns of stories created for them by others without realizing their own power to change the story.

The problem with dominantly established mindlessness is that it does not allow people to see anything except the direction given to them: once you get yourself locked into some information, you may not be able to see anything else except the given information.

Clients can be subjugated to dominant therapeutic discourses too. Once they are labelled as depressed, for example, they would move in line with that dominant discourse: they keep themselves distant from people; they listen to sad music, and people around them see them as depressed too and act towards them accordingly.

Narrative therapy challenges the domineering psychotherapeutic discourses and questions their universality.

In doing so, narrative therapy may be well-embedded within Langerian doctrine of mindfulness where mindfulness requires understanding the specific contexts of the action, behaviors, feelings and stories of a client.

The contextual understanding of clients would require an in-depth exploration of their uniqueness. To examine the context would also take place through the rigorous and mindful understanding of the client's language: *what is it that clients tell themselves and others, what is maximized or minimized in their stories, how does their language contribute to their empowerment or disempowerment, how is their language influenced by a macro language coming from their culture, upbringing, education, political and economic system? What is the language that they have been using or what language have they been subscribed to use?*

Labels bring mindlessness (see Langer 2009). Clients can be mindlessly subjected to a passive mode of living through complying with labels attributed to them either in macro or micro levels. From a Langerian perspective, dominant therapeutic discourses can also impose mindlessness through creating a reference point where client's context is marginalized and his/her voice is lost.

Language plays a pivotal role in creating mindfulness (see Fatemi 2018). Language is not just an instrument or a device to make transactions: it entails a mode of being. When mindless, people are incarcerated within a language that seems to be unchangeable and unavoidable. For people with depression, this language produces sadness, fear, anxiety and helplessness (Davidson 2000). This language unfolds itself in the paramount emotions of people with depression. The use of a counterproductive language epitomized in the barrage of negative emotions would impede the process of deconstructing the language from the user of the language: the person strongly identifies himself/herself with the language, and he/she cannot disengage himself/herself from the emotions generated by the underlying negative emotions.

Langerian mindfulness starts off with helping the clients notice perspectives that may not be available in the repertoire of the person with depression. The client is encouraged to explore possibilities of alternative modes of perspectives. When depressed or stressed, people experience negative interpretation bias: they see more negative aspects than any positive sides. This may lead to their acting from a single perspective that does not allow them to see any other modes of possibilities except what they are enmeshed in.

Langerian mindfulness commencement point lies in delineating the relationship between one's perspective and one's mode of existence. Mindlessly lived stories do not leave any room for attention to variability. Helping clients understand how perspectives can be limited and limiting would allow them to see the implications of their phenomenologically lived stories.

Stories entail *a what* and *a how*. In discussing the what of stories, clients examine the events, their sequential order and their syntagmatic analysis and focus on what is it that has occurred, namely, the content of their stories.

In focusing on how stories are told, clients are encouraged to fathom the discourse of their stories: how the stories are told, their modes of display and their modes of presentation are pronounced here.

In understanding the differences, clients learn to see the discourse of their own stories (how they are told) and its implications. Stories' discourse can be limiting, oppressive and paralyzing. Langerian mindfulness would help clients realize how the content and the discourse of their stories can mindlessly impede the process of looking into the unnoticed features of their stories. When fraught with depression, anxiety, fear and doubts, clients may neglect the realm of alternative possibilities that may be available to them. Mindlessness would circumscribe the horizon of possibilities by narrowing down the agency behind people's stories.

Langerian mindfulness would help clients understand the process of separating themselves from the dominant discourse of their stories. This separation is facilitated through an increase of mindfulness where the client is encouraged to see the difference between what he/she is experiencing as a problem and his/her power of making a choice to act differently towards the problem.

Clients' perceptual, cognitive, behavioral and emotional experiences learned from the past may limit, distort and constrict their phenomenological access to the present moment. Therefore, they may be emotionally or cognitively blocked to see any other alternative way of looking at the story that they have lived through.

Hence the mindfulness we are discussing brings a shift of attention where clients can get out of their socially and culturally constructed world and look for modes that may have been easily unnoticed.

When people are mindlessly drowned into accepting the unchangeability of their stories, they abide by the frequently repeated discourse of the same stories.

Practicing mindfulness allows people to realize that anxiety and depression can be choices one *may* accept. Deep down the foundational prerequisites of the mindful management of depression and anxiety, there lies the power of *choices*.

One way to facilitate the shift of attention for exploring the possibility of multifarious layers and features in a story can transpire through reading and examining stories. Stories can provide a rich platform through which one may come to realize the changeability of one's story. Art, in its broadest sense, can also provide a significant medium where the observer may become mindful of the constructional nature of his/her mode of living through the power of words, images and discourse (see Langer 2009).

In line with the value of understanding the textual and subtextual configuration of stories, Langerian mindfulness highlights the vitality of the deconstruction of stories. When people fail to express their lived story or they are prevented from expressing their story or they are surrounded by people who insist on adopting a pretentious stance instead of relating and connecting to their story, stories appear to operate in a wide variety of infiltrating and indirect contexts: Unexpressed stories do not cease to operate; they appear in different levels of one's intrapersonal and interpersonal relationships.

Langerian mindfulness underlines the role of nonjudgmental, open and flexible listening of therapists in helping clients to freely and comfortably express their lived stories. This is also associated with the therapists' attunement and intersubjectivity and mindful presence where they help the clients experience a sense of empathy, support and flexibility in their therapeutic relationships.

Along with the experiential presence in the therapeutic relationships, clients are encouraged to step outside the experience and observe their lived stories. This often happens through a combination of open questions where the clients are invited to examine and realize how their stories can be deconstructed into elements and features. Through this *mindful deconstruction and decomposition*, clients are encouraged to describe the experience and see how that description may have an impact on their feelings and behaviors. The bottom line here is to help clients understand the *externalization* of the problem: they are not the problem; the problem is separate from them. Through an increase of mindfulness, clients learn to see how mindlessness may have contributed to their identifying themselves with the problem. This may also take place through the therapists' explication of the role of internal vs. external attribution. An in-depth understanding of the role of attribution would help clients realize how their mind-sets may impose a relationship where change is not possible.

Mindfulness help clients to break themselves free from the problem and realize their own power of control, sensibility, choice and power in creating a new meaning, a new story for themselves. This may happen through a work of art or paying attention to a story, parables, metaphors and poems where the act of noticing can turn out to be an art where the observer makes a discernment of his/her novelty in paying attention to multiple potential layers of a story.

Mindlessness paralyzes people's power of searching for otherwise in their stories (Fatemi 2018). Mindlessness imposes a tunnel vision where the person is placed only in a circumscribing mode where possibilities are denied. This denial would maximize the negativity, weak point and problems in the person's life while ignoring, marginalizing and neglecting his/her strengths. Langerian mindfulness would facilitate the process of finding the dominant stories and their discourses and their power to dictate the impossibility of change, the certainty of the person's identification with the problem situations.

The dialectical journey of noticing new aspects of one's life along with attention to variability would provide the clients to see how their stories can be changeable: There are dimensions, features and aspects in the story that may not have been taken into consideration due to the heavy deluge of negatively induced mindlessness.

When depressed, people may be mindlessly and automatically embedded within the negative repertoire of their recollection, associations, etc. Langerian mindfulness would help clients examine the bright side of their life without denying the dark side. So for a depressed person, the questions would be: *Are there times in your life where you have not experienced what you are experiencing now? What does that suggest? If you have not been always at the mercy of what you are now, does that not suggest that the experience is not equated with you: you are not what you experience?* The goal is to help clients understand how mindlessness would lead people to equate themselves with their mind-sets and thus lose their power of choices.

Through helping the clients explore novel aspects of their situation, we would invite clients to extend their quest, in their own stories, for locating positive sides. Deconstructing the dominant negative stories, their negative predilections and their effects would help clients understand that they can re-author their own story through implementing mindful creativity in constructing a new horizon of possibility.

Helping the clients in action to see the differences between mindlessness and mindfulness and their praxis in giving rise to different modes of realities would serve as a preamble in illustrating the relationship between one's story and one's perspective.

Language can give rise to Langerian mindfulness. This mindfulness would help clients to be vigilant of the language that they can mindfully use and its perlocutionary impacts. Language may imprison or emancipate people as it can revitalize or paralyze people's power of choices.

A phenomenologically based experiential openness towards art and its manifestations or a practical connectedness to stories may help people observe the subtle and rigorous impact of language in creating, shaping, transforming and recreating realities.

A discovery of one's voice, its power and its impact unfolds itself in the process of a mindful therapeutic conversation.

The medium for leading the attention towards the process may vary from a focus to traditionally articulated stories in the collective consciousness where attention towards different layers would espouse finding something fresh in the context of those stories or it can be exemplified in accessing or activating different works of art. The latter may also open up the interactive process of the "I" as the agent and "I" as the actor in the dialectically opulent rich relationships of emergent mindfulness.

With an abundantly experiential exposure to a mindful examination of one's agency, the power of choices may transpire in the diachronic and synchronic observation of one's own narratives. The generative sagacity of the process may contribute to the power to recompose one's narrative with composure and equanimity.

Implications and Guidelines for Mental Health Professionals

Understanding the theoretical and practical implementations of Langerian mindfulness would help psychotherapists to develop a more creative, caring, open and meaningful relationship with their clients.

Applying Langerian mindfulness may facilitate the process of understanding the relationship between performative "I" and the reflective and reflexive "I" in the context of art and psychotherapy.

Psychotherapists are invited to apply such mindfulness in helping clients to freely and comfortably express their lived experiences and stories.

Through increasing the power of mindful expressiveness, clients may learn to distinguish between the dominant story of their life and the often ignored discursive layers of their narratives.

Voice is an essential component of implementing Langerian mindfulness. Therapists need to help clients look for "missing voices" in their story and to search for the unexpressed voices or the ones that have been lost in the dominant discourses of oppressive and disempowering narratives.

A change in language may lead to an existential transformation. Through a recondite implementation of Langerian mindfulness, clinicians need to help clients experience the infinite power of language in creating and constructing novel realities. This may entail an ontologically mindful leap beyond the borders of ordinary discourse where signification of signifiers and signified may have been mindlessly established. Visual arts, poetry, films, stories and visualization can be creatively explored in the context of Langerian mindfulness to put this goal into effect.

References

Davidson, J. R. (2000). *Anxiety, Depression and Emotion*. New York: Oxford University Press.

Fatemi, S. M. (Ed.). (2016a). *Critical Mindfulness*. Cham: Springer.

Fatemi, S. M. (2016b). Langerian Mindfulness and Liminal Performing Spaces. In A. L. Baltzell (Ed.), *Mindfulness and Performance (Current Perspectives in Social and Behavioral Sciences)* (pp. 112–124). New York: Cambridge University Press.

Fatemi, S. M. (2016c). Mindfulness and Perceived Control: Controlling the Impossibility of Controllability. In J. W. Reich & F. J. Infurna (Eds.), *Perceived Control: Theory, Research, and Practice in the First 50 Years* (pp. 131–146). New York: Oxford University Press.

Fatemi, S. M. (2018). *The Psychological Power of Language*. New York: Routledge.
Fatemi, S. M., Ward, E. D., & Langer, E. J. (2016). Peak Performance: Langerian Mindfulness and Flow. In A. L. Baltzell (Ed.), *Mindfulness and Performance (Current Perspectives in Social and Behavioral Sciences)* (pp. 101–111). New York: Cambridge University Press.
Hayes, S., Masuda, A., Bissett, R., Luoma, J., & Guerrero, L. (2004). DBT, FAP, and ACT: How Empirically Oriented are the New Behavior Therapy Technologies? *Behavior Therapy, 35, 35–54.*
Kabat-Zinn, J. (2003). Mindfulness-based Interventions in Context: Past, Present, and Future. *Clinical Psychology: Science and Practice, 10*(2), 144–156.
Kabat-Zinn, J. (2005). *Coming to Our Senses: Healing Ourselves and the World Through Mindfulness*. New York: Hyperion.
Langer, E. J. (1975). The Illusion of Control. *Journal of Personality and Social Psychology, 32*, 311–328.
Langer, E. J. (1989). *Mindfulness*. Reading: Addison- Wesley.
Langer, E. J. (2000). *Mindful Learning. Current Directions in Psychological Science, 9*, 220–223.
Langer, E. J. (2005). *On Becoming an Artist: Reinventing Yourself Through Mindful Creativity*. New York: Ballantine Books.
Langer, E. J. (2009). *Counterclockwise: Mindful Health and the Power of Possibility*. New York: Ballantine Books.
Lieblich, A., Tuval-Mashiach, R., & Zilber, T. (1998). *Narrative Research: Reading, Analysis and Interpretation*. Thousand Oaks, CA: Sage.
Linehan, M., Dimeff, L., Reynolds, S., Comtois, K., Welch, S., Heagerty, P., & Kivlahan, D. R. (2002). Dialectical Behavior Therapy Versus Comprehensive Validation Therapy Plus 12–Step for the Treatment of Opioid Dependent Women Meeting Criteria for Borderline Personality Disorder. *Drug and Alcohol Dependence, 67*(1), 13–26.
Segal, Z. V., Williams, J. M. G., & Teasdale, J. D. (2002). *Mindfulness-Based Cognitive Therapy for Depression: A New Approach to Preventing Relapse*. New York: Guilford Press.
White, M. (2007). *Maps of Narrative Practice*. New York: Norton & Company.
White, M., & Epston, D. (1990). *Narrative Means to Therapeutic Ends*. New York: Norton & Company.

4

Film, Mental Health and Therapy

Gurvinder Kalra, Dinesh Bhugra, and Antonio Ventriglio

Introduction

For more than a century now, films have played a crucial role in shaping the social, political and cultural psyche of our world. And, through film, much can be learnt about cultural norms and cultural differences, increasing our understanding and awareness of cultural influences, cultural sensitivities and commonalities. Films not only are a source of endless entertainment

G. Kalra (✉)
Flynn Acute Adult Inpatient Psychiatric Unit, Latrobe Regional Hospital Mental Health Services, Traralgon, Victoria, Australia

D. Bhugra
Health Service & Population Research Department, Institute of Psychiatry, Psychology and Neuroscience, King's College London, London, UK
e-mail: dinesh.bhugra@dineshbhugra.net

A. Ventriglio
Institute of Clinical and Experimental Medicine, University of Foggia, Foggia, Italy

B. Kirkcaldy (ed.), *Psychotherapy, Literature and the Visual and Performing Arts*, Palgrave Studies in Creativity and Culture, https://doi.org/10.1007/978-3-319-75423-9_4

but have a potential educational and therapeutic impact as well. Most importantly films which depict personal and family dynamics, social norms and mental illness can shape the public's attitudes to mental illness.

It is important to note that cinematic portrayals of mental disorders often reinforces stereotypes and may not have a positive effect on destigmatizing mental illness. But when films portray mental illness in a humane and empathetic manner, they can help to foster better understanding of many conditions and disorders, including dementia, depression, bipolar disorders and so on. Teaching with film can also be incorporated into medical studies to create a positive impact on medical students and other health professionals.

Our chapter discusses this important role that films have played and continue to play in society as a whole and also particularly in relation to the field of psychiatry with a specific focus on how they portray mental illness and therapy and shape our perception of these issues. We begin by outlining how each one of us got personally interested in the field of films as arts in relation to the field of psychiatry.

GK

As a child, I have grown up in a family that used to immerse itself in movie watching every weekend or when a new blockbuster hit nearby cinema theatres. Films have always lured me as a person, due to the dramatization of various issues, from their storylines, the characters playing these issues and the overall centre stage that they enjoyed through such portrayals. The very experience of getting immersed along with my family in these portrayals was such a pleasure that I forgot much of the dismays of life growing up. I saw first-hand how this entire experience of getting ready to go movie watching, watching the movie and then having endless discussions on them consumed so much of our time. In this process, I also realized how some characters caught my attention more than the others, and these portrayals lingered in my mind for longer periods than I would have expected them to. Many such characters, I soon realized, were mirroring what I was actually seeing in real life around me on a day-to-day basis. They were depicting real-life relationships between parents, relationships between parents, spouses and siblings. They depicted social issues such as love marriages or love relationships between the rich and the poor and questioned the social mores that surrounded these issues in the Indian society. They seemed to give voice to those who didn't have any! Amidst all these melodramatic portrayals, I noticed that by investing all that time and energy in watching these films and then discussing them afterwards, my attitudes towards these social issues were getting subtly affected. This was also, not surprisingly, true for those who I watched these films with, my family.

This childhood experience gave birth to an interesting curiosity in me regarding how films and film characters do what they do. With this curious mind and wanting to care for others, I landed in the discipline of health care and then, later, psychiatry. Taking up psychiatry increased my curiosity about human suffering and how we could help those who are suffering. One way that I could see was to interview these individuals and allow them to open a window for me into their suffering. However understandably this was not always feasible. This is where the artistic portrayals of mentally ill and their struggles in films came in handy for me, and I started to see films more for education than for entertainment.

AV

My interest in arts, film and music dates back to my earlier professional training. I trained as a musician and obtained academic degrees in the disciplines of organ and harpsichord. In my training and teaching, I implement films and arts as a medium. I have written on Italian films and how they portray mental illness and their potential in increasing stigma, on the one hand, but if used vigilantly, such medium can help illustrate psychopathology and offer guidelines for the management of mental illness.

DB

As a practising psychiatrist, I have always been intrigued and amazed by the way mentally ill characters have been portrayed in films. Coming from a country that views cinema as a major source of entertainment, no doubt, I have always had interest in cinema. Having had my early training in medicine in the East, India, and then psychiatric training in the West, the UK, I have also been curious about how culture impacts on mental illness and its presentation to mental health professionals. This also meant an interest in how mental illness was represented in films which I believe form a significant part of a culture. Films can give us an in-depth insight into the sociocultural mores of a society and how that society deals with various issues. Hence they can be used as an important learning tool for anthropological studies. Through my first in-depth work on Hindi cinema, *Mad Tales from Bollywood: Portrayal of Mental Illness in Conventional Hindi Cinema*, I looked at how we as mental health professionals could read a film in order to understand how culture, mental illness and cinema impact on each other. Having taken a sabbatical to allow me to delve into this project, I could have the leisure of time on my side, in which I realized how films not only are an art form that reflect what happens in the society they are set in but also act as an art form to which the society reacts in a variety of ways.

Films and Society

Films are not only a powerful tool for providing entertainment but also effective means of transmission of important sociocultural and political messages. A film in its entirety delivers both verbal and visual messages contemporaneously often reinforced with congruous background music. This marriage of the visuo-verbal messages is quite a strong medium in which one can expect learning to happen. Films can also provide a window into the unique experiences of individuals that they portray in their storylines. One can look at films as an integral part of any culture since they often portray important sociocultural issues and in this process reflect the prevailing sociocultural mores from the societies in which they are produced. The relationship between films and society is thus often bidirectional. Films portray various social issues and in this process may impact on these issues or the way they are perceived or dealt by the viewers and the larger society. The 1970s film, *One Flew Over the Cuckoo's Nest* is a classic example of a film that portrayed the condition of psychiatric institutions in the early twentieth-century society. It not only gave a face to the general view that the society held towards psychiatry as a discipline of medicine but also affected this view. This was around a time when the recovery movement in psychiatry began through the civil rights and disabilities movements (Davidson et al. 2010).

Along with portraying issues, films can be a powerful messenger and shape the perceptions of the audience on a range of subjects (Pautz 2015). Pautz (2015) used two films *Argo* and *Zero Dark Thirty* as case studies to see how they affect the opinion of viewers about government and found about a quarter of viewers' opinions about government were positively affected after watching these two films. Kalra (2013) used the movie club approach to see how film viewing impacted on the attitudes of psychiatry trainees towards male homosexuality and found a positive change that sustained over a period of one year.

Although most of us watch films for entertainment, part of the process also involves contemplation or reinforcing of the issues that are portrayed on screen (Lehman and Luhr 2003). The differences in our perceptions of these issues in films, as what Lehman and Luhr (2003) argue, are key to the assumptions that underlie such perceptions. To highlight this, the authors use a scene from *Dragon: The Bruce Lee Story* (1992), where Bruce Lee (Jason Scott Lee) is watching *Breakfast at Tiffany's* (1961) in a theatre with his girlfriend. A particular scene from the *Breakfast at Tiffany's* is perceived differently by Bruce Lee to other audience members. This scene uses the character of an Asian man, Mr. Yunioshi, to bring in a comic feel, showing him banging his head on a lamp, jumping up and stumbling into things in his apartment. While the scene does evoke a comic relief for the entire audience, Bruce Lee feels the opposite to the point that he leaves the theatre getting upset. Thus a single and a simple scene leads to different reactions in the audience. It is then easy to understand why and how portrayal of complex societal issues such as infidelity, extramarital affairs, extremist ideologies or homosexuality lead to multiple reactions in not only the audience members who watch the film but also those who do not. A classic example of this can be found in the reactions to the portrayal of female homosexuality in the 1996 film *Fire* by Indo-Canadian filmmaker Deepa Mehta, which was the first mainstream Hindi film to touch upon this issue. While a section of the Indian society praised the film for the way it handled a sensitive issue in Indian society, the remaining section rejected the theme claiming it was against the existing cultural mores. It is easy to see how this could happen, given that we ourselves may feel quite differently about different themes in different films.

It is also important to understand that it is not just about the reactions that films or film scenes evoke in us as viewers but also about how they shape our ideas or opinions about various issues. Bollywood films, for instance, have a high influence on shaping social attitudes in not only the Indian subcontinent but also different parts of the world among the Indian diaspora (Akthar 2005). Films are often a source of connection for people with their culture, ancestral history and ideology. It is likely that an Australian Aboriginal person living in the present could become more aware of the past Aboriginal history by watching films like *Rabbit-Proof Fence* (2002). In a similar vein, an Indian migrant may feel (re)connected to the Indian culture by watching a film that portrays celebrations like festivals or weddings (e.g., *Vivah*, 2006, English translation: Marriage) or films with themes of migration and Indian diaspora (e.g., *Aa Ab Laut Chalen*, 1999, English translation: Come, Let Us Return Now; *Dilwale Dulhania Le Jayenge*, 1995, English translation: The Big-Hearted Will Take Away the Bride).

Films and Psychiatry

Psychiatry has long been a favoured discipline for many filmmakers, who have used various mental illnesses or mentally ill characters as the main theme of their films' storylines. One can find an endless list of films that portray issues ranging from schizophrenia, bipolar disorder to substance use disorders, grief and suicide. While the use of psychiatric themes in films has successfully evoked curiosity and interest in the viewers, it is also known to influence broader public attitudes to mental illness (McDonald and Walter 2009). It has been stated that the film *One Flew Over the Cuckoo's Nest* (1975) can be a keystone of a future archaeological reconstruction project to understand a twentieth-century psychiatric institution (Collins 2017). This observation by Collins clearly underscores the impact that this film from the 1970s has made on the history of psychiatry. Watching films can also have an impact on viewers' attitudes towards less-discussed social issues such as medical ethics (Alexander et al. 2005), grief (Furst 2007), homosexuality (Mazur and Emmer-Sommer 2002) and transgenderism (Kalra 2015). However, this may not be as simplistic as viewers watching a film with a psychiatric theme and taking in all that is seen. It is complicated by the fact that most cinematic portrayals of mental illness are complex, often negative and influenced by general social stereotypes about mental illness (Bhugra 2005). Often the way mental illness is represented in these films can be an important determinant of how the viewers will receive and perceive those with mental illness. The film director's notions of mental illness and mentally ill are likely influenced by the sociocultural milieu in which the director lives or has grown up. This will affect how the director then handles these issues in his/her work. Unfortunately, in this process, the director loses control over how these issues will be perceived by those who watch this work. Much of this will be, as discussed below, affected by the viewers' own life story and cognitive capacity.

Most films deal with the following themes in psychiatry: *mental illness and the mentally ill*, the *power differentials* in the profession of psychiatry and *boundary violations* in psychotherapeutic relationships.

Readers can easily find a list of films on mental illness from various sources (Kalra 2011; Wedding and Niemiec 2014). What is interesting about these films is that most of them tend to sway towards using psychotic spectrum disorders in their storylines, mainly because directors can play with such themes in a multitude of ways often to their own advantage, including (but not limited) to create suspense (e.g., *Shutter Island*, 2001) and comic stances (e.g., *One Flew Over the Cuckoo's Nest*, 1975), and evoke empathy or simply as a narrative of the mentally ill portraying their experiences with their illnesses (e.g., *The Snake Pit*, 1948; *A Beautiful Mind*, 2001). Possibly using psychotic spectrum disorders provides the filmmakers with the 'other-ness' to their stories that other psychiatric disorders may not be able to provide. This 'other-ness' is the lesser known of psychiatric illnesses, is usually more stigmatized and is feared by the viewers. It is also within such films that filmmakers bring in the angle of treatment or therapy in mental illness. This could be subtly portrayed as with the side effects of antipsychotic medications in *A*

Beautiful Mind (2001) or more deeply dealt with such as in *Side Effects* (2013). Again the viewer has to be quite astute in order to understand these portrayals before accepting them in entirety. While the former deals with actual side effects of antipsychotic medications and how this impacts on individual functioning, the latter film goes beyond what could be expected and uses a range of thrilling and dramatic side effects to portray collateral damage done by psychotropic medications.

Out of all the films till date, *One Flew Over the Cuckoo's Nest* (1975) is probably the most relevant to the history of psychiatry as a discipline. It came at a time when psychiatry saw the deinstitutionalization movement as a result of the failure of 'moral therapy' model from the 1800s, inhuman conditions in regimented asylums and discovery of psychotropic medications in the 1950s. This film gave an insight into the often repressive and overcrowded conditions of psychiatric hospitals and the power differences between patients and psychiatric professionals. This was also the time when the current recovery movement in psychiatry was at its nascent stage and people with long-term mental illnesses were beginning to write about their experiences of coping with their symptoms, getting better and gaining an identity despite their mental illness. The outcome of this was a reconsideration of the notion of outcome and expertise in psychiatry as we see it today. The protagonist in this film, Randle McMurphy (Jack Nicholson), feigns mental illness in order to escape prison sentence. Although he gets sent to the mental hospital, he soon realizes the similarities of mental health system to the prison system. As much as this film highlighted power differentials, it also brought to the fore discussions about some basic ethical principles in health care, such as autonomy, beneficence and non-maleficence.

Many subsequent films have continued to play with another similar related theme, for example, *Dressed to Kill* (1980). A thriller by genre, this film follows the story of Liz Blake (Nancy Allen), who is the only witness to Kate's murder, and raises some serious boundary violation themes. Dr. Robert Elliott (Michael Caine) is the psychiatrist for both the murdered victim (Kate) and the witness (Liz), and a prevalent theme in his consults with both these women is that of sexual boundary violation with them. Although at first it appears that the theme is just about sexual boundary violations in psychiatric consultation, it soon becomes clear (as the suspense becomes clearer) that it is related to psychopathology in the consulting psychiatrist. Dr. Robert is portrayed as a transgender patient with possible underlying dissociative identity disorder. Going by the clusters described by Schoener and Gonsiorek (1989), Dr. Robert appears to most aptly fall in the cluster of psychotic personality or sociopathic/narcissistic character disorder. The exact prevalence of such boundary violations is difficult to know due to under-reporting but is generally considered to be somewhere between 2% and 6% in psychiatry (Gartrell et al. 1986; Quadrio 1996). Although the boundary violation portrayals in *Dressed to Kill* (1980) appear being initiated by the two female clients, the motives behind these are not discussed in any detail and are best left to the imagination of the viewer. The gendered dyads that are used in this film to represent these violations are reflective of what studies show about them: majority of such violations having occurred between male psychiatrists and female patients (Gartrell et al. 1986). Looking at the rarity of such violations and the associated themes that the filmmakers tend to throw in their film storylines, one can only imagine what the lone viewer watching such films thinks about psychiatry or psychiatrists.

To add to the above list of psychiatric themes in films, Bhugra and Kalra (2015) note that one could look at film storylines through a psychoanalytic lens. In their chapter on psychoanalysis in Bollywood cinema, Bhugra and Kalra (2015) note that psychoanalysis and cinema have evolved in parallel and that the former has influenced the latter in a significant manner (Bergstrom 1999). They discuss a few Hindi films that portray the Indian notions and perceptions of Oedipal complex (for details, see Bhugra and Kalra 2015). Again from the perspective of the director, this may not have been the initial goal (when making the film), but as Bhugra and Kalra (2015) stress, this could interestingly and definitely be an angle to watch films from.

Therapy in Films

As observed earlier in this chapter, films with psychiatric themes of mental illness and the mentally ill may also touch upon treatment issues, which may include both psychopharmacological and psychotherapeutic interventions. Interestingly but not surprisingly, these portrayals may be weaved together with the other two themes, power differentials and boundary violations, making an easy recipe for a film that will maintain curiosity in the viewers. In the era when psychiatry as a discipline did not have many medications to choose from its repertoire, a lot of treatment involved using existing medications in higher doses to the point that they made patients appear like zombies. *One Flew Over the Cuckoo's Nest* (1975), while using some mentally ill patients in the asylum to create a comic stance (such as patients maintaining odd postures and staring through the windows), also showed many of them being given medications in an asylum ritualistic way, patients queuing up daily for their medications at the same time. The focus is not so much on the reasons for them being administered these pills or their side effects. This becomes clear when Mr. McMurphy asks the reason why he was being given the pills and is told by the nurse that they will help him feel better. Similarly, one can only see patients with medication side effects in the background in several scenes with the foreground being occupied with another issue that is given a higher importance. An example of this is the first time that Nurse Ratched conducts a group session with the ward patients. While the entire focus is on issues related to Mr. Harding that she discusses from the last meeting with a possible intention (in the film plot) to introduce these to the viewers and also to Mr. McMurphy, one can see a patient sitting in the background almost blankly staring through the window while his left hand shows what one could interpret as severe tardive dyskinesia. The film also subtly touches upon other issues in psychiatric treatment such as enforced medication in an asylum setting, patient choices, autonomy, non-adherence (e.g., when Mr. McMurphy 'cheeks' his medications and later on shows them to Mr. Harding), medication sharing between patients and so on.

The most striking impact of *One Flew Over the Cuckoo's Nest* appears on the use of ECT as a treatment modality, where it is used as a means of controlling the uncontrolled Mr. McMurphy. Obviously this portrayal of ECT is nowhere close to the advances that it has seen over the last four decades. However, unfortunately such inaccurate portrayals of ECT continue in both Hollywood and Bollywood films (Sharma and

Malik 2013). Andrade et al. (2010) reviewed depiction of ECT in Hindi cinema from 1967 to 2008 and found 13 Hindi films with referrals or depictions of ECT, almost all of which were inaccurate and overly dramatized. Interestingly, both in Hollywood (McDonald and Walter 2009) as well as in Bollywood films (Andrade et al. 2010), ECT administration has been used as a punitive measure for questionable clinical indications. This possibly reflects the wider public attitude (Teh et al. 2007; McFarquhar and Thompson 2008; Chakrabarti et al. 2010) in the societies that these films come from, both the West (Hollywood) and the East (Bollywood).

In the same scene of Nurse Ratched's group session in *One Flew Over the Cuckoo's Nest* (1975) discussed earlier, although at first sight it appears a general discussion of Mr. Harding's suspicions on his wife, it soon appears to spiral down in a chaotic disarray where each of the patients involved start yelling at the other. While it appears that the intention of the director would have been to portray a common group discussion session in a mental health ward, it alludes more to a group psychotherapy type setting. What gives it more of a comical stance for both the viewer of the film and Mr. McMurphy is the way the session is started off by Nurse Ratched but left to spiral down in its own predictable way without any intervention by anyone including herself or other team members. She is thus rendered a mere passive spectator to the entire session similar to Mr. McMurphy and the film viewers.

Within the area of psychotherapy, Bhugra and Kalra (2015) discuss a few realms of psychotherapeutic relationships including transference, countertransference and boundary issues in Hindi films and point out how these interesting snippets are used as a dramatic device within a clinical context in film storylines. Such snippets not only generate an element of curiosity and interest in the viewer but also provide a common strand through the story and help move the story from the start to the climax which seems to hold some sort of a resolution of the issue at hand. The use of such psychotherapeutic elements is not infrequent in Hollywood cinema as discussed earlier and has been a favourite there too.

In common parlance, we as viewers go to see films for various reasons. It could be for sheer entertainment, for pleasure or for merely killing time. What is likely to happen in these cinema viewings is a subtle process of adult learning as described by Kolb (Kolb 1984). Kolb's 'experiential learning model' is one of the best-known models of adult learning that describes adult learning as happening in four stages, beginning with 'concrete experience' and passing through 'reflective observation', 'abstract conceptualization' and 'active experimentation', after which the cycle is often repeated. The viewer watching a film probably participates quite 'concretely' in the entire experience of on-screen portrayal of issues and characters. Given the wide gamut of issues that are part of the storylines of scores of such films, it is highly likely that many such portrayals may be actual representations of life experiences of viewers themselves. It is then inevitable for the viewer to see his/her own reflection in these portrayals and hence identify with the characters in the storylines, the so-called heroes and villains. This identification and possible introjection is also likely to impact on viewer's cognitive processing of the issues that on-screen characters are dealing with. It is thus likely to lead to a conceptual analysis of the experience, wherein the viewer analyses how the on-screen character dealt with an issue in focus in order to get a particular set of consequences. This reflection and analysis may then allow the viewer to apply this in real-life situation outside of the cinematic theatre, resulting in either the same (as the on-screen) or an entirely different set of consequences.

It is thus easy to draw parallels between this process of film viewing and the process of psychotherapy. Prior to going to see a film, the viewer has to plan and (possibly) purchase tickets. During the screening, there is always an introductory segment of the film, where the viewer is introduced to the theme of the film and the characters who will be playing this theme. Various complexities treading these themes and characters are then portrayed in a way that is best suited to the needs of the film's director, most crucial of which is entertainment since that is most likely the basic aim of the director. However, there is no control over how these themes are taken in by the viewers, who are likely to perceive and interpret them based on their own life stories and cognitive processing abilities. Nevertheless, within this theatrical setting, adult learning can and does happen as discussed in the earlier section. This learning can pave way for therapeutic outcomes where viewers can look at the on-screen characters, relate to them and how they deal with their issues and apply it in their own lives. Films can thus be used in therapeutic sessions to catalyse the process of understanding one's problems, finding hope, and sometimes to come to reality with one's repressed emotions (Hesley and Hesley 1998). Hesley and Hesley (2001) also argue that this can enhance traditional therapy outcomes, although they also caution readers to be sensitive and make informed use of this modality. The primary author (GK) of this chapter has similarly and successfully used films in a therapeutic context in both his routine work such as with clients presenting with simple adjustment disorders (e.g., portrayal of resilience in *The Diving Bell and the Butterfly*, 2007) and also in his work with sexual minorities, especially with individuals presenting with gender-related concerns. One example of such use by him has been the film *Ma Vie En Rose* (English translation: My Life in Pink, 1997), which follows the family of Ludovic, who is biologically born as a boy but feels like a girl. As much as the film portrays the trials and tribulations of the family, it also shows how they come to terms with the reality of their child, providing food for thought to many such parents who struggle with gender issues in their own children.

Guidelines for Health Practitioners

It is thus clear that psychiatry has been the girlfriend of filmmakers since the start of cinematic era and that this status quo will be maintained into the future. This fact is important for mental health-care providers to know for the simple reason that films will continue to reflect societal attitudes and also shape them. Hence it is relevant for them to know whether these films portray mental health issues positively or negatively, as either of these will likely impact help-seeking attitudes of individuals struggling with mental illness. Pathways into mental health care are seemingly open to influence from films as well. Consider, for example, an on-screen portrayal of a character with possible mental illness who is shown to visit informal or traditional sources of care such as shamans or even exorcists and demonologists (e.g., in *Insidious*, 2010) versus another who visits an on-screen psychiatrist (e.g., *A Beautiful Mind*, 2001). The outcome in each of these cases is highly likely to influence the pathway that the viewer will take into mental health care if required. Other factors that will influence this decision include the type of portrayal, attitude of characters towards mental illness and help seeking from a mental health professional, severity of the mental illness, use of fear or comic elements in this portrayal, professionalism of the on-screen mental health professional and lastly sociocultural factors in which the viewer experiences this portrayal.

Being aware of myths and misconceptions that films promulgate is also helpful to mental health professionals as it would inform their clinical practice and mental health advocacy efforts. Films such as *Peacock* (2010) and *Split* (2016) portray mentally ill individuals as being inherently violent and base their storylines on thrilling dramatics rather than on evidence. But again the use of violence in cinema has been an integral ingredient since its inception and is less likely to completely disappear from the basket of themes for filmmakers. Health-care professionals need to be mindful of violence in any film character versus violence in a mentally ill character as the latter is likely to strengthen negative stereotypes of mentally ill individuals. Alternately, any normalization of help-seeking process in mentally ill by filmmakers is bound to be positive both for the viewer and also for the profession of psychiatry, presenting them in a positive light.

For mental health professionals, engaging and collaborating with filmmakers to influence their understandings and hence how they handle mentally ill characters in their work could be the first step in helping film portrayals become positive. A successful example of this initiative is that of Broadcast Thought, a group of three psychiatrists—Eric Bender, Praveen Kambam and Vasilis Pozios—who provide expert consultation to the entertainment industry regarding portrayals of mental health–related issues (http://www.broadcastthought.com/what-is-broadcast-thought/). Some authors have also suggested interdisciplinary training collaborations between psychiatry residency and journalism training programmes to enhance positive representations and destigmatize psychiatry in the wider media (Campbell et al. 2009).

References

Akthar, S. (2005). *Freud Along the Ganges: Psychoanalytic Reflections on the People and Culture of India*. New York: Other Press.

Alexander, M., Lenahan, P., & Pavlov, A. (2005). *Cinemeducation: A Comprehensive Guide to Using Film in Medical Education*. Abingdon: Radcliffe.

Andrade, C., Shah, N., & Venkatesh, B. (2010). The Depiction of Electroconvulsive Therapy in Hindi Cinema. *Journal of ECT, 26*(1), 16–22.

Bergstrom, J. (1999). Introduction: Parallel Lines. In J. Bergstrom (Ed.), *Endless Night: Cinema and Psychoanalysis* (pp. 1–23). Berkeley: University of California Press.

Bhugra, D. (2005). *Mad Tales from Bollywood: Portrayal of Mental Illness in Conventional Hindi Cinema*. Oxford: Taylor & Francis.

Bhugra, D., & Kalra, G. (2015). Applying Psychoanalysis to Hindi Cinema. In L. Huskinson, & T. Waddell (Eds.), *Eavesdropping: The Psychotherapist in Film and Television*. New York: Routledge. ISBN: 978-0-415-81409-6.

Campbell, N. N., Heath, J., Bouknight, J., Rudd, K., & Pender, J. (2009). Speaking out for Mental Health: Collaboration of Future Journalists and Psychiatrists. *Academic Psychiatry, 33*(2), 166–168.

Chakrabarti, S., Grover, S., & Rajagopal, R. (2010). Perceptions and Awareness of Electroconvulsive Therapy Among Patients and their Families: A Review of the Research from Developing Countries. *Journal of ECT, 26*(4), 317–322.

Collins, A. (2017). One Flew Over the Cuckoo's Nest: Dean Brooks - Psychiatry in the Movies. *British Journal of Psychiatry, 210*(4), 297.

Davidson, L., Rakfeldt, J., & Strauss, J. (2010). *The Roots of the Recovery Movement in Psychiatry: Lessons Learned*. Hoboken: Wiley-Blackwell.

Furst, B. A. (2007). Bowlby Goes to the Movies: Film as a Teaching Tool for Issues of Bereavement, Mourning and Grief in Medical Education. *Academic Psychiatry, 31*, 407–410.

Gartrell, N., Herman, J., Olarte, S., Feldstein, M., & Localio, R. (1986). Psychiatrist-Patient Sexual Contact: Results of a National Survey. I: Prevalence. *American Journal of Psychiatry, 143*(9), 1126–1131.

Hesley, J. W., & Hesley, J. G. (1998). *Rent Two Films and Let's Talk in the Morning: Using Popular Movies in Psychotherapy*. Wiley: University of California.

Hesley, J. W., & Hesley, J. G. (2001). *Rent Two Films and Let's Talk in the Morning: Using Popular Movies in Psychotherapy* (2nd ed.). Wiley: University of Michigan.

Kalra, G. (2011). Psychiatry Movie Club: A Novel Way to Teach Psychiatry. *Indian Journal of Psychiatry, 53*, 258–260.

Kalra, G. (2013). Sensitizing Psychiatry Trainees Towards Male Homosexuality: A Movie Club Approach. *Journal of Contemporary Medical Education, 1*(2), 106–112.

Kalra, G. (2015). Hijras in Bollywood Cinema. *International Journal of Transgenderism, 16*, 160–168.

Kolb, D. (1984). *Experiential Learning as the Source of Learning and Development*. Englewood Cliffs: Prentice Hall.

Lehman, P., & Luhr, W. (2003). *Thinking About Movies: Watching, Questioning, Enjoying*. Malden: Blackwell.

Mazur, M. A., & Emmers-Sommer, T. M. (2002). The Effect of Movie Portrayals on Audience Attitudes About Non-Traditional Families and Sexual Orientation. *Journal of Homosexuality, 44*(1), 157–179.

McDonald, A., & Walter, G. (2009). Hollywood and ECT. *International Review of Psychiatry, 21*(3), 200–206.

McFarquhar, T. F., & Thompson, J. (2008). Knowledge and Attitudes Regarding Electroconvulsive Therapy Among Medical Students and the General Public. *Journal of ECT, 24*(4), 244–253.

Pautz, M. C. (2015). *Argo* and *Zero Dark Thirty*: Film, Government, and Audiences. *Political Science & Politics, 48*(1), 120–128.

Quadrio, C. (1996). Sexual Abuse in Therapy: Gender Issues. *Australian and New Zealand Journal of Psychiatry, 30*, 125–133.

Schoener, G. R., & Gonsiorek, J. C. (1989). Assessment and Development of Rehabilitation Plans for the Therapist. In G. R. Schoener, J. C. Gonsiorek, J. H. Milgrom, E. T. Luepker, & R. M. Conroe (Eds.), *Psychotherapists' Sexual Involvement with Clients: Intervention and Prevention* (pp. 401–420). Walk-In Counseling Center: Minneapolis.

Sharma, B., & Malik, M. (2013). Bollywood Madness and shock Therapy: A Qualitative and Comparative Analysis of Depiction of Electroconvulsive Therapy in Indian Cinema and Hollywood. *International Journal of Culture and Mental Health, 6*(2), 130–140.

Teh, S. P., Helmes, E., & Drake, D. G. (2007). A Western Australian Survey on Public Attitudes Toward and Knowledge of Electroconvulsive Therapy. *International Journal of Social Psychiatry, 53*(3), 247–273.

Wedding, D., & Niemiec, R. M. (2014). *Movies and Mental Illness: Using Films to Understand Psychopathology* (4th ed.). Boston: Hogrefe Publishing.

5

The Power of the Performing Arts in Healthcare

Bruce Kirkcaldy and Ahmed Hankir

One of the contemporary pioneers in disclosure of one's mental health issues has been Kay Jamison, nominated by the *Time* as 'Hero of Medicine' and herself a sufferer of psychological distress (bipolar affective disorder), which resulted in an attempted suicide when she was 28 years old. Currently she lectures in psychiatry at John Hopkins University School of Medicine (the USA) as well as being an honorary professor in English at the University of St Andrews (the UK). This fusion of interests and passion towards the arts and medicine are eloquently expressed in her utterance:

B. Kirkcaldy (✉)
International Centre for the Study of Occupational and Mental Health, Düsseldorf, Germany

A. Hankir
Bedfordshire Centre for Mental Health Research in association with the University of Cambridge (BCMHR-CU), Cambridge, UK
e-mail: ahmedzakaria@doctors.org.uk

B. Kirkcaldy (ed.), *Psychotherapy, Literature and the Visual and Performing Arts*, Palgrave Studies in Creativity and Culture, https://doi.org/10.1007/978-3-319-75423-9_5

> *They [artists] learn in suffering what they teach in song. An artist survives, describes and transforms psychological pain into an experience with more universal meaning so that his or her own journey becomes one that others thus, better protected, can take.* (Jamison 1993)

Over the last decade there has been an array of publications directed at gathering insights from health professionals who have themselves experienced serious illness whether physical or psychological (e.g. Kirkcaldy 2013). Sparked by an anonymous letter in *The Psychologist* (Dec. 2015), a psychological health practitioner reported experiencing sudden intense emotions coupled with intense fear and hopelessness as a young man and feelings of shame and terror and self-harming. Later he had been cautioned that speaking openly about his borderline personality disorder (BPD) would imply 'a career death'. He felt that there is a dire need to break down the barriers between us (normal professionals) and them (ill patients) which have led to increased compassion he has experienced in his work. Another revelation followed by the former British Psychological Society President J. Hughes (2016) exclaiming that he had been drawn towards clinical psychology in part because of early experiences of panic attack and post-traumatic stress. Moreover, five years after graduation and qualifying as a clinical psychology practitioner, he suffered from 'debilitating bouts of depression' and a diagnosis of bipolar disorder. He too felt encouraged to speak openly about psychological distress to attenuate the associated stigmatisation, and underlined the value of empathy with clients when we ourselves are wounded by psychological health problems.

Personal Motivation in Writing This Chapter

Why did we decide to write this chapter? My decision (BK) to write this chapter was after a career stretching 40 years, almost half of which was spent in clinical research and the latter half in clinical practice focussing on anxiety and depressive disorders. It may be that my decision to enter the helping professions, and further an insatiable appetite to author scientific publications, including book chapters and edited/authored books, arose out of a deep-seated 'demand' on myself to gain an increased insight into my own cultural and family heritage conflicts which seemed associated with my subsequent chronic desire to meet the expectations of others and gain the approval of others. We are born into a family structure coupled with idiosyncratic dynamics, and this appears the singular universe of discourse for a young child. When we approach early adulthood and leave the nuclear family, the exposure to others leads us to question the legitimacy and value of our family of origin's belief systems and values. Looking back, I am certain that my family was dysfunctional—a mother (exposed to the traumatic effects of war) who was anxious and possibly depressive, and a father whom, in hindsight I describe as 'infantile, hysterical and personality disordered with an almost obsessive religious mania', and yet both parents loving in their own way. Family discord was felt daily, and my own problems, which included a speech impediment and social anxiety, an intense fear of death, and an introverted and compulsive neurotic tendency, seemed overlooked by my parents and teachers. Recalling my publications and clinical experience, I have learned much about life and relationships and, more especially, the value of the arts and literature in coping with the daily hassles of life and the more traumatic events that we are confronted with, including serious illnesses of close family members, death of parents and extended family members, tension and disruption of communication among siblings and so on. In my attempts to resolve these problems (and those of my clients), I felt an increasingly sceptical attitude towards the more conservative, rigid medical models of psychological disorders (Kirkcaldy 2013 Kirkcaldy and Siefen 2011) and, more recently, a strong inclination towards the creative arts.

One of the co-authors (AH) constructed a Wounded Healer Program to challenge mental health stigma and to encourage care seeking for psychological problems. The Wounded Healer (TWH) has been described as an innovative method of pedagogy that blends the performing arts with psychiatry and it also utilises the power of storytelling. Through the vehicle of TWH, AH shares his remarkable recovery journey from having been an impoverished and homeless 'service user' to receiving the 2013 Royal College of Psychiatrists Foundation Doctor of the Year Award, which marks the highest level of achievement in psychiatry in the UK.

TWH pays tribute to *Knight's Move Thinking*. Knight's Move Thinking in psychiatry is a thought disorder characterised by discourse that consists of a sequence of unrelated or remotely related ideas. However, Nancy Andreasen argues that Knight's Move Thinking in the context of creativity is not a hallmark of mental illness but rather can be used synonymously with lateral thinking (Andreason 1979).

AH invites audiences to 'our world of metaphor, intrigue, fantasy and deceit' (i.e. the mind of a medic with manic-depressive illness) by providing them with an insight into the subjective experience of Knight's Move Thinking in the context of an artistic temperament. He then re-enacts scenes from films (i.e. *Pulp Fiction*, *The Message*, *The Dark Knight*, *The Last of the Mohicans* and *Blade Runner*) and recites passages from polymaths (Gerard de Nerval) and stanzas from romantic poets (Edgar Allen Poe).

AH has been fortunate enough to deliver TWH to over 50,000 people in 12 countries in five continents worldwide. TWH has also been integrated into the medical school curriculum of four UK universities. Documentary makers from the London College of Communication at the University of the Arts in London also successfully secured funding from the Institute of Inner Vision to commission the production of the Wounded Healer film which is being submitted to film festivals worldwide. Preliminary unpublished research has revealed that the Wounded Healer film is associated with immediate reductions in stigma variables.

Background

Application forms for medical school invariably contain a 'white space' for prospective students to enter a personal statement about why they want to study medicine. A motif or recurrent theme of these statements, no doubt, is that prospective students want to 'help people' (whether applicants genuinely want to 'help people' or not is certainly disputable. Raymond Tallis, in the preface of his magnum opus *Hippocratic Oaths: Medicine and Its Discontents*, argues that 'there are those who use the moral high ground as a platform for self-advancement') (Tallis 2003).

Those who experience disease, inherited or acquired, are often in distress, and as healthcare professionals we are in the unique position to alleviate patients of their suffering with our knowledge, experience, expertise and empathy. There is a disparity of esteem, however, in the policy and provision of mental and physical healthcare, and this not only influences the allocation of resources but also impacts perceptions of illness and disease (https://www.theguardian.com/society/2013/oct/23/mental-health-bed-cuts-ashamed-nhs). People—healthcare professionals and the 'layman'—perceive that mental health conditions are not 'real diseases' (Smith 2002) and as such those who experience them are not really suffering. Take, for instance, what the twentieth-century multi-award-winning American novelist and essayist William Styron had to say in his poignant autobiographical narrative *Darkness Visible* about his first-hand experience with depressive illness:

> *When I was first aware that I had been laid low by the disease, I felt the need, among other things, to register a strong protest against the word "depression". Depression, most people know, used to be termed "melancholia," a word which… crops up more than once in Chaucer, who in his usage seemed to be aware of its pathological nuances. "Melancholia" would still appear to be a far more apt and evocative word for the blacker forms of the disorder, but it was usurped by a noun with blank tonality and lacking any magisterial presence, used indifferently to describe an economic decline or a rut in the ground, a true wimp of a word for such a major illness. … Told that someone has evolved a storm – a veritable howling tempest in the brain, which is indeed what clinical depression resembles like nothing else – even the uniformed layman might display sympathy rather than the standard reaction that "depression" evokes something akin to "So what" or "You'll pull out of it" or "We all have had bad days".* (Styron 2004)

In this compelling excerpt, Styron movingly and evocatively describes, through the medium and the power of the written word, the flaws of reductionism by intimating that the term 'depression' can deprive people who experience this condition the validation that they warrant from genuine suffering. Styron's authoritative account commands the attention of all those who stake a claim in wanting to better understand the subjective experience of depressive illness by providing a precious qualitative insight into this condition. Succinctly put, those who experience mental illness suffer in the same way (if not more since they must fight a crippling battle on two fronts: dealing with the debilitating symptoms of the mental illness itself and enduring the egregious effects of stigma and discrimination that invariably ensue) as those who experience physical illness do and as such are just as deserving of the empathy we unreservedly give to the latter (https://www.time-to-change.org.uk/blog/trishas-story).

We, the authors, argue that working in mental health provides people with the opportunity to help those who are in distress and to alleviate them of their suffering. In a vivacious interview with the President of the World Psychiatric Association, the ever-effervescent Dinesh Bhugra discusses and describes why he decided to become a psychiatrist. Bhugra emphatically exclaims that an orthopaedic surgeon would preoccupy himself or herself with mending broken bones, which never appealed to him (in fact he stated this preoccupation was rather dull). But as a psychiatrist you heal broken minds and broken hearts, and there is no other medical specialty that could be more thrilling, rewarding and challenging than that (Hankir 2014).

But how do we help and serve the most vulnerable people in our society, namely, those who are under psychological distress? In a scintillating interview article for *The Lancet Psychiatry* with mental health systems expert Graham Thornicroft, he authoritatively asserts that the design, development and delivery of mental health services should be service user/consumer led (Langford and Thornicroft 2014). Indeed, Patrick Corrigan, an authority on mental health stigma, conducted a systematic review and meta-analysis of 13 randomised controlled trials on challenging public stigma and revealed that social contact with someone who has first-hand experience of mental illness is the most effective way of reducing public stigma (Corrigan et al. 2012). In other words, *it's the people who have experienced psychological distress who have the power to reduce the stigma associated with it.* Corrigan issues a clarion call to psychiatrists aloft in their ivory towers proclaiming that consumers are 'experts by experience' and as such they should operate at the vanguard of any campaign to challenge mental health stigma and that psychiatrists need to take a back seat. This, of course, is a bitter pill to swallow for some psychiatrists who enjoy the prestige and authority that their profession confers upon them, and to relinquish that power requires humility, a virtue that mental healthcare professionals tend to lack according to service users.

People with mental illness are suffering and are among the most vulnerable in our societies. If you genuinely want to be of service to humankind and humanity, choose a career in psychiatry or mental healthcare

(Hankir and Zaman 2015). If you sincerely desire to help those who are under psychological distress, you must recognise and respect that service users/consumers/patients/experts by experience can play a critical role in the design, development and delivery of mental healthcare services. To guide our approach to the policy and provision of mental healthcare, we must show humility and earnestness and turn to the patients for advice on how best to assess, treat and support them.

The Stigma Attached to Mental Illness

People under psychological distress fear being labelled as 'mad' or being viewed as a person who has 'lost his or her mind'. As such, they may mount a fierce resistance against receiving a diagnosis of mental illness. Diagnoses such as schizophrenia and bipolar affective disorder are loaded with psychopathological connotations which can have far-reaching effects (i.e. it is an established fact that employers are far less likely to recruit someone with a history of mental illness. Moreover, landlords often deny tenancy to a person who suffers from psychopathology. Homelessness and unemployment have both been identified as social determinants for physical and mental ill health) (Corrigan et al. 2003).

Terms such as 'auditory hallucinations' exude stigmatising nuances. Eleanor Longden, an academic affiliated with the Psychosis Research Unit at Manchester University, the UK, has first-hand experience of psychosis. She eventually graduated top of the country in psychology for both her bachelor's and master's degrees, and this remarkable achievement should contribute to debunking the myth that people who experience an 'enduring' mental illness will never recover or succeed in life. Her TED talk, 'Learning from the Voices in My Head', is consciousness raising. She dissects and dismantles psychiatric constructs with her eloquence and erudition. Moreover, she is reluctant to use stigmatising terms such as 'auditory hallucinations' and prefers 'hearing voices' since the latter is more descriptive and less likely to be construed as pejorative. Eleanor vociferously argues that if an individual is (1) not under distress, (2) has insight and (3) is not experiencing any impairment in functioning other than hearing voices, he should not be perceived as pathological or problematic (Longden 2013).

In a recent study, Ellison et al. (2015) explored the effect of renaming mental disorders in order to reduce iatrogenic stigmatisation: *bipolar disorder* was perceived with less fear and social distance than the term 'manic depression', in much the same way that *integration disorder* (rather than 'schizophrenia') was associated with a pronounced endorsement of a biopsychosocial cause coupled with a reduction in dangerousness.

As enumerated above, people experiencing mental illness often lack insight and are in denial. It should come as no surprise then that psychiatrists encounter resistance when they want to initiate a patient on psychotropic medication. The patient might perceive adhering to such treatment as conceding that they are 'mad' or that they have 'lost their mind'. Psychotropic medication also has adverse side effects such as weight gain, hyper-prolactinaemia, troublesome extrapyramidal side effects, sedation and fatal agranulocytosis to name but a few. People on psychotropic medication do not necessarily respond well to treatment and can remain symptomatic (Cuijpers et al. 2014). There is a culture of prescribing pills to treat mental illness which is discussed and described below in the following section.

Kinderman (2017) purports, 'Mental health problems are fundamentally social and psychosocial issues … replace diagnosis with straightforward descriptions of our problems, radically reduce use of medication, and use it pragmatically rather than presenting it as a cure…instead, we need to understand how each of us has learned to make sense of the world, and tailor help to our unique and complex needs.'

Overprescribing of Psychotropic Drugs to Treat Psychological Problems

The prescribing of mind-altering chemicals is both widespread practice (one in five adults in the USA is now taking at least one psychotropic medication) and big business (Americans spent more than $34 billion on drugs for their mental health issues in 2010 alone) (http://www.apa.org/monitor/2012/06/prescribing.aspx).

However, although psychopharmacology has been hailed as 'one of the success stories of modern psychiatry' (Datta 2009), the American

Psychological Association and other reputable organisations have expressed deep concerns that many people with mental health issues are being inappropriately prescribed psychotropic drugs. Indeed, according to a study conducted by the Centers for Disease Control and Prevention (CDC), patients often receive psychotropic medications without ever being evaluated by a mental health professional (http://www.apa.org/monitor/2012/06/prescribing.aspx).

There are multiple theories that have been postulated that attempt to fathom and explain the culture of prescribing psychiatric drugs. Helman proposed that the use of psychotropic drugs is 'embedded in a matrix of social values and expectations' (Helman 2001). Kirkcaldy and colleagues conjecture that '[i]n many Western industrialised societies, "chemical coping" (Pellegrino 1976) and chemical comforters—including tobacco, alcohol, vitamins, marijuana and psychotropic drugs—are consumed to enhance one's emotional state and social relationships and, as such, form a method for dealing with the vicissitudes of daily living' (Kirkcaldy et al. 2011).

The anti-psychiatry movement and other organisations and individuals have not been reticent about their sentiments towards pharmacotherapy. 'Psychiatric drugs do more harm than good,' proclaimed Peter Gøtzsche, professor and director of The Nordic Cochrane Centre in Denmark. In a *British Medical Journal* debate, Gøtzsche attempts to substantiate his controversial claim by reporting that '*more than half a million people over the age of 65 die because of the use of psychiatric drugs every year in the western world*' (Gøtzsche et al. 2015).

Gøtzsche is not alone when it comes to being sceptical about the 'popping of pills' as the most appropriate treatment option for people with mental health problems. After reviewing the published literature, the National Health Service in England adopted cognitive behavioural therapy as a first-line treatment for mild and moderate depression because the risk-benefit ratio is, to quote, 'poor' for antidepressants (http://www.apa.org/monitor/2012/06/prescribing.aspx).

It was perhaps timely, then, that the President of the World Psychiatric Association Professor Dinesh Bhugra and colleagues collectively issued the clarion call that '[t]he mental health of the nation was unlikely to be improved by treatment with psychotropic medication alone' after conducting a large-scale (n = 25,522) national study on psychiatric morbidity in Great Britain (Brugha et al. 2004).

US-based psychiatrist Vivek Datta passionately states in his article entitled 'Neurohawks fight back' (also, to their credit, published in the *British Journal of Psychiatry*) that 'research on psychopharmacology is extremely expensive and may be occurring at the cost of social, epidemiological and psychological research for which it is increasingly difficult to secure funding… such research has created evidenced-based interventions for mental illness. For example, the finding that high expressed emotion in families is associated with greater relapse in schizophrenia led to the development of family intervention (Kuipers et al. 2002)' (Datta 2009).

Lest there be any ambiguity about our position, we, the authors, would like to make it explicitly clear that we do not advocate a 'dichotomous' approach to treating and managing mental illness (indeed, we are ardent supporters of a 'personalised' approach to mental healthcare). We are merely stating that 'one size does not fit all'. There is evidence in favour of both pharmacotherapy and psychosocial interventions in the treatment of mental illness, and what works for one condition might not necessarily work for another. Indeed, most often the best evidence points to the combining of medications with psychosocial interventions.

In a recent study, Cuijpers and co-workers reported that '[t]he differences in effects between psychotherapy and antidepressant medication were small to non-existent for major depression, panic disorder and Seasonal Affective Disorder. We also found evidence that pharmacotherapy was significantly more efficacious in dysthymia, and that psychotherapy was significantly more efficacious in Obsessive Compulsive Disorder' (Cuijpers et al. 2014).

The advancement in neuroimaging techniques has contributed to the 'biologisation' of psychiatry and possibly has fostered a disproportionate amount of attention and resource allocation to psychotropic medication for research on the treatment of mental illnesses. Indeed, there has been significant decline to non-existent provision of arts and dramatherapy in mental health units across the UK. We argue that arts-based therapies can act in synergy with psychiatric medications and should, at the very least, be held with higher regard than it currently is. The performing arts, under which dramatherapy falls under, possesses an extraordinary power. The following section provides a brief overview of dramatherapy and closely aligned narrative and expressive writing as adjuncts to effective therapeutic change.

A Brief Overview of Dramatherapy

> *In the aftermath of September 11th, I witnessed the enormous benefits of these modalities [creative arts therapies] in helping people to express their emotions and have seen Capitol Hill exhibits illustrating the meaningful gains through artistic process*. (Hillary Rodham Clinton) (http://www.nadta.org/what-is-drama-therapy.html)

Before we offer a contemporary definition of dramatherapy, we will go further back in time to antiquity to trace the origin of this 'artform'. Drama ('action') and therapy ('service, healing') are both words of Greek etymology. It should come as no surprise, then, that descriptions of drama and its power to heal are replete in Greek mythology.

Considered as a genre of poetry in general, the dramatic mode has been contrasted with the epic and the lyrical modes ever since Aristotle's *Poetics* (c. 335 BCE)—the earliest work of dramatic theory (Destrée 2016).

Definition of Dramatherapy

The North American Drama Therapy Association (NADTA) was incorporated in 1979 to establish and uphold rigorous standards of professional competence for drama therapists. NADTA defines dramatherapy as:

> *the systematic and intentional use of drama/theatre processes and products to achieve the therapeutic goals of symptom relief, emotional and physical integration, and personal growth. Drama therapy is an active, experiential approach that facilitates the client's ability to tell his/her story, solve problems, set goals, express feelings appropriately, achieve catharsis, extend the depth and breadth of*

inner experience, improve interpersonal skills and relationships, and strengthen the ability to perform personal life roles while increasing flexibility between roles.... Participants can expand their repertoire of dramatic roles to find that their own life roles have been strengthened. (http://www.nadta.org/what-is-drama-therapy.html)

The two masks associated with drama are symbols of the ancient Greek muses, *Thalia* and *Melpomene*. *Thalia* was the muse of comedy (the laughing face), whilst *Melpomene* was the muse of tragedy (the weeping face).

Participants benefiting from dramatherapy span the life spectrum. Client populations may include persons recovering from addiction, dysfunctional families, developmentally disabled persons, abuse survivors, prison inmates, homeless persons, people with AIDS, older adults, at-risk youth and the general public (http://www.nadta.org/what-is-drama-therapy/faq.html).

Research on Dramatherapy

A review of the relationship between art and healing (Stuckey and Nobel 2010) suggests a belief that 'creative expression can make a powerful contribution to the healing process has been embraced in many different cultures. Throughout recorded history, people used pictures, stories, chants as healing rituals ... much philosophical and anecdotal discussion about the benefits of arts and healing, but less empirical research'. They go on to review the field and conclude 'despite methodological and other limitations, the studies ... appear to indicate that creative engagement can decrease anxiety, stress and mood disturbances ... does not contradict the medical view in bringing emotional, somatic, artistic and spiritual dimensions to learning. Rather it complements the biomedical view by focusing on not only sickness and symptoms themselves but the holistic nature of the person' (p. 263).

Sajnani (2014) in an interview of theatre and trauma claimed 'tremendous pressure to redefine what we do in the language of dominant paradigms: instead of building creativity and spontaneity, we are engaged in resilience enhancement; instead of physicality, we are doing stress management; instead of dramatic enactment, we are employing imaginal exposure; instead of embodied, exuberant play, we are improving attachment; instead of witnessing and re-storying we are applying cognitive restructuring'.

There are several areas in which dramatherapy has proven particularly useful. For example, in the treatment of domestic violence. Jennifer Kirk (2015) implemented a multimodal model of dramatherapy which combined drama with art, movement and music. This approach to the arts therapies is also known as an 'integrated arts approach' involving two or more expressive therapies to cultivate awareness, emotional growth and improved relationship to self and other (Kirk 2015). The results revealed significant positive changes in a subset of CORE system scores: for these women, dramatherapy was more effective in reducing psychological distress than key worker sessions.

Kipper and Ritchie (2003) conducted a meta-analysis of 25 experimental design studies examining the effectiveness of 'psychodrama' techniques and concluded, 'Observers of psychodrama have been torn between the favourable clinical impression of the method … and the absence of empirical validation for its multifarious interventions.' Overall, there was a large effect size improvement of the same or better order of magnitude to group psychotherapy. They tried to identify which specific facets of therapy ('role reversal, doubling, and role playing enactment, singularly or together') could add to the therapeutic endeavour.

Daykin et al. (2008) offered a systematic review of research findings in the decade 1994–2004 on the impact of performing arts on health among adolescents (focusing on drama intervention and performance), for example, obesity, coronary heart disease and sexual health. They searched through 17 electronic databases filtering 3670 articles, of which 104 met the criteria. The strongest finding was the influence of drama on peer interaction and social skills. Favourable changes in behaviour among at-risk adolescents and enhancement of social skills, for example, self-confidence and cooperation, improved sexual knowledge and shifts in attitudes associated with availability and access to contraception and increased resistance to drug usage.

Dramatherapy focuses on the importance of contact and connection, and is less based on cognitive ability, making it particularly appropriate for the dementia sufferer. Mechaeil and colleagues conducted a small-scale, quantitative study to explore the effects of dramatherapy on older people suffering from dementia. Positive therapeutic effects were first observed in the evaluations examining the pre- to post-therapy differences. Dramatherapy influence was greatest on levels of *attention and engagement.* Additionally, it was more pronounced in the last stage of therapy, comprising sessions 9–13. A similar pattern was evident on all other factors, in which scores on the final stages of therapy reflected better performance in individuals assigned to dramatherapy. However, the study did reveal that for the factors of happiness and social contact, the sustained effects were in favour of the control group (Mechaeil et al. 2010).

Overall, as Blank (2010) argued, dramatherapy is often a chance to change one's life narrative using diverse modalities such as visual arts, music, poetry and dance and movement. It employs techniques encompassing improvisation, storytelling, theatre games and enactment. 'It provides a context for participants to tell their stories, set goals, solve problems, express feelings, or achieve catharsis.'

Feldman et al. (2010) commented, '[S]ocial-emotional education, spearheaded by Daniel Goleman (1995) have been instrumental in increasing awareness of the important link between social emotional functioning and academic achievement … social-emotional education seems to share quite a few goals with drama therapy, such as building self-awareness, developing social awareness, and relationship skills, improving self-management, fostering responsible decision-making skills, developing the capacity for empathy and effecting behaviour changes' (p. 286).

Some would argue that there lacks a sound theoretical underpinning for dramatherapy, and Frydman (2016) commented, '[S]cope of drama therapy stands to benefit from a continued and critical dialogue with neuroscientific subfields (cognitive affective, developmental, behavioural, neuropsychological, etc) … provides a structural basis for the link between drama therapy and neuropsychology, by enlisting role theory and executive functioning as cooperative and interchangeable frameworks' (p. 41).

Therapeutic Effect of Writing

Furnham (2013) in a short article examined whether 'scribbling may be better than therapy' and claimed, 'This is much more than simply trying to write pretty sentences. It is about singling out experiences, events and people that contributed to one's life. Seeing cause and effect, understanding psychological processes can significantly increase self-understanding. Suddenly things become apparent: patterns observed, explanations obvious. Writing is also often redemptive. And it helps because nearly always it involves some commitment to change.'

Perhaps one of the key figures in inaugurating therapeutic writing was the Jungian psychotherapist Ira Progroff, who used writing exercises to enable individuals to facilitate self-growth and development. He suggested that it increased awareness on diverse aspects of life, promoted connection with the person's real self, and aided in the development of a more meaningful self (cf. www.intensivejournal.org).

Almost a decade earlier, George Kelly (1955) had introduced the concept of a self-disclosure technique, 'self-characterisation', which entailed *writing a character sketch* of oneself in the third person *as if* representing the principal character in a theatre play, and as if he is actually experiencing some form of stress in his current life phase. It was underlined that they should write as if it had been written by a sympathetic and compassionate friend. Kelly was focused on taking an 'inner outlook' that basically was an attempt to capture the language and meaning (constructs) that an individual uses—a non-invasive approach—and thus took a view opposed to the prevalent scientific methodology and diagnostic terminology which remain so pervasive today.

In the article 'Key themes in the study of therapeutic uses of storytelling', Ingemark (2013) suggests that '[t]he most basic proposition—ground zero, so to speak—is that the verbalisation of experience is in itself therapeutic'. And then goes on to cite some of the pioneer work of expressive writing by James Pennebaker:

> [A]ct of disclosing trauma is seen to have beneficial effects, in the form of both health benefits and peace of mind. Inhibiting memories and thoughts of the trauma requires a mental effort that affects the body as well, and

> disclosing them releases this tension, resulting in greater health: blood pressure and heart rate drops, and immune function is improved (Pennebaker 1997, pp. 30–56). Writing also imposes structure on our thoughts and experiences ... elaborating on the same event repeatedly contributes to the organisation of the experience into a coherent narrative; the writing focuses on the most salient features of the trauma, which are crystallised and contemplated in the narrative.

In a book entitled *The Therapeutic Potential of Creative Writing*, Gillian Bolton (2013) asserts, '[W]riting is different from thinking or talking ... act of writing creates and object to which the writer can relate tangibly, visually and aurally. The writing is seen, it can be heard, it can be touched on the page – framed, filed with care, screwed up in a ball, or burnt. And this tangibility lasts over time, to be re-experienced in different frames of mind, different stages of life' (pp. 213–214).

Michael White (2005) in his innovative model of narrative therapy asserted that the person is not the problem; rather the 'problem is the problem itself' and proposed the concept of 'externalising the problem', as the most effective way of dealing with the problem leading us to learn to re-author the problem. This involves generating stories and metaphors to perceive from a different perspective. In this way more value is placed on the personal history (underlining personal resources, strength and social networks) rather than the therapist. He would focus on cues countering the deficit-oriented ('problem-saturated') stories, oppressive stories that dominate our lives. The aim would be to generate liberating stories, offering space and novel avenues for 'alternative stories'.

In a tribute to White's contribution, van Wyk (2017) summarised,

> The narrative therapist would regard psychiatric illnesses as problems outside individuals, who have to learn to cope with these problems and create alternative landscapes of action in which they can function against the problem, not as part of the problem. Unlike the medical psychiatrist, the narrative therapist would take the stance of a nonexpert, in a not-knowing fashion, so that the client is the expert and not the therapist (Anderson and Goolishian 1992; Semmler and Williams 2000). ... approach would aim at deconstructing the limiting boundaries enforced by definitions of psychiatric illnesses, building a rich description that functions against the

general notions of diagnosed psychiatric illnesses. The re-construction defeats problem-saturated stories that entrap individuals, re-storying them into alternative richer stories. (White 1989)

Anderson (personal communication 2015) does not identify her work as narrative therapy, but her approach as *collaborative dialogue*, focussing on a specific kind of relationship and conversation that invites possibilities for newness in meaning and understanding. The distinction is the focus on therapist and client as conversational partners who are in a more rather than less equitable relationship. Together, they jointly create the imagined destination and the paths to reach it. The journey is filled with uncertainty and unpredictability; however, once the destination is reached, it is one with relevance and usefulness for the client because of their participation in creating it. In other words, it is not a therapist led process. With regard to listening, it is not listening in the usual sense as it is referred to in psychological literature but a responsive listening in which professional responses—for example, questions and comments—are informed by a client's story and maintaining coherence with the client's story. It is a listening to try and understand as best as one can, a client's reality, what a client wants the professional to understand. Therefore, understanding from a client's sense-making map/logic rather than from a professional.

These ideas challenge the professional model, an issue addressed by Mattingly (1998) underlining that '[n]arrative studies of patient-doctor communication have addressed power through examination of a subordinate (patient) voice which is in contest with a prevailing and powerful medical voice. Analysis of interchanges between doctors and their patients often show patient narratives as neglected or re-organised through the doctor's "medicalising" discussion … (doctor talk) … gains its perlocutionary power precisely through a set of discursive moves which suppress personal narrative, such as adoption of the passive voice and consequent elimination of agency' (p. 12).

Consistent with these ideas, Anderson and Goolishian (2002) suggest abandoning paradigmatic models that evaluate a client's experience compared to a concept of normality, rather familiarising ourselves with the 'expertise report' of the afflicted individual to gain an 'insight' into the client's perception ('listening' as opposed to 'diagnostic formulation'), that is, client's hypotheses as opposed to 'professional hypotheses'. Hence the role of collaborative therapist ('not-knowing and client-as-expert'), with 'therapist's expertise is in creating a space for and facilitating a process for collaborative relationships and dialogical conversations'. The generative process is more like a process of 'transformation' rather than 'change', 'call(ing) our attention to and not lose sight that the client has a wealth of expertise on his or her own life', and further 'caution us to not value, privilege and worship the expertise of the therapist as a better knower of the client's life and how it should be lived than the client does'.

Practical Tips for Mental Health Practitioners

- Mental health practitioners must take the time to listen to their patients with empathy, earnestness and humility and explore the suffering behind a symptom.
- Narratives from people who have first-hand experience of psychological distress offer precious qualitative insights into these conditions. Reading these narratives may increase empathy towards people with mental health problems.
- Getting to apply expressive writing techniques—'Making room for and giving the client the choice to tell their story in their manner and at their pace … (and) being genuinely interested and curious about the client's story' (Anderson 2009, 2015).
- Use techniques offered by Pennebaker of getting clients to write for four consecutive days, for a fixed period of 15 minutes about the problem that brought them into therapy.
- Wherever and whenever possible, service providers must work in partnership with service users to formulate a management plan that is 'patient centred' and 'evidence based'.
- Healthcare professionals are a common source of stigma reported by people with mental illness. Mental health stigma is like mental illness in the sense that those who *suffer* from these 'conditions' often lack insight and are in denial. Healthcare professionals must be honest with themselves and question if they are a possible source of stigma, and if so challenge it.

- Social contact with people with mental health problems is the most effective way of reducing stigma.
- Mental health practitioners must be careful when communicating with patients and refrain from using terms that patients may construe as stigmatising, that is, 'schizophrenic', 'bipolar', 'auditory hallucinations'. Whenever and wherever possible use descriptive language instead, that is, 'hearing voices' , 'oscillations in mood'.
- Health professionals should advocate a personalised approach to healthcare. 'One size does not fit all'.
- Drugs can have troublesome adverse effects, and patients often resist being started on medication for their mental health.
- Psychotropic medication is overprescribed in the management of mental health problems. Mental health practitioners with prescribing powers should consider all treatment options available before initiating a patient on medication.
- Dramatherapy, which falls under the remit of art therapy, has been defined as *the systematic and intentional use of drama/theatre processes and products to achieve the therapeutic goals of symptom relief, emotional and physical integration, and personal growth.*
- A growing body of evidence is lending support to the use of dramatherapy as an adjunct for treating mental health problems such as dementia. Mental health providers should discuss these treatment options with their patients and educate them about their potential merits and drawbacks.
- Mental health practitioners should offer support and advice to people who must make the difficult decision between concealment and disclosure about their mental illness.
- Service users have also been described as 'experts by experience', and there are case studies of people who have first-hand experience of psychological distress who have been energised to campaign against the stigma attached to mental health problems.

Acknowledgement Thanks go to the personal communication and comments from Harlene Anderson.

References

Anderson, H. (2009). Collaborative Practice: Relationships and Conversations that Make a Difference. In J. Bray & M. Stanton (Eds.), *The Wiley Handbook of Family Psychology* (pp. 300–313). New York: John Wiley & Sons, Inc.

Anderson, H. (2015). Collaborative Therapy. In E. Neukrug (Ed.), *Sage Encyclopedia of Theory of Counseling and Psychotherapy*. Thousand Oaks: Sage Publishing.

Anderson, H., & Goolishian. (1992). The Client is the Expert. A Not Knowing Approach to Therapy. In S. McNamee & K. J. Geren (Eds.), *Therapy as a Social Construction* (pp. 25–29). London: Sage.

Anderson, H., & Goolishian, H. A. (2002). Narrative and Self: Postmodern Dilemmas for Psychotherapy. In D. Fried Schnitman & J. Schnitman (Eds.), *New Paradigms, Culture and Subjectivity* (pp. 217–228). Creskill: Hampton Press.

Andreason, N. C. (1979). Thought, Language and Communication Disorders. A Clinical Assessment, Definition of Terms and Evaluation of Their Reliability. *Archives of General Psychiatry, 36*(12), 1315–1321. PMID 496551.

Blank, B. T. (2010). Theater Processes Therapeutic Drama Therapy. *The New Social Worker.* Spring.

Bolton, G. (2013). *The Therapeutic Potential of Creative Writing: Writing Myself.* London/Philadelphia: Jessica Kingsley Publishers.

Brugha, T. S., Bebbington, P. E., Singleton, N., Melzer, D., Jenkins, R., Lewis, G., Farrell, M., Bhugra, D., Lee, A., & Meltzer, H. (2004). Trends in Service Use and Treatment for Mental Disorders in Adults Throughout Great Britain. *British Journal of Psychiatry, 185*, 378–384.

Corrigan, P. W., Watson, A. C., & Ottati, V. (2003, June). From Whence Comes Mental Illness Stigma? *International Journal of Social Psychiatry, 49*(2), 142–157.

Corrigan, P. W., Morris, S. B., Michaels, P. J., Rafacz, J. D., & Rüsch, N. (2012, October). Challenging the Public Stigma of Mental Illness: A Meta-Analysis of Outcome Studies. *Psychiatric Services, 63*(10), 963–973. https://doi.org/10.1176/appi.ps.201100529.

Cuijpers, P., Sijbiandij, M., Koole, S. L., Andersson, G., Beekman, A. T., & Reynolds, C. F., III. (2014, February). Adding Psychotherapy to Antidepressant Medication in Depression and Anxiety Disorders: A Meta Analysis. *World Psychiatry, 13*, 56–67.

Datta, V. (2009). Neurohawks Fight Back. *The British Journal of Psychiatry, 195*(3), 268–269. https://doi.org/10.1192/bjp.195.3.268b.

Daykin, N., Orme, J., Evans, D., Salmon, D., McEachran, M., & Brain, S. (2008). The Impact of Participation in Performing Arts on Adolescent Health and Behaviour: A Systematic Review of the Literature. *Journal of Health Psychology, 13*(2), 251–264.

Destrée, P. (2016). Aristotle on the Power of Music in Tragedy, Greek & Roman Musical Studies. *4*(2), 2016; Gregory L. Scott, *Aristotle on Dramatic Musical Composition The Real Role of Literature, Catharsis, Music and Dance in the Poetics*, ISBN: 978-1530500772

Ellison, N., Mason, O., & Scior, K. (2015, April). Renaming Schizophrenia to Reduce Stigma: Comparison with the Case of Bipolar Disorder. *The British Journal of Psychiatry, 206*(4), 341–342. https://doi.org/10.1192/bjp.bp.114.146217.

Feldman, D., Sussman Jones, F., & Ward, E. (2010). The Enact Method of Employing Drama Therapy in Schools. In D. Read Johnson & R. Emunah (Eds.), *Current Approaches in Drama Therapy*. Springfield Illinois: Charles Thomas.

Frydman, J. (2016). Role Play, Executive Functioning: Constructing Cooperative Paradigms of Drama Theory and Cognitive Neuropsychology. *The Arts in Psychotherapy, 47*, 41–47.

Furnham, A. (2013, August 29). Writing as Therapy. Scribbling May Be Better than Therapy. *Psychology Today*. https://www.psychologytoday.com/blog/sideways-view/201308/writing-therapy

Golemann, D. (1995). *Emotional Intelligence*. London: Bloomsbury.

Gotzsche, P., Young, A. H., & Crace, J. (2015). Head To Head Maudsley Debate Does Long Term Use of Psychiatric Drugs Cause More Harm than Good? *British Medical Journal, 350*, h2435.

Hankir, A. (2014). Interview with Dinesh Bhugra MA, MSc, MPhil, MBBS, PhD, FRCPsych, Professor of Mental Health and Diversity at the Institute of Psychiatry at King's College London. President Elect of the World Psychiatric Association. *World Journal of Medical Education and Research*, Issue 8, Special Issue on Mental Health. Volume 8, Issue 1, DAUIN 20140069.

Hankir, A., & Zaman, R. (2015, September). Global Strategies Targeting the Recruitment Crisis in Psychiatry: the Doctors Academy Future Excellence International Medical Summer School. *Psychiatria Danubina, 27*(Suppl 1), S130–S135.

Helman, C. G. (2001). *Culture, Health and Illness* (4th ed.). London: Arnold.

Hughes, J. H. (2016, November). Experiencing What Clients Experience. *The Psychologist, 29*, 810–815.

Ingemark, C. A. (2013). Key Themes in the Study of Therapeutic Use of Storytelling. In C. A. Ingemark (Ed.), *Psychotherapeutic Uses of Storytelling* (pp. 7–17). Lund, Sweden: Noric Academic Press.

Jamison, Kay Redfield (1993): *Touched with Fire: Manic-Depressive Illness and the Artistic Temperament,* New York, The Free Press. ISBN: 0-02-916030-8

Kelly, G. (1955). *The Psychology of Personal Constructs*. New York: Norton.

Kinderman, P. (2017). *Our Turbulent Minds*. Lecture Presented at BPS Annual Conference, Brighton. https://thepsychologist.bps.org.uk/our-turbulent-minds

Kipper, D. A., & Ritchie, T. D. (2003). The Effectiveness of Psychodramatic Techniques: A Metaanalysis. *Group Dynamics, 7*(1), 13–25.

Kirk, J. C. (2015). Dramatherapy with Women Survivors of Domestic Abuse: A Small-Scale Research Study. *Dramatherapy, 37*(1), 28–43. https://doi.org/10.1080/02630672.2015.1101480.

Kirkcaldy, B. D. (2013). *Chimes of Time: Essays by Wounded Healers*. Leiden: Sidestone Publishers.

Kirkcaldy, Furnham, & Siefen. (2011). Transcultural Psychopharmacology: Impact on Psychological Health Related Variables. In B. D. Kirkcaldy (Ed.), *The Art and Science of Health Care. Psychology and Human factors for Practitioners*. Göttingen/New York/Vienna: Hogrefe Publishers.

Kuipers, E., Leff, J., & Lam, D. (2002). *Family Work for Schizophrenia: A Practical Guide* (2nd ed.). Gaskell. London: RCPsych Publications.

Langford, A., & Thornicroft, G. (2014, November). *Lancet Psychiatry, 1*(6), 425–426. https://doi.org/10.1016/S2215-0366(14)00016-9. Epub 2014 Nov 5.

Longden, E. (2013). *Learning from the Voices in My Head* (50 pp.). New York: Ted Books. ISBN: 978-1-937382-37-7.

Mattingly, C. (1998). *Healing Drama and Clinical Plots. The Narrative Structure*. Cambridge: Cambridge University Press.

Mechaeil, R., Graybow, A., & Cobham, P. (2010). Towards a Purposeful Ending: A Study Exploring the Impact of Dramatherapy on the Quality of Life of People Suffering from Dementia. *Dramatherapy, 31*(2), 27–34. https://doi.org/10.1080/02630672.2009.9689775.

Pellegrino, E. D. (1976). Prescribing and Drug ingestion symbols and substances. *Drug Intelligence and Clinical Pharmacy, 10*(11), 624–630.

Pennebaker, J. W. (1997). *Narrative and Psychotherapy*. London: Sage.

Rüsch, N., Abbruzzese, E., Hagedorn, E., et al. (2014). Efficacy of Coming Out Proud to Reduce Stigma's Impact Among People with Mental Illness: Pilot Randomised Controlled Trial. *The British Journal of Psychiatry, 204*, 391–397. https://doi.org/10.1192/bjp.bp.113.135772. Epub 2014 Jan 16.

Sacks, O. (1985). *Preface to* The Man Who Mistook His Wife for a Hat. London: Picador. ISBN: 8601200580358.

Sajnani, H. (2014, November). *Theater and Trauma Addressing the Wounds of the Soul.* https://canysynthesis.wordpress.com/2014/11/04/dr-theatre-dressing-the-wounds-of-the-soul/

Semmler, P. L., & Williams, C. B. (2000). Narrative Therapy. As storied Context for Multicultural counselling. *Journal of Multicultural Counselling and Development, 28*, 51–62.

Seymour, A. (2015). Editorial. *Dramatherapy, 37*(2–3), 75–77. | Published Online: 19 Oct 2016.

Smith, R. (2002). In Search of "Non-disease". *British Medical Journal, 324*(7342), 883–885. PMCID: PMC1122831.

Stuckey, H. L., & Nobel, J. (2010). The Connection Between Art Healing and Public Health: A Review of Current Literature. *American Journal of Public Health, 100*(2), 254–263.

Styron, W. (2004). *Darkness Visible.* London: Vintage Books. ISBN: 9780099285571.

Tallis, R. (2003). *Hippocratic Oaths. Medicine and Its Discontents.* London: Atlantic Books Ltd. ISBN: 9781782396512.

White, M. (1989). *Selected Papers*. Adelaide: Dulwich Centre Publications.

White, M. (2005). Workshop Notes. Dulwich Centre. https://dulwichcentre.com.au/michael-white-archive/writings-bymichael-white/

van Wyk, R. (2017). *Narrative House; A Metaphor for Narrative Therapy: Tribute to Michael White* (Downloaded on 11th July, 2017). https://www.researchgate.net/profile/Rene_Van_Wyk/publication/316274668_A_metaphor_for_Narrative_Therapy/links/5903094eaca2725bd722ebac/A-metaphor-for-Narrative-Therapy.pdf

Part II

Theater and Dance Perspectives

6

Theater and Psychology: A Symbiotic Relationship

Jeff Zinn

Personal Interest in Theater and Psychology

There seems to be a real affinity between the worlds of psychology and the theater. Each uses the other as a lens through which to better understand its own core concerns. Jargon from each realm is borrowed by the other and freely used to explain core principles. Actors delve deep into the psychological history of a character to discern motivations. Psychologists speak in terms of roles adopted and employed. Role-playing is a common therapeutic device. While I had, as a young actor and director, routinely explored the psychology of characters in plays and employed the common vocabulary noted above, it was not until I went looking for clues to a character in an Ionesco play I was directing that I found myself intensely engaged in a new line of inquiry, one that led directly to people like Irvin Yalom, Sheldon Solomon, and, above all, Ernest Becker. When I thought I might begin to write about the new connections I was making between

J. Zinn (✉)
Gloucester Stage, Gloucester, MA, USA
e-mail: jz@jeffzinn.com

B. Kirkcaldy (ed.), *Psychotherapy, Literature and the Visual and Performing Arts*, Palgrave Studies in Creativity and Culture, https://doi.org/10.1007/978-3-319-75423-9_6

my own field—the theater—and the unfamiliar universe of psychological theory, I briefly considered going back to school to get a second degree. How, I wondered, could I write intelligently about something I knew relatively so little about? In the end, I decided not to go down that particular academic wormhole and instead settled for a more informal, if not less rigorous, course of self-study.

One of the major figures I encountered along the way was sociologist Ervin Goffman. In his exhaustive study of everyday human interaction, *The Presentation of Self in Everyday Life*, Goffman (1959) leaned heavily on the metaphor of performance. In the preface he states, "[T]he perspective employed in this report is that of the theatrical performance; the principles derived are dramaturgical ones." He goes on to speak of the individual "sustaining his performance" and maintaining "belief in the part one is playing." He makes careful distinctions between persons who genuinely believe in their performances and those who "put on a show" for reasons both cynical and altruistic. The overriding message of Goffman's work is that the ordinary transactions that dominate everyday life are freighted with psychological significance. We care about what other people think of us.

This insight became a key element in my own attempt to arrive at a workable toolbox of techniques for directors, playwrights, and actors whose job it is to create, interpret, and/or reveal character in an accurate and truthful way. In my book, *The Existential Actor: Life and Death, Onstage and Off*, I named that element *transaction*, and it functions in a way that supports, and is supported by, three other essential elements: *action*, *shape*, and *surrender*.

I arrived at these four elements after a process of exploring the path of my theatrical forebears who all struggled with unraveling just what it is we do as actors and what it is we are doing when we do it well. Some of the early attempts at this—and when I say early I mean starting 4000 or so years ago—resulted in huge compendiums of "how-to's" such as that produced by the Egyptians and Indians to codify their theatrical religious rituals. Two thousand four hundred years ago, Aristotle set down his *Poetics*, which outlined more than a dozen essential elements whose purest execution might result in great drama. He was trying to figure out what had worked so well in the tragedies of Aristophanes, Socrates, and

Euripides, whose great works were already hundreds of years old and holding up very well, thank you. He distilled that dozen to six even more essential: plot, character, action, song, theme, and spectacle. Right there in second position—character—we find Aristotle, perhaps for the very first time, joining the worlds of theater and psychology. His protégé, Theophrastus, homed in on that element and teased out over 30 essential types (now referred to as "stock characters"). Much later, in France and Italy just following the Middle Ages, character/shape was still front and center in the theater in the form of commedia dell'arte's dozen or so archetypes. In fact, it would not be until Shakespeare arrived (at least according to Harold Bloom) that "the human"—that is, a rendering of complex characters that transcended archetypal *shapes* such as the captain, the lover, the professor, and so on—was born in dramatic literature.

Once dramatists began creating complex characters—Shakespeare, yes, but not again really until Strindberg, Ibsen, and Chekhov—the search for truth and authenticity in character led theater practitioners in all realms digging through the trunks of the then nascent field of psychology for ideas, theories, and techniques. Even Aristotle relied upon the psychological theory of his day. The *humours* provided straightforward psychological underpinnings for various characters who were variously sanguine, choleric, melancholic, or phlegmatic. But a theory that simplistic would not be sufficient to handle the inner workings of a Hedda Gabler.

The theorists of the new modern theatrical age realized that the old *shape* dominated approach to portraying character, where actors were not called upon to do more than present an external form (buttressed by a singular "psychological" adjective such as "choleric") and declaim their lines, would no longer do. Techniques were needed to call forth authentic human emotion on stage. Of course, in life such emotions are triggered freely in response to events and experience. But how to harness it in order to bring it forth on cue, under artificial circumstances? That's when we start looking over the shoulders of the psychologists to see what they are up to and if there are any useful tips and tricks we might steal.

Around 1800 a theory of brain structure, first called *organology* and later *phrenology*, was developed by the German physician Franz Joseph Gall and became a cultural phenomenon. We can guess that actors of the time were gossiping about it in the dressing rooms. Gall argued that the brain is divided into a large number of functional organs, each responsible for particular human mental abilities and dispositions: hope, love, spirituality, greed, language, the ability to detect the size, form, and color of objects, and so on. Almost 100 years later Stanislavski would incorporate into his system the "affective memory" experiments of French psychologist Théodule-Armand Ribot. Rebranding it *emotional memory*, Stanislavski hoped to offer a scientific basis for unlocking the secrets of releasing authentic emotion onstage. Ribot found that stimulating the brain in specific places had the effect of triggering memories and eliciting emotions. Stanislavski seized on this promising experiment and surmised that if one could consciously "go into" the brain with directed thought, it might be possible to tease out those "emotional memories" and trigger authentic emotion on demand. To do so he devised "sense memory" and "affective memory" exercises. This capacity to both experience and release authentic emotion is what I have labeled *surrender*.

Armed now with centuries worth of tried-and-true shapes, and new scientific techniques for unlocking emotion, and in the context of a culture newly infatuated with "scientific" approaches and systems, the theater world exploded with techniques and approaches laden with jargon and comprised of multiple technical elements. Stella Adler famously visited Stanislavski in Moscow and came away with a hand-drawn chart detailing over 50 distinct elements.

My own personal journey as a theater maker—first as an actor and later as director—led me to the conclusion that 50 distinct elements were too many to carry around in one's head as one navigated the moment-to-moment experience of actually playing a part onstage or in front of a lens. Consider everything the actor has to carry around in his head as he steps out onto the stage: he's waiting for his cue, the precise moment when he is to take that step pegged to a specific line or a subtle shift in lights, to music, or to a sound effect. Memorized lines must now be spoken in a particular way, conveying meaning and character. Weeks of rehearsal have imbued those lines with subtext, the meaning under the meaning. There is blocking, furniture to navigate around and onto. Then there are other actors with whom the actor interacts. What are those relationships?

All of this is within the world of the play, but underneath it, or perhaps just outside of it, is a relentless stream of information from the real world: "I'm in a theater. There's an audience. Who's in the audience? Why didn't my scene partner say that line right? Oh no, she skipped a page. No she didn't. I don't feel good; I think I might be coming down with something. Focus. What's my intention in the scene? Get back in the play. Remember to breathe…" and so on.

Somehow we do manage to absorb it all and still perform. The human capacity to hold vast quantities of information in memory and put that knowledge and insight to work on the fly is more than impressive. To put it into perspective, scientists in the field of artificial intelligence have found it enormously difficult to write code that would allow a robot to enter a room and improvise a route around unknown obstacles. After some of those experiments, they concluded, "Our systems are pathetic compared to biological systems" (Selman et al. 1996). Yet the actor lives with the gnawing feeling that she is not quite getting it, that perfection lies somewhere just beyond what she is achieving. We strive to *live in the moment* and to *become the character*. Then, when our own consciousness asserts itself in the scene (as it must, since we are not robots), we feel that we have failed.

James Rhodes (2013) describes similar challenges he faces as a concert pianist:

> Playing 120,000 notes from memory in the right order with the right fingers, the right sound, the right pedaling while chatting about the composers and pieces and knowing there are critics, recording devices, my mum, the ghosts of the past, all there watching and perhaps most crushingly, the realization that I will never, ever give the perfect recital. It can only ever, with luck, hard work and a hefty dose of self-forgiveness, be 'good enough'.

How might we go about formulating a technique for doing "it" better? The impulse to organize experience is utterly human—the world is too big, too chaotic for us to take in all at once. We look for patterns and for systems that will allow us to make sense of it all. We look for a way to manage the terror that comes from overload.

In *Consilience: The Unity of Knowledge*, Edmund O. Wilson (1999) talks about the importance of reduction to the scientific process: "… the breaking apart of nature into its natural constituents… reductionism is the primary and essential activity of science. It is the search strategy employed to find points of entry into otherwise impenetrably complex systems." Should we use a reductionist approach to understanding something as complex as the theater? "Complexity is what interests scientists in the end, not simplicity. Reductionism is the way to understand it." The same can be said for artists. The artist's technique is the pathway toward that complexity. What then are the techniques that work? How can we successfully manage all the nuts and bolts of such a technique and somehow deliver a performance that is effective, truthful, moving, and even transcendent?

Starting with the Greeks we see a succession of systems whose one unifying feature might be an acceptance that the actor's task is too large, too complex to take in all at once. Some reduction is needed to focus the mind. If you are standing in the wings mentally bombarded with all the lines, cues, blocking, meanings, relationships, and so on, and with the added burden of self-doubt that comes from caring what others think—your parents, the director, your peers—the response might well be total paralysis. A good strategy might be to identify a few key elements that can serve as focal points, centers of attention, guideposts.

As Stanislavski formulated his system, he was clearly influenced by an awareness of contemporaneous psychological theory and practice. Indeed, Freud's theory, which emphasized the importance of the unconscious mind, was well established in the cultural zeitgeist by the time Stanislavski began formulating his own system. The 50 distinct elements of the Stanislavski system are neatly divided, with half of them labeled "Complete Internal/Inner Feeling" and the other half labeled "Complete External." The "Internal" side of the chart includes elements such as *imagination*, *emotional memory*, *feeling of truth*, and *fluid exchange of emotion*, as distinct from more shape-oriented elements on the right side of the chart, such as *external tempo and rhythm*, *placement of voice*, *diction*, and *rules of speaking*.

When the Stanislavski system migrated to America in the 1930s, it found a receptive audience in young firebrands like Harold Clurman,

Robert Lewis, Sanford Meisner, Elia Kazan, and Lee Strasberg—all members of the Group Theatre—who were already impatient with the calcified theatrical conventions of declamation and representation that were still the norm, and ready for a more realistic approach. But as they incorporated Stanislavski into their own theater labs, classes, and workshops, there was a natural impulse to simplify (as per E.O. Wilson above) and focus on what they intuited might be the most essential elements to carry onstage. Bobby Lewis decided that *intention*—a sense of a clear object or goal in a given scene—was the most important and useful element. Meisner seized on Stanislavski's "exchange of sentiments" to build an entire technique and school (the Neighborhood Playhouse) around careful connection and listening via his "repetition exercise." Most famously, Lee Strasberg built his Actors Studio curriculum upon the foundation of "emotional memory" employing "sense memory," and many other exercises, to help actors get to the root of feeling and expressing truthful emotion.

As late as the 1970s, when I made my way to New York City after college and started taking acting classes, the ethos of the Group Theater espoused by Strasberg and Meisner was still dominant. There were certainly other emergent strains, in some cases influenced by non-Western theatrical practices and philosophies less driven by realism and an insistence on "psychological truth." Notably, theorists and practitioners such as Peter Brook, Robert Wilson, Elizabeth LeCompte, Mary Overlie, and Richard Foreman were all forming companies and producing more experimental work that played in opposition to the forms that dominated, and still dominate, most work seen onstage and on screens of all sizes. These "downtown" artists—they tended to perform in lofts, churches, and other converted spaces below 14th Street—injected energy and excitement into the theater scene, but to my eye, there was a disconnect between the non-naturalistic, *shape*-driven approaches of the downtown artists and the naturalistic, "psychological" approach of the Actors Studio and Meisner-influenced mainstream. I wondered if there might be a way to unite the two worlds in a new paradigm that would somehow infuse the most extreme, non-naturalistic shapes with a sense of emotional truth.

My journey as a scholar/practitioner eventually led me to the burgeoning field of terror management theory advanced by social psychologists Sheldon Solomon, Jeff Greenberg, and Tom Pyszczynski. Their experiments had been heavily influenced by Ernest Becker, whose main thesis, extolled in works such as *The Birth of Meaning* and *The Denial of Death*, was that human identity (character or *shape*) was built in response to the anxiety brought on by mortality salience—death awareness. This notion, that our culturally determined shapes provide a psychological buffer to protect us from the Kierkegaardian paralysis that might arise from death awareness, suggested to me a theoretical framework that might serve in the creation and interpretation of characters in the theater and other media.

One of the things that make us human is that we know we are alive. We are absolutely conscious of the fact that we exist. This awareness is literally awesome, exhilarating, and potentially joyous. But as Adam and Eve learned the hard way, knowledge is a bitter fruit. Cast out of Eden, their initial euphoria and sense of themselves as godlike creations of God are replaced by the understanding that they are nothing more than animals or, as Solomon and colleagues have put it, "…breathing, defecating, urinating, vomiting, expectorating, perspiring, menstruating, ejaculating, exfoliating, postnasal dripping, pieces of meat, no more significant or enduring than cockroaches or cucumbers" (Solomon et al. 2003).

It was Kierkegaard who used the Eden myth to capture this tension in our natures. He observed that if we were either completely of the spirit or completely animal, we might live in blissful innocence. But because we are aware of our dual status as "godlike" creatures, we experience both joy and dread. The word Kierkegaard used was *angst*, usually translated as "anxiety," but a more complete definition includes feelings of both anxiety and exaltation. Simply being alive and fully feeling that aliveness can induce feelings of ecstasy, but as the temporary nature of our existence becomes salient, a sense of dread creeps in behind the exaltation.

Exactly when does the awful knowledge of our mortality assert itself? It is there in the cry of the baby—feed me, hold me, love me, or I'll die. Then, if we are lucky and have someone who will feed us, hold us, love us, and protect us from whatever is awful, we are able to live awhile in the safe cocoon of young childhood. Eventually, though, we start asking and we are told: "Yes, things die. People die. Parents die. YOU will die, but not for a long, long time." Except that it is a lie. The hard truth about death is that it really can and does come at any time. So we lie. We lie to our children as we teach our children not to lie.

That we will not die is the vital lie that all cultures construct for themselves. It is at the center of huge edifices of belief and worldview that we inherit and in which we participate all our lives. These belief systems help us feel that we are not so vulnerable, not quite so mortal. They help us feel that we are at least symbolically, if not literally, immortal. We construct these lies because the angst named by Kierkegaard is too intense for us to carry around in every moment.

No matter how well constructed the lies, there are times when the full awareness of our impossible status as mortal gods comes crashing down upon us. This awareness may intrude at times that are unexpected and unwelcome. There are also times when we deliberately seek it out. What does this have to do with the theater? Plenty. We go to the theater, we go to the movies, we read novels and watch TV, and we tell stories and listen to stories because we are, all of us, insatiably curious about *us*. We want to understand why we do what we do. We identify with characters. They are like us and they are not like us. They get into jams and they get out of jams.

When we go to the theater, we prefer the stakes onstage to be life and death even when the circumstances appear to be relatively low key. Why? Because if they are not, we lose interest. We turn away. Our own lives mostly lack drama, which is to say that the life-and-death struggle lurking in the background has been put safely out of view. Theater is most effective when it brings back into view that which we have conveniently blocked out: the inevitability of death. The theater is a place where we can temporarily break through the buffers and engage these hardest of truths head-on.

In the real world, death awareness can elicit a kind of stage fright. What if you believed—not just intellectually but viscerally—that just outside your door the chances were even that an anvil would drop from the sky, or a sniper would fire at you from a hidden vantage point, a car would run you down, a passing meteor would veer off course and smash into the earth, annihilating not just you but all of life? The result would be paralysis. Catatonia and agoraphobia are only the most extreme forms of stage fright, a sense of being frozen in the wings that sometimes renders us unable to step out onto the stages of our lives. Events like 9/11 and the Boston Marathon bombings remind us that these fears are real and only reinforce how vulnerable we are.

The solution, according to Ernest Becker and others, is to wrap ourselves in layers of psychological armor. *Culture* provides that armor: a ready-made framework, a worldview complete with rules for how to walk, talk, dress, and behave. Biological factors are determinative, of course, and none of us chooses our parents or the complicated stew of genes and chromosomes that shape us. But once we have drawn the lottery ticket that is handed out at birth, culture takes over with that "set of beliefs about the nature of reality people share in groups." It is culture that reduces anxiety associated with the awareness of death by accomplishing two important functions: First, it lends meaning by providing us with answers to universal cosmological questions about the nature of life—answers that reassure us that the world we live in is a stable, orderly, meaningful place. Second, it allows us to feel that we ourselves are valuable people who play significant roles in that universe.

We can imagine how these culturally devised solutions might have begun: Casting ourselves back in time to the earliest moments of self-aware humanity, we can picture our ancestors tenuously perched in a rugged and inhospitable environment, gazing at the stars and confronting the mysteries of their universe. It must have been discombobulating to exist in a harsh terrain confronted by the fact of a natural world capable of dispensing incredible bounty but also utter devastation and sudden death. They must have wondered:

> *Where do we come from?*
> *What are we supposed to do while we are here?*
> *Where do we go after we die?*

Today we may congratulate ourselves for knowing so much more than they did, for having so many answers whose truths would have been inconceivable to their primitive brains. Yet the answers to those basic questions allowed our forebears to feel that the universe was an orderly place with rules for living. Observing those rules conferred meaning and acceptance. The questions still resonate because the answers devised by cultures are, even today, works in progress. Contemporary philosophers and psychologists still grapple with them. Martin Heidegger (2014) famously rephrased the first question as "Why are there beings at all instead of just nothing?" (p. 1).

We do not come up with answers to the three questions on our own. In fact, we do not really come up with anything on our own. We know that infants are aware of others even before they are aware of themselves (Rochat 2003). The construction of the human self is something that happens from the outside in. We only know what we know about ourselves because of what we receive from the outside world. This simple idea of validation from others will take on huge importance when we start to explore *transaction.*

The Three Questions

Every culture answers the first question, "where do we come from?" in its own way. "In the beginning God created the heavens and the earth…." A quick Google of creation myths, however, returns a long list of fabulous tales from the Babylonian to the Yoruba:

- The Boshongo, a Bantu tribe, believe that "in the beginning, Bumba was all alone in the water. Then he got sick and vomited the sun, moon, stars and land…."
- The Yokut believe that life on earth began with a great flood, "…then out of the sky one day glided an enormous eagle with a black crow riding upon its back, searching for a place to light…."
- Greek myth begins with Chaos ruled by the goddess Eurynome. She mates with the wind to produce Earth and sky who themselves mate to create a race of Titans led by Cronus. Cronus devours his young to escape the prediction that he will be overthrown and replaced by a son, but the infant Zeus survives to fulfill the prophecy.

You and I may find these stories amusing. But who's to say that one worldview—ours—is true and the others false? Does it even matter? Sheldon Solomon answers:

> Culture really has nothing to do with the truth. If anything, its function is to obscure the horrifying possibility that we live in a random and indeterminate universe in which the only certain outcome is death and destruction. (Lecture)

The answers to the second question, "What do we do while we are here?" are too numerous to be contained in a simple story told by the fire or in the opening chapter of a Bible. Those answers require libraries, museums, and educational, legal, and political institutions. They reside in endless catalogs of science, art, and law. Each culture generates its own versions of these things and communicates them to its members in a million ways: parent to child, peer to peer, through educational systems, and through the media. Thousands of years before the birth of Christ, oral histories handed down through generations of lyric poets found their way into some of the first written narratives of Western culture. The *Iliad* and the *Odyssey* spelled out intricate codes of conduct, ways of being in the world. Buried inside those fabulous tales was almost everything one might need to know about how to behave in the realms of love, war, property, marriage, friendship, loyalty, and generosity, how to grieve death properly, and what constitutes heroism.

Within each culture exist subcultures that include separate religions, nations, political parties, "isms," sports teams, and professions, each with their own rules and regulations, jargon, dress, and codes of behavior. All of them provide the individual with a blueprint for answering question number two: the question of what we are to do while we are here and even *how* we are to do it. Adherence to the code of any culture or subculture helps define success and failure and provides an essential sense of self-worth. These culturally determined codes of behavior, which include how we dress, how we dance, the languages we speak, the dialects and regional accents within those languages, are what go into the broad category I call *shape.*

The third question, "What happens to us after we die?" goes to the very heart of this business of immortality. By and large, society confers either literal or symbolic immortality upon those members who conform to and abide by the roles and rules of those cultures. Literal immortality is promised by various religions, with different versions of life after death.

We may be tempted to relegate this notion of *literal* immortality to primitive and/or prehistoric cultures until we consider that 74% of all Americans believe in an afterlife.

Literal belief in life after death requires "faith." Symbolic immortality, however, is available to all and can be acquired through the works we do, especially creative works, which remain after we are gone. Builders of pyramids, bridges, and skyscrapers derive satisfaction in knowing that their works will outlive them. Shakespeare, Leonardo, and Picasso are artists whose work, most would argue, will live forever. It is not only the pharaohs, architects, and master builders, however, who participate in symbolic immortality. Bricklayers, iron workers, carpenters, computer programmers, and anyone who fashions something out of nothing can derive a sense of satisfaction from the knowledge that their labors will outlive them. Consider the medieval church builders who did not finish their work in their lifetime. Symbolic immortality, a culturally devised solution to the certainty of our own death, is available—and essential—to us all.

Heroism

In a very real way, all of us are actors—and heroes. Everyone is playing the leading role in the story of his or her own life, the heroic narrative in which each of us is the protagonist. The classical hero goes into battle, faces death, and survives. Compared with the exploits of, say, Achilles, simply surviving our day-to-day existence might seem an egregious lowering of the heroism bar. Henry David Thoreau (2005) wrote, "Most men lead lives of quiet desperation," which does not sound especially heroic. But all of us, even in our quietest shapes, are living heroically, or trying to. We must. Every day we get out of bed and we *act*. I do not mean that we put on a show or pretend anything. I mean that we take *action*. We *do*. According to Jean-Paul Sartre (1946), we only exist through what we do. He said, "There is no reality except in action. Man is nothing but the sum of his actions.... There is no love apart from the deeds of love; there is no genius other than that which is expressed in works of art." The idea is ancient. *Karma* is the Sanskrit word for *action*. You are what you do. You become what you do. You are who you are because of what you have done.

Another great modern philosopher, Louis C.K., has a great riff on *action* as character. In one of his bits, he talks about how when he is flying first class and a soldier comes onto the plane he imagines himself giving up his seat, but he never does. That does not prevent him from luxuriating, briefly, in the warm feeling of what a great guy he is for just having the thought. By poking fun at himself in this way, Louis reminds us that we are what we *do*, and if we don't do anything, we are basically just jerks. Descartes had a different view: "I think therefore I am," which makes us wonder if Descartes is the guy who manages to continue to believe what a great guy he is just for thinking that he *might* give up his first-class seat for a soldier. I'm definitely on the side of "I *act* therefore I am." I vote for *karma*.

To act—and I mean this in every sense of the word—is to be heroic. When you thrust yourself into the open and take a stand, when you allow yourself to stick out, when you proclaim to the world that you have something to say and you are going to say it, you make yourself something of a target. You invite people to take shots at you—and they will. That is heroism. That is *individuation*.

The very powerful and necessary urge to individuate is something we all share, but we also have the equally powerful urge to disappear into the crowd, to merge. If individuation lifts us up and makes us stick out from the masses, there is also a kind of gravity that pulls us down and makes us want to merge. We merge with mommy. We merge with our friends and our peers, our families, our lovers. We merge, daily, with our coworkers, our sports teams, our political parties—all those *isms*—that define us and give us *shape*. This is the erotic urge. To individuate and to merge—these are the *twin ontological motives* (cf. Becker 1973), which is a fancy way of saying that no matter what you are doing, you are always in the process of doing one or the other.

Culture responds to the unknowable mysteries of existence by answering the three basic questions and passing those answers along to us. Those answers provide the blueprint—the *shape*—of the heroic narrative. The creation and subsequent lifelong maintenance of this project of self-invented identity is, in theatrical terms, the central *action* of every human being. The accomplishment of that action provides us with a sense of ourselves as heroic figures, as symbolically immortal. Conversely, failing to accomplish that action threatens a loss of self-esteem and a symbolic death.

We shield ourselves from the truth of existence so that we may *act*—so that we may move forward with agency and without paralysis. All of us throughout our lives cling to our heroic narratives, whether modest or grandiose. We drive cars, live in houses, go shopping, and educate our children. It is right and fitting that we do so. The paradox of psychological health is that to function with any equilibrium at all, we must engage in a vital lie. We must deny the fact of death in our everyday existence. Ironically, mental health means shutting out the truth. Mental health means narrowing down our capacity for feeling *everything*. Mental health requires us *not* to surrender to the awful truth of our cosmic insignificance.

The artist, however, *must* surrender. To be creative the artist must have the capacity to strip away his or her psychological armor. The actor, in particular, must be able to take on the shape of whatever character she is portraying, complete with all the death-denying armor that character carries around. The most interesting characters, the most challenging, the ones we most want to play, and the ones we most want to watch are those who come to a moment in the narrative when the vital lie is pierced. In that moment the actor must have the capacity to strip away her own armor so as to convey the experience truthfully. The actor who can do no more than suggest the shape of that moment and merely present a simulacrum of that experience is, to use a piece of theatrical jargon, just *indicating* the emotion.

This may explain why the need for art and artists runs so deep and why art is found in every culture. Art offers opportunities for stripping away culturally constructed veneers in a relatively safe environment. The function of the artist is to stay available, stand ready to remove the armor, stay exposed, and surrender to the mortal truth of existence. Removing the armor and standing exposed is itself an act of heroism. *Surrender* represents the possibility of unleashing an explosion of creativity and emotion in a splitting of the creative atom when we crack through the shell of our culturally constructed armor and when the buffering shape of things gives way to the truth of our existence. Acknowledging these human dynamics and embedding them in our work as artists are the beginning of *raising the stakes.* When we find the courage to individuate, to stand boldly on the stage and ask that we be watched, when we have the heroism to *act*, what we create will have the potential to carry within it a sense of the largeness of life and death.

Guidelines for Mental Health Professionals

In our never-ending quest to interpret and portray complex characters, we theater practitioners will surely continue to freely borrow from the world of psychological theory. If I were to offer any guidance to mental health professionals who feel the need to borrow from the collection of techniques developed over time by our side of the equation, I would respectfully submit the following:

- Psychological armor (*shape*) is there for a reason. Maybe it is OK to acknowledge that the protective identities we choose may be, as Ernest Becker says, "vital lies," but the key word in that construction is "vital."
- Talk (therapy?) is cheap. *Action* is everything. *Do* something!
- Be present in the *transaction*. Audiences know when actors are phoning it in. So do clients.
- We all need to allow ourselves to *surrender* once in a while, to let go and release the emotions that we are experiencing.

References

Becker, E. (1973). *The Denial of Death*. New York: The Free Press.

Goffman, E. (1959). *The Presentation of Self in Everyday Life*. New York: Anchor Books.

Heidegger, M. (2014). *Introduction to Metaphysics* (2nd ed.p. 1). New Haven: Yale University.

Rhodes, J. (2013). *Find What You Love and Let It Kill You*. http://m.guardiannews.com/music/musicblog/2013/apr/26/james-rhodes-blog-find-what-you-love

Rochat, P. (2003). Five Levels of Self-Awareness as They Unfold Early in Life. *Consciousness and Cognition, 12*, 717–731.

Sartre, J. P. (1946). *Existentialism Is a Humanism*. https://www.marxists.org/reference/archive/sartre/works/exist/sartre.htm

Selman, B. (1996). *Challenge Problems for Artificial Intelligence.* In Proceedings of AAAI-96, Thirteenth National Conference on Artificial Intelligence, Portland, August 1996. pp. 1340–1345. https://www.aaai.org/Papers/AAAI/1996/AAAI96-201.pdf

Solomon, S., Greenberg, J., Schimel, J., Arndt, J., & Pyszczynski, T. (2003). Human Awareness of Mortality and the Evolution of Culture. In *The Psychological Foundations of Culture* (pp. 15–40). Mahwah: Lawrence Erlbaum Associates.

Thoreau, H. D. (2005). *Civil Disobedience and Other Essays.* Digireads.com

Wilson, E. O. (1999). *Consilience: The Unity of Knowledge* (p. 58). New York: Vintage Books.

7

The Dance of Presence: Mindfulness and Movement

Sarah de Sousa and Shauna Shapiro

Personal Motivation and Passion Toward Dance and Psychotherapy

We have been dancing since we were young girls: classical ballet, competitive ballroom, Argentine tango, Cuban salsa, swing, and ecstatic dance. As dancers and healthcare professionals, we find that the dance of human relationship is not merely a metaphor but an opportunity for embodied practice. Our meditation practice has deepened our capacity to speak the language of the body's signals and improved the ability to attune to the movements of our partners. Likewise, years of training as dancers have enhanced our mindfulness practice and therapy skills. This lived experience forms the basis of our ongoing inquiry into the relationship between mindfulness, movement, and psychological well-being. Hence the fusion of our passion for dancing and movement with our professional focus on

S. de Sousa (✉) • S. Shapiro
School of Education and Counseling Psychology, Santa Clara University, Santa Clara, CA, USA
e-mail: sarah@insight-education.net; slshapiro@scu.edu

B. Kirkcaldy (ed.), *Psychotherapy, Literature and the Visual and Performing Arts*, Palgrave Studies in Creativity and Culture, https://doi.org/10.1007/978-3-319-75423-9_7

mindfulness and attentiveness can best be formulated in Rumi's astute observation that "[i]n order to understand the dance one must be still. And in order to truly understand stillness one must dance" (Rumi).

It is tempting to conceive of mindfulness as a practice that takes place in the mind, but mindfulness is both a state of mind and an embodied way of being in the world. Though much of the literature focuses on the "mental" dimensions of mindfulness training, preliminary research evidence offers insight into the benefits of mindful movement as informal mindfulness practice. Below, we seek to explore these benefits with particular attention to the physiological and interpersonal dimensions of mindfulness that are enhanced by mindful movement. Research from multiple social science disciplines is beginning to show that dance training, for example, holds the potential to encourage prosocial behavior and improve emotional coherence. In a way that physical exercise alone does not, dance offers the opportunity to experience the embodied harmony of physical and emotional expression. We offer this exploration of mindful movement within the context of an intervention for patients/clients to increase mental well-being and social connectedness, and as a tool for therapists to develop skills essential to psychotherapy, including somatic awareness, empathy, and presence.

Defining Mindfulness

We begin our exploration of mindful movement and its clinical applications by offering an operational definition of mindfulness. Mindfulness is a "consciousness discipline," a way of training the mind and body to be fully present with life. It involves bringing our full awareness to the present moment, and not just awareness of mental experiences but also training the mind to be fully present of somatic experiences. In his short story collection, *Dubliners*, James Joyce says of one character, "Mr. Duffy lived a short distance from his body" (Joyce 1914). Indeed, it is quite possible and common in the midst of our modern lives to be so absorbed in the life of the mind that one loses touch with the body, its signals, and its wisdom. Although often associated with mental training, mindfulness is much more than a mental exercise. Awareness of the body and somatic practices to help train this awareness have always been at the heart of mindfulness. In fact, the Buddha is quoted as stating that all of his teachings could be found in this "fathom long body" (Rohitassa Sutta, T. Bhikkhu Trans., 2013).

Although mindfulness is trained through formal meditation practices, it is a way of being, a way of living. As the poet David Whyte puts it, "The template of natural exchange is the breath, the autonomic giving and receiving that forms the basis and the measure of life itself. We are rested when we are a living exchange between what lies inside and what lies outside" (Whyte 2015, p. 181). This capacity to be fully alive and fully awake is at the heart of being human—and at the heart of working in a healing profession. A mindful clinician is one who is committed to listening deeply to her client, as well as to the embodied wisdom that arises when she senses what is beyond the words by listening in ways that transcend what ears alone can hear.

As we deepen our understanding of mindfulness and our ability to bring mindfulness into psychotherapy, it is imperative that we include an embodied lens as well as a mental one. Also important is exploring somatic practices that will help deepen our mindfulness of the body.

Three Core Elements of Mindfulness

In the model of mindfulness offered by Shapiro and Carlson (2009), mindfulness comprises three core elements: intention, attention, and attitude. *Intention* involves knowing *why* we are doing what we are doing: our ultimate aim, our vision, our aspiration. *Attention* involves attending fully to the present moment and to both our inner and outer experiences. *Attitude*, or *how* we pay attention, enables us to stay open, kind, and curious. These three elements are not separate—they are interwoven, each informing and feeding back into the others. Mindfulness *is meeting all of our experience with wisdom and compassion. We commit to opening rather than closing, being rather than changing, engaging rather than rehearsing.*

Intention

The first core component of mindfulness is *intention*. Intention is simply knowing why we are doing what we are doing. When we have discerned our intentions and are able to connect with them, our intentions help motivate us, reminding us of what is truly important. Discerning our intention involves inquiring into our deepest hopes, desires, and aspirations, listening deeply for the answers, and allowing them to arise organically. This deep listening, with trust in the process and the timing, allows one's truth to emerge at its own pace. Mindful attention to our own intentions helps us begin to bring unconscious values to awareness and decide whether those values are really the ones we want to pursue.

Intention, in the context of mindfulness, is not the same as (and does not include) striving or grasping for certain outcomes for our patients or ourselves. Those who have practiced a form of mindful movement such as yoga might recognize intention as the conversation between the ideal that any one pose represents and the embodiment of that pose in one's unique body. As Jack Kornfield puts it, "Intention is a direction not a destination" (personal communication 2012). We step readily in the direction our intention points, but we step lightly, with open eyes, ears, and heart as well as the consciousness that life has its own say in the matter (whatever the matter may be) and that there is much we have yet to learn.

Attention

The second fundamental component of mindfulness is *attention*. Remember, mindfulness is about seeing clearly, and if we want to see clearly, we must be able to pay attention to what is here, now, in this present moment. Paying attention involves observing and experiencing our moment-to-moment experience. And yet, this is not so easy. Recent research demonstrates that our mind wanders approximately 47% of the time (Killingsworth and Gilbert 2010). The human mind is often referred to as a "monkey mind," swinging from thought to thought as a monkey swings from limb to limb. Mindfulness is a tool that helps us tame and train our mind so that our attention becomes stable and focused. In formal mediation practice, the breath is often treated as the anchor of our attention; we train our attention by returning the mind's focus to the breath each time it wanders off. This practice already suggests the intimate connection between mind and body that is at the heart of mindfulness. However, other forms of mindfulness practice take the body directly as an anchor for attention, such as walking meditation in which one trains the mind to observe the movement of walking in exquisite detail.

Whatever the focus of our attention, what is essential is that the mind remains in a state of "relaxed alertness." Often, as we try to pay attention, our attention becomes tense and contracted. This is because we mistakenly think we have to be stressed or vigilant to focus our attention in a rigorous way. However, the meditation traditions teach us of a different kind of attention, one that involves clarity and precision without stress or vigilance (Wallace and Bodhi 2006). Mindful attention is also deep and penetrating; as Bhikkhu Bodhi notes, "[W]hereas a mind without mindfulness 'floats' on the surface of its object the way a gourd floats on water, mindfulness sinks into its object the way a stone placed on the surface of water sinks to the bottom" (Wallace and Bodhi 2006, p. 7).

Attitude

Attitude, the third core component of mindfulness, comes into play once we have learned to intentionally pay attention in the present moment. When we do so, we may notice something: our mind is constantly judging. The attitude with which we pay attention is essential to mindfulness. For example, attention can have a cold, critical quality, or an openhearted, compassionate quality. In fact, the Japanese symbol for mindfulness combines the symbol for presence with a symbol that can mean *mind*, *spirit*, or *heart* depending on the context—in other words, the familiar concept of mindfulness could also be translated *heart*fulness. To be mindful is also to have presence of heart.

The transformation from mind*less* to mind*ful* is catalyzed by the lovelight we shine on the dark corners of our inner world. If we want the bud to open, to smell, taste, live the benefits of mindful practice, the light of our own mind must be like the soft warmth of the sun. The invitation of mindfulness is not simply to pay attention, but to attend with kindness. This quality of kind attention is what brings out the best of our humanity and enhances our clinical work.

Attending without bringing the attitudinal qualities of *curiosity, openness, acceptance, and love* (COAL; Siegel 2007) into the practice may result in an attention that is condemning or shaming of inner (or outer) experience—our own or our client's. This may well have consequences contrary to the intentions of the practice; for example, we may end up cultivating patterns of criticism and striving instead of equanimity and acceptance.

These attitudes of mindfulness do not alter our experience, but simply contain it. For example, if while we are practicing mindfulness impatience arises, we note the impatience and see if we can bring an energy of acceptance and kindness to the impatience. We do not try to substitute these qualities for the impatience, or use them to make the impatience disappear. The attitudes are not an attempt to make things be a certain way, but an attempt to relate to whatever *is* in a certain way. By intentionally bringing the attitudes of COAL to our awareness of our own experience, we relinquish the habit of striving for pleasant experiences, or of pushing aversive experiences away. Instead, we attend to whatever is here. Doing so within a context of curiosity, openness, acceptance, and love not only makes it much easier to stay present, it can also transform our capacity to foster well-being in those who seek our clinical care.

Cultivating Mindfulness

What we practice becomes stronger (Shapiro 2017). When we practice mindfulness, we strengthen our capacity to be present moment by moment in a curious, accepting, and loving way. Mindful practice can be categorized into *formal* and *informal* practice; each kind of practice supports the other. The formal practice will support the ability to practice mindfulness in day-to-day life, and informal practice is meant to generalize to everyday life what is learned during the formal practice.

Formal practices, like sitting meditation, are geared toward cultivating mindfulness skills in focused and systematic ways. These can involve relatively brief daily meditation woven into one's day, or intensive days- or weeks-long retreats involving many hours of formal sitting and walking meditation based on centuries-old traditions. Informal practice involves intentionally bringing an open, accepting, and discerning attention to whatever we are engaged in—for example, reading, eating, dancing, or practicing therapy.

Both formal and informal practices have a role to play in clinical work. Below, we review research investigating how dance and other forms of movement when treated as informal mindfulness practice can enhance our somatic awareness, visceral awareness, and emotional coherence, in turn supporting our efficacy as clinicians. In addition to the role that mindful movement can play as a specific intervention, it is worth considering that all therapy and clinical work can be approached as informal mindfulness practice. Setting the intention at the beginning of each therapy session, each group, each clinical training or supervision to "intentionally pay attention with kindness, discernment, openness and acceptance" is a powerful and effective practice that can transform the clinical experience.

Dance as Informal Practice

Informal mindfulness practice offers one way to bring mindfulness into our day-to-day activities. Intentionally choosing activities that can cultivate mindfulness through our bodies in addition to our minds can be especially fruitful. Dance can be an informal mindfulness practice and offers a way to access our felt sense of equanimity, interconnectedness, heartfulness, and presence through the body. As Rumi says, "You dance inside my chest where no-one sees you, but sometimes I do, and that sight becomes this art" (Barks 1995).

Another benefit of choosing dance as an informal mindfulness practice is that it can explicitly help cultivate interpersonal mindfulness, as in partner dancing. Mindfulness is often narrowly conceived of as a purely intrapersonal practice. And yet, our interconnectedness as living beings is a central tenet of the wisdom traditions that inform mindfulness practice. Through the systematic cultivation of compassion, sympathetic joy, loving kindness, and acceptance, we come to understand that our sense of a separate self is an illusion that perpetuates unnecessary suffering. As Bien (2006) writes, "One great paradox of the spiritual life is rooted in the notion of nonself or interbeing: *If you set out to heal the world, you will lose yourself. If you set out to heal yourself, you heal the world.* The best way to take care of yourself is to cultivate…a calm, spacious, accepting, open awareness of what is happening in the impermanent, ever-changing world inside and outside our skin. By taking care of yourself in this way, you are at the same time of the most help to others" (p. 31).

Finding informal practices that help cultivate mindfulness within interpersonal relationships is important, especially for clinicians. The journey of becoming a mindful clinician is a rewarding one, but it is also of little use if we do not learn how to integrate the awareness and insights from our intrapersonal practice back into our work with clients. As Sharon Salzberg says, "The path may lead to many powerful and sublime experiences, but the path begins here with our daily interactions with each other" (Salzberg 1995, p. 171). Mindful movement such as dance not only enhances our awareness of what is happening in our own skin, but it enhances our awareness of energetic exchange between bodies in space and other forms of nonverbal communication, thus supporting our capacity as therapists to listen with our whole bodies to what is communicated by our clients.

Though psychological research on this topic is limited, research from multiple social science disciplines indicates that dance training holds the potential to encourage prosocial behavior and improve emotional coherence. Dance as a mindfulness practice offers the opportunity to experience the embodied harmony of physical and emotional expression.

Summary of Dance Research

In a study that investigated synchrony and cooperation in groups, behavioral scientists at Stanford found that "acting in synchrony with others can increase cooperation by strengthening social attachment among group members" (Wiltermuth and Heath 2009, p. 1). As Wiltermuth and Heath (2009) point out, synchronized movements including dance, chanting, singing, and marching are ancient cultural rituals that may have served an evolutionary function by promoting prosocial behavior. In experiments that required groups of three members to engage in varying degrees of synchronous and asynchronous behavior, Wiltermuth and Heath (2009) found that participants in the synchronous conditions felt more connected to their other group members, exhibited greater cooperation, and were more willing to engage in potentially costly social interaction for the collective benefit of the group (Wiltermuth and Heath 2009). Remarkably, participants in this study were merely asked to walk, march, or clap in synch, rather than more complex movements required by yoga or dance, and yet even these simple activities enhanced prosocial behavior.

In a novel mindfulness-based intervention aimed to enhance relationship quality for well-functioning, non-distressed couples, Carson, Carson, Gil, and Baucom (2004) adapted the yoga component of Mindfulness Based Stress Reduction (MBSR) to a partner format. Though the effects of this aspect of the intervention were not evaluated independent of the intervention's other components (meditation, mindful touch, and other mindfulness skills training), a study by Carmody and Baer (2008) found that the yoga component of MBSR was associated with more changes in measures of mindfulness and well-being than body scanning or sitting meditation, providing support for the hypothesis that partner yoga may offer similar benefits to couples. For those who may not be willing to engage in a practice such as partner yoga or other practices with obvious nonsecular roots, dance may offer a rewarding and more accessible alternative.

Dance may, in fact, offer something more than partner yoga does to couples and individuals who engage in group dance classes and dance events. Haidt et al. (2008) propose that the highest levels of individual well-being require occasional opportunities to transcend the self and merge with a larger social organism. According to the hive hypothesis proposed by Haidt et al. (2008), the self—particularly the modern Western self plagued by isolating tendencies and the pressures of capitalism—poses an obstacle to the fullest realization of human happiness. In the language of mindfulness, clinging to our concept of a distinct and separate self obscures our access to the deeper fulfillment available through realizing the fundamental interconnectedness of all life. As mentioned above, the loss of self through group rituals involving dance, music, and other forms of synchronized movement is an ancient and perhaps evolutionarily advantageous facet of collective human experience. Durkheim (1915) described this phenomenon as "collective effervescence" and "considered the intense passion and joy generated by these periodic events to be essential in the long-term maintenance of a cohesive group" (Haidt et al. 2008, p. 140).

We know from positive psychology that positive emotions such as joy, connection, awe, and a sense of purpose are both indicators and causes of well-being (Shapiro and Carlson 2009). The benefits of collective effervescence may accrue to the individual directly through the cultivation of these states, or indirectly through the "social capital" and sense of belonging that engagement in collective action generates (Haidt et al. 2008). One implication among others of the hive hypothesis is that in the context of dance, synchronized styles of dance should offer greater benefits than freestyle dancing in which individuals move according to their own desires. However, the study by Wiltermuth and Heath (2009) found that large motor movements were not superior to singing alone and other subtler forms of synchronization in facilitating increased cooperation.

Furthermore, the merging of the self with a larger social organism is not the only mechanism by which dancers experience a transcendent state. As Tessa Cook, a former dancer with Nederlands Dans Theater, so eloquently expressed, "Through dancing I have experienced how fantastic it is to give. You are full of love and then you are given something, music, dance, and you are able to give that to other people. In dance you can express all your emotions. When I danced, I felt always relieved. I never needed to express myself with words" (Tessa Cook; Aalten 2004, p. 273). In an article examining embodied experiences in ballet, anthropologist Anna Aalten studied the practices, training methods, and life stories of a group of professional ballet dancers. Though in the corps de ballet, perfect synchronization is in fact a physical and aesthetic ideal, ballet is not generally conceived of as a group activity. Rather, the training and daily striving for perfection of a ballet dancer is more often compared to a lone runner racing against her own best time. And yet, her observations led Aalten to conclude that "even ballet with its technical rules and regulations… offers women the possibility to exceed the discontinuity of body, mind and emotions…In ballet women learn to control their bodies, but they also experience, even for a moment, the synchronizing of physicality, willpower and emotionality" (Aalten 2004, p. 274). This is what several dancers in Aalten's (2004) study referred to as when "it all comes together." Dance, as a mindfulness practice, offers us the opportunity to bridge our inner and outer worlds, to experience and embody the felt sense of interconnection between mind and body, self and other that enhances well-being and our capacity to facilitate transformation and healing in others.

Dance as Therapy

While dance has much to offer both practitioners and clients as an informal practice to cultivate mindful awareness of the body and mind, there is also evidence to suggest that it can be an effective therapeutic intervention for specific psychological disorders. Such potential can come from the evolution of somatic education and somatic therapy (Eddy 2009). As Eddy (2009) notes, "The goal of the somatic movement professional is to heighten both sensory and motor awareness to facilitate a student-client's own self-organization, self-healing, or self-knowing" (p. 8). Among the pioneers in somatic therapies are the founders of the Feldenkrais Method and Rolfing, both alternative therapies that leverage the mind-body connection to facilitate healing. Though these approaches are not what is meant when we speak of dance as a therapeutic intervention, it is the intersection and cross-pollination of thought between somatic healers, dancers, and the world of psychotherapy that gave rise to various body-oriented psychotherapy modalities, including dance movement therapy (DMT) (Eddy 2009, p. 24; Röhricht 2009).

DMT was first founded in the 1950s by dancer and choreographer Marian Chase. By the 1970s, Chase and others had founded the American Dance Therapy Association (ADTA), and today DMT is regarded as an effective evidence-based intervention for the treatment of anxiety, depression, eating disorders, somatoform disorders, and chronic pain (Koch et al. 2014). In practice, DMT encompasses multiple dance styles and disciplines; it is not itself a unique "dance" or "technique" to be learned, but rather a process "viewing the human body as the vessel or container, and rhythmic movement as the medium, [wherein] the receptor systems—kinesthetic, proprioceptive, vestibular, auditory, visual—can be systematically manipulated for therapeutic ends" (Berrol 1992). As such, DMT practitioners work within a variety of dance styles, including modern dance, ballroom dance, social dances, and improv. Whereas in talk therapy, the client's verbal and nonverbal communications are interpreted by the therapist in an effort to offer insight into the client's behavioral and cognitive patterns, DMT takes movement as the source of such insight.

Mindful Dance

Though DMT could perhaps be described as a form of "mindful movement," in practice mindfulness is not an explicit component of DMT. Likewise, "dance" has not often been incorporated into mindfulness-based interventions as a form of mindful movement. And yet, research exploring the benefits of such practices can help us understand what the union of mindfulness and dance can offer as a therapeutic intervention. In a study evaluating the effects of movement-based courses on self-regulatory self-efficacy, mood, stress, and sleep quality in college students, Caldwell et al. (2010) found that movement classes produced significant increases in mindfulness as measured by scores on the Five Facet Mindfulness Questionnaire (FFMQ). Moreover, changes in mindfulness were associated with improved mood, lower perceived stress, and better sleep quality (Caldwell et al. 2010). The movement-based courses included in the study (GYROKINESIS, Taiji Quan, Pilates) each offered an explicit component of mind-body awareness training, though the mechanisms of action by which these courses increased mindful awareness were not explored in greater depth. Nonetheless, these findings provide support for mindful movement as a possible intervention for a range of psychological disorders and as a form of self-care for practitioners.

Approaching dance as an informal mindfulness practice may significantly enhance the benefits of dance interventions, because mindfulness offers a kind, open, accepting attitude. The effects of dance on psychological well-being may be limited or confounded by the negative internal and external pressures that dancers can face at all levels. Rather than enhancing mind-body awareness, dance training can just as easily widen the gap between mind and body through the objectification of the dancer's body as a "tool" for achieving a certain set of aesthetic and artistic ideals. In the pursuit of aesthetic ideals often at odds with the body's natural structure and range of motion, dancers can develop harsher rather than kinder relationships to their own bodies. As neuroplasticity and mindfulness teach us, what we practice grows stronger (Shapiro 2017). Practicing dance does not promise to enhance psychological well-being if it reinforces rather than diminishes engrained habits of self-judgment, anxiety, perfectionism, and striving.

One innovative RCT sought to compare the effects of Argentine tango and mindfulness meditation to determine whether dance training could be as effective as mindfulness training in the treatment of depression (Pinniger et al. 2012). Participants were assigned to one of three groups: tango, mindfulness, and a wait-list control group. After six weeks of training, both the tango and mindfulness groups reported significant reductions in self-reported depression. However, the tango group also reported significant reductions in stress when compared to the other two groups. As Pinniger and colleagues (2012) note, "This suggests that dynamic physical activities may be more effective in reducing psychological stress than static activities such as mindfulness meditation" (p. 6). Another surprising result from the study found that the tango group reported greater increases in mindfulness than either the mindfulness or control group, suggesting that it may not be necessary for mindfulness meditation to be an explicit component of a movement practice for it to confer some of the same benefits.

A study by Sze et al. (2010) further explored the different effects of mindfulness meditation and dance, comparing experienced meditators to experienced dancers on measures of coherence between emotional experience and physiology. Sze et al. (2010) found that meditators exhibited greater levels of self-reported visceral awareness and higher levels of coherence between subjective emotional experience and heart period. Dancers displayed higher levels of coherence than did control group participants, and results for the control group were consistent with the assumption that a certain amount of coherence is built-in (Sze et al. 2010). The implication is that our inherent levels of emotional coherence may be improved by training such as dance, which tends to improve somatic awareness (muscle, tension, balance, posture), but are more likely to be maximized by training that also includes meditation's focus on visceral awareness (breath, heartbeat). The benefits of such training offer fertile ground for future research.

The role of emotional response coherence in human relationships is the focus of a growing body of work demonstrating that "greater coherence is associated with increased positive affect and well-being" (Sze et al. 2010, p. 811). Mauss and colleagues (2011) argue that effects of emotional coherence on psychological well-being are mediated by social connectedness, a hypothesis supported by the results of a prospective longitudinal study evaluating 135 participants over a period of six months.

Benefits of Mindful Dance for Clinicians

We know that when therapists practice mindfulness it can improve patient outcomes and enhance practitioner effectiveness (Grepmair et al. 2007). Mindful movement may offer similar benefits beyond self-care that extend to patient outcomes insofar as such practices enhance qualities that are essential to effective therapy. Though this emerging field of research offers much territory yet to be explored, it suggests that movement training specifically designed to enhance both visceral and somatic awareness may not only increase positive affect, but may also improve the accuracy with which internal emotional states are communicated to others. This is especially important for those in the helping professions.

The client-therapist relationship is often described as a dance. It is an apt metaphor in that it captures the organic, unpredictable, fluid, and interdependent nature of the therapeutic relationship. As dancers must, both therapist and client are compelled to be equal partners in building the trust, intimacy, and connection that foster healing and create the art of a life well lived. It is the coming together with each other, but also with ourselves, that mindful movement offers, an opportunity to merge our inner and outer worlds—nurture the container and its contents—to achieve the integration that underlies an authentic and fulfilling life.

Future Directions and Conclusion

Expanding our understanding of mindfulness to include somatic as well as mental processes is essential. As we've discussed, one possible area of future exploration is to study informal practices of mindful movement. We offered dance as one such practice and reviewed the pioneering research suggesting its potential benefits for both patients and clinicians. There are a number of important future directions and research paths that merit attention in this new area.

It will be helpful to explore ways of integrating dance into already existing mindfulness-based intervention programs. It will also be helpful to develop dance-based therapies that integrate mindfulness. Future research could also investigate the impact of mindfulness and dance-based therapy on both patients and clinicians. Of particular interest is the extent to which mindfulness and dance can be used to help health professionals develop core clinical skills, and the impact on clinical outcomes. Also important is research investigating the mechanisms through which these effects occur.

Mindfulness-informed dance therapy has not been tested empirically. Studies that investigate the outcomes associated with mindful dance and other mindful movement in the therapeutic setting are needed.

Further research also needs to focus on the impact of mindful movement and mindful dance on self-care for healthcare professionals. We know that self-care is critical for health professionals, both in terms of protecting practitioners' own health and well-being and for optimizing outcomes for patients. Accordingly, it is important to attend specifically to this dimension of clinician well-being.

The potential applications of mindful movement and dance for clinicians and patients are far-reaching. We are hopeful that continued research and exploration in this area will bring greater awareness of the richness and dimensionality of mindfulness as an embodied practice.

References

Aalten, A. (2004). The Moment When It All Comes Together': Embodied Experiences in Ballet. *The European Journal of Women's Studies, 11*, 263–276.

Barks, C. (1995). *The Essential Rumi*. San Francisco: Harper.
Berrol, C. F. (1992). The Neurophysiologic Basis of the Mind-Body Connection in Dance/Movement Therapy. *American Journal of Dance Therapy, 14*(1), 19–29.
Caldwell, K., Harrison, M., Adams, M., Quin, R., & Greeson, J. (2010). Developing Mindfulness in College Students Through Movement-Based Courses: Effects on Self-Regulatory Self-Efficacy, Mood, Stress, and Sleep Quality. *Journal of American College Health, 58*(5), 433–442.
Carmody, J., & Baer, R. (2008). Relationships Between Mindfulness Practice and Levels of Mindfulness, Medical and Psychological Symptoms and Well Being in a Mindfulness-Based Stress Reduction Program. *Journal of Behavioral Medicine, **31***, 23–33.
Carson, J. W., Carson, K. M., Gil, K. M., & Baucom, D. H. (2004). Mindfulness-Based Relationship Enhancement. *Behavior Therapy, 35*, 471–494.
Durkheim, E. [1915] (1965). *The Elementary Forms of the Religious Life* (J. W. Swain, Trans.). New York: Free Press.
Eddy, M. (2009). A Brief History of Somatic Practices and Dance: Historical Development of the Field of Somatic Education and Its Relationship to Dance. *Journal of Dance and Somatic Practices, 1*(1), 5–27.
Grepmair, L., Mitterlehner, F., Loew, T., & Nickel, M. (2007). Promotion of Mindfulness in Psychotherapists in Training: Preliminary Study. *European Psychiatry, 22*(8), 485–489.
Haidt, J., Patrick Seder, J., & Kesebir, S. (2008). Hive Psychology, Happiness, and Public Policy. *The Journal of Legal Studies, 37*(S2), S133–S156.
Joyce, J. (1914). *Dubliners (Illustrated)*. Cork: BookBaby.
Killingsworth, M. A., & Gilbert, D. T. (2010). A Wandering Mind Is an Unhappy Mind. *Science, 330*(6006), 932–932.
Koch, S., Kunz, T., Lykou, S., & Cruz, R. (2014). Effects of Dance Movement Therapy and Dance on Health-Related Psychological Outcomes: A Meta-Analysis. *The Arts in Psychotherapy, 41*(1), 46–64.
Mauss, I., Shallcross, A., Troy, A., John, O., Ferrer, E., Wilhelm, F., & Gross, J. (2011). Don't Hide Your Happiness! Positive Emotion Dissociation, Social Connectedness, and Psychological Functioning. *Journal of Personality and Social Psychology, 100*(4), 738–748.
Pinniger, R., Brown, R. F., Thorsteinsson, E. B., & Mckinley, P. (2012). Argentine Tango Dance Compared to Mindfulness Meditation and a Waiting-List Control: A Randomised Trial for Treating Depression. *Complementary Therapies in Medicine, 20*(6), 377–384.

Rohitassa Sutta: To Rohitassa (AN 4.45). (2013). (T. Bhikkhu, Trans.). *Access to Insight (Legacy Edition)*.

Röhricht, F. (2009). Body Oriented Psychotherapy. The State of the Art in Empirical Research and Evidence-Based Practice: A Clinical Perspective. *Body, Movement and Dance in Psychotherapy, 4*(2), 135–156.

Salzberg, S. (1995). *Lovingkindness: The Revolutionary Art of Happiness*. Boston: Shambhala.

Shapiro, S. L. (2017, March). *Shauna Shapiro: The Power of Mindfulness: What You Practice Grows Stronger* [Video File]. Retrieved from https://www.youtube.com/watch?v=IeblJdB2-Vo

Shapiro, S., & Carlson, L. (2009). *The Art and Science of Mindfulness: Integrating Mindfulness into Psychology and the Helping Professions*. American Psychological Association.

Siegel, D. (2007). *The Mindful Brain*. New York: W. W. Norton.

Sze, J., Gyurak, A., Yuan, J., & Levenson, R. (2010). Coherence Between Emotional Experience and Physiology: Does Body Awareness Training Have an Impact? *Emotion, 10*(6), 803–814.

Wallace, A. B., & Bodhi, B. (2006). *The Nature of Mindfulness and Its Role in Buddhist Meditation: A Correspondence Between B. Alan Wallace and the Venerable Bhikkhu Bodhi* (Unpublished Manuscript). Santa Barbara Institute for Consciousness Studies, Santa Barbara.

Whyte, D. (2015). *Consolations: The Solace, Nourishment and Underlying Meaning of Everyday Words*. Langley: Many Rivers Press.

Wiltermuth, S., & Heath, C. (2009). Synchrony and Cooperation. *Psychological Science, 20*(1), 1–5.

8

Benefits of Theatrical Improvisation in the Training of Psychotherapists

Daniel J. Wiener

Introduction

Theater improvisation ("improv") is a method of stage acting characterized by spontaneous invention and distinguished by the minimal use of prearranged structures such as scripts, plots or props. As performed, improv has both an individual component (spontaneity) and, equally important, a relational one (cooperative engagement with others). As expressed by Knoblauch (2001), improvisation can be defined as "an unpremeditated spontaneous activity emerging within an interactive context" (p. 786). According to Lowe, "Improv[isation] is a relationship. It is a relationship with oneself and with others" (Lowe 2000, p. 38). Viola Spolin, an early originator of improv games who employed them therapeutically, stated: "improv[isation] is not an exchange of information between players; it is communion" (Spolin 1963, p. 45).

D. J. Wiener (✉)
Central Connecticut State University, New Britain, CT, USA
e-mail: wienerd@ccsu.edu

B. Kirkcaldy (ed.), *Psychotherapy, Literature and the Visual and Performing Arts*, Palgrave Studies in Creativity and Culture, https://doi.org/10.1007/978-3-319-75423-9_8

Improv has, over the past 40 years, acquired visibility in popular Western culture primarily as a form of entertainment, a descendent of the *commedia dell'arte* that flourished in sixteenth-century Italy. From a still broader perspective, improv can be classified as a specific branch of non-scripted theater that has its roots in pre-literate oral storytelling traditions (Fox 1994).

Improv should be distinguished from clinical role playing, which "refers to [goal-directed] behavior expressed as a result of a conscious decision on the part of the player or at the request of others" (Kipper 1986). McReynolds and DeVoge (1977) delineate a hybrid practice, "improvisational role playing," which they describe as "a subclass of role playing in which the subject, given that he accepts the circumstances with which a role-play opens, makes up his behavior as he goes along – he is thus simply himself dealing with a somewhat novel problem situation" (p. 224). While clinical role playing may involve a degree of improvisational performance, both its explicit pre-assignment of client and therapist roles and its implicit rules to practice realistic, purposive and ethically conforming conduct constrain its practitioners from partaking fully in the far-less-bounded spontaneous and playful spirit characteristic of improv.

My Personal and Professional Journey into Improv

My use of improv in therapy developed out of a hobby—stage-improvising with other actors who were also drawn to the "risky fun" of public performance without preparation for what was going to happen next. I also enjoyed the opportunity to explore playing characters very different from my usual social persona, including uninhibited, colorful, even antisocial ones who could then have all kinds of (mis)adventures on stage without any real-life consequences. The cardinal rule of improv is to "accept all offers," which means that the actors co-create a stage reality by an ever-shifting, moment-to-moment consensus instead of struggling to control or explain what is to happen next. The result of following this rule is a cooperative flow that brings the actors emotionally closer to one another as they launch (at times) into absurd, fantastic and vivid onstage adventures.

After about a year of stage-improvising, I noticed that some improvisers, who were performing capably most of the time with their stage partners, became strangely "de-skilled" when they were paired with certain other stage partners. The parallel with the functioning of certain couples I was treating clinically was striking. That is, for these couples, each individual partner presented to me as socially considerate, respectful and attentive. However, when interacting in my presence with their life partners, each exhibited competitive, dismissive, even hurtful behavior toward the partner. It then dawned on me that good improvising has a lot in common with *good relationship functioning*: both require cooperation, support, attending closely to one's partner and making the partner look good. Following this epiphany, I began to use certain improv exercises that I had adapted from stage performance to *assess* relationship functioning in my clinical practice, first with couples, then with families and later with groups. Regularly, I would find a correspondence between their difficulties in improvising together and their problems in social relating. Soon after, I began also to utilize improv exercises as *interventions* to teach clients how better to connect and cooperate with others.

Core Rules of Improv

As noted above, the cardinal rule of improv is to "accept all offers" (sometimes phrased as "Yes And"), meaning that everything proposed or implied to one player by another is to be taken as valid and contributing directly to the stage reality being co-created in that moment. In what follows, a person who is on stage and takes on dramatic character is termed a "player."

If Player A holds out her hand toward Player B, saying, "Here are your keys," Player B must accept the stage reality that (a) there are keys that Player A is holding out and (b) that he is being offered the return of these keys, implying that Player A's character believes them to belong to his character. By miming the taking of keys from Player A's character, Player B is fulfilling the "Yes" part of the rule, agreement with that reality; he then must fulfill the "And" part, perhaps by saying in a grateful manner, "Thanks, Sally, I'm always forgetting things lately," indicating that he knows her and recognizes that he is often forgetful. This addition by Player B provides an offer for Player A to accept; in this way the scene evolves through its co-creation by both players. If, instead, Player B were to say, "What keys? That's a matchbox," he would be violating the "Yes" part (which is termed "blocking") by negating the stage reality of the keys, while if he merely took the keys without saying or doing anything additional, he would be failing the "And" part of the rule by giving nothing to Player A upon which to develop the scene further (for a fuller explanation, see Wiener 1994, pp. 59–63).

An additional rule is that you are to attend closely to everything, both internal and external: to your stage partners; to objects and place features introduced in the scene; and to details of your own character as it is being developed in the unfolding scene (so that you are fully aware of and responsive to all offers). Aligning with this rule sharpens the here-and-now focus on the present moment. Gale (2004) refers to this rule as "contextual amplification." A third rule is to build and maintain trust among players by validating one another on multiple levels. Halpern et al. (1994, p. 37) state: "Support and trust go hand in hand for performers; they must trust that their fellow performers will support them. The only star in improv is the ensemble itself; if everyone is doing his job well, then no one should stand out. *The best way for an improviser to look good is by making his fellow players look good* [original emphasis]."

While successful improvising builds upon skills that most adult persons have acquired effortlessly, it should not be thought that "we are all born improvisers." "Improvisational enactment, where players 'make it up' as they go along, is far from an artless, random, or haphazard activity. To improvise well, players must be fully attentive and responsive to cues on multiple levels both from their stage partners and from their own impulses, all while remaining oriented to those time, place, and plot elements already introduced in the scene. Perhaps hardest of all, players need to overcome the deeply ingrained habits of trying to control and anticipate where the scene is going" (Wiener 1999, p. 52).

Since 1985, I have applied, modified and developed a variety of improv exercises that I use in (a) conducting psychoeducational workshops on relationship; (b) clinical practice (primarily with couples, but also with groups and families); (c) demonstrations of applied improv to audiences of mental health professionals and (d) the training of psychotherapists. I have named this application "Rehearsals for Growth," or RfG (Wiener 1994). RfG training for therapists, described further below, also includes distinctive techniques and procedures which I have devised for incorporating improv enactments effectively into relationship therapy.

Life, Improv and Psychotherapy: Perspectives

A broad explanatory paradigm, dramaturgy, surfaced in academic sociology in the 1950s. Dramaturgy is constructed around the fundamental principle that "the meaning of people's doings is to be found in the manner in which they express themselves in interaction with similarly expressive others" (Brissett and Edgley 1990, p. 3). In one extreme version, all social behavior can be understood as theatrical performance; persons are always "on stage" and selectively display only part of themselves to others (Goffman 1959). In numerous ways, "theater is lifelike and life is theater-like" (Wiener 1994, p. 3).

Most psychotherapists are familiar with either or both psychoanalytic and behaviorist paradigms and are comfortable with using reductive analysis to "explain" intrapsychic or interpersonal phenomena. By contrast, a consequence for psychotherapists adopting a dramaturgical perspective is that it is unhelpful to attempt any such analysis; what is meaningful is only that which is experienced in the present moment. Analogously, improvised activities are meaningful in the moment of their (co)creation.

Uses/Benefits of Improv

1. Improv Trains Clients in Life Skills

A major goal of psychotherapists using improv is to enhance their clients' life skills via theatrical training to improve their performance. "Performance," it should be noted, has the dual connotations of "productive action" and "artistic display of oneself"; improvement in both aspects benefits clients. Improv training as a subset of theatrical training is particularly challenging, though it offers numerous practical benefits. Among these is putting our conceptual "truths" to the test of experience. Jean Escow, a noted acting teacher, pointed out that "[t]ruth can be discovered or predicted; discovery comes through improvisation… There lies the great value of improv[isation]; to expose the fact that we often predict actions that we never take. We tell ourselves things that we would, but never do."

A comprehensive listing of skills, the attainment of which improv training is believed to be helpful for, would be quite lengthy. The specific life skills most often cited as enhanced by improv are developing active listening skills, promoting interpersonal trust, accessing and restoring playfulness (especially to adults), opening to creativity, experiencing and acting on spontaneity, reducing the fear of making mistakes, gaining more nuanced perspectives on one's habitual choices, unmasking one's subconscious judgments of self and others, learning to laugh at oneself and gaining confidence in one's own resiliency in the face of the unexpected. To these, Gale (2002) adds the following benefits: better accommodating and adjusting to the fluidity of rules and roles of daily living; assisting in experiencing the boundaries of familiar behaviors as one practices novel behaviors; assisting in learning that one's identity beliefs are not intractable scripts, but composed in social performances; engaging in problem-solving experiences which help practice one's culture's taken-for-granted rules and testing their boundaries.

In order to teach clients life skills through improv, therapists must themselves be able to improvise, both to function as effective instructors and to serve as authentic role models.

2. Improv Benefits the Personal Lives of Therapists

If clients benefit from performing improv techniques in their therapy, it follows that therapists obtain these same benefits when they train in and practice improv, though the context of their own learning is different. Improv taught to clients in therapy is "packaged" at the initiative of the therapist, who is somewhat aware from an external perspective of some of the clients' deficits in life functioning. Consequently, a therapist can make connections between a client's improv skills and his/her life functions during therapy. Also, the therapist can effectively monitor the immediate impact of improv training on clients during sessions, pace the introduction of new challenges and supportively provide the client with encouragement to face these challenges. The therapist who learns improv outside of the client role needs to be more self-directed, though clinical improv training programs can lessen the differences between the contexts of learning in therapy sessions and learning through improv classes.

3. Improv Techniques Serve as Clinically Useful Tools in Therapy

As described above, the practice of improv is guided by certain rules/principles. "In improvisational theater, these practices were developed to help actors shift from an individualistic (and sometimes competitive) perspective on performance and success, to collaborative performances based on trust, acceptance and the shared accomplishment of meaning" (Gale 2004, p. 2). When improv is practiced in accordance with these rules, the resulting performances conform with good interpersonal functioning (Wiener 1994). Consequently, the offering of improv exercises to clients in therapy serves as an assessment tool, a situational test of clients' ability to interact according to these rules. While there is some benefit in conducting assessments of individual functioning (see Wiener 1999), the most useful applications of improv tasks to clinical assessment are to relationships, as the interaction of the improvisers then becomes the focus of observation.

Beyond its uses in assessment, improv tasks can be employed as training methods that teach clients those specific individual and interpersonal skills which prior assessment has identified as deficient. When conducting relationship therapy (with families and couples), such improv enactments serve as interventions directed at improving the relationship itself (Wiener 1994).

While there has been widespread anecdotal evidence for the effectiveness of improv training in improving mental health, only recently has there also been published empirical evidence. In a recently published study (Kreuger et al. 2017), four 2-hour sessions of group improv training over an eight-week period were used to treat 31 outpatient psychiatric patients presenting with symptoms of anxiety, depression and low self-esteem. Significant improvement was found for all three, with medium effect sizes for anxiety and depression.

4. Improv Training Enhances Therapist Effectiveness

A considerable number of clinicians, representing both a diversity of theoretical orientations and writing over a 50-year span, have advocated therapists taking an improvisational approach in conducting therapy to obtain, among many others, the following benefits: self-playfulness as an example to clients (Winnicott 1971); flexibility, activeness and directness (Knoblauch 2001; Satir 1967); spontaneity (Moreno 1987); moment-to-moment creative engagement with clients (Ringstrom 2011; Kindler and Gray 2010); generating excitement (Pagano 2012); modeling risk-taking to potentiate client growth (Wiener 1994). However, far fewer have proposed specific methods during the training and supervision of therapists by which these benefits may be attained.

The RfG Training Program for Therapists

Development of RfG Training

While I offered sporadic one-day demonstration and practice workshops in RfG starting in 1991, by 1999 I had begun a Certificate Program to train practitioners to offer RfG to clients. The program consisted of 60 hours of direct instruction, assigned readings and demonstrated skill in conducting therapy sessions using RfG. Since 2013, these 60 hours of direct instruction have been divided into four levels of 15 hours each (Wiener 2017b). Trainees in the current RfG Certificate training begin with experiencing improv enactments in the role of client/participant, progress to taking the role of therapist/director offering to others, move on by learning to process client enactments verbally immediately afterward and culminate in offering case material from their practices for consultation (such cases are simulated in role plays by the training group). Trainees also review videotapes of their performances from workshops and study a training video of a simulated couples therapy case (Wiener 2010).

As of mid-2017, 47 therapists have completed this training and approximately another 300 have experienced partial training in RfG or are in process of completing their RfG training. Perhaps another 2000 have gained exposure to RfG through my demonstrations or brief workshops ranging from three hours to two days' duration at about 200 professional conferences and mental health agencies over the past 27 years.

Beginning in 2014, I developed an advanced training for a few RfG Certified Practitioners wishing to offer RfG training; to date there are four RfG Certified Trainers who have qualified to lead RfG training workshops independently.

Description of RfG Training

All RfG exercises are enactments that have both structured and improvisational components. The structure (or premise), offered by the therapist before the enactment begins, orients the clients to some activity, location, character, relationship, attitude and/or outcome. (For example, when working with a couple, the therapist says: "The two of you are to have a Tug of War with this imaginary rope. One of you will be the winner and the contest will last no more than thirty seconds. When I give the signal, pick up the rope lying on the floor between you and begin. Remember to make the rope look real during your contest. OK...begin!") The improvisational component is manifested by the choices the clients make during the enactment, reflected in their ongoing bodily, emotional and verbal interaction.

Note that the RfG therapist is not her/himself improvising when offering structures or when providing a context for the clients to improvise within the premises and rules set forth. The skills needed to function effectively as an RfG therapist include choosing an RfG exercise that is appropriate to and timely for the clinical context of the moment; being encouraging, though not pushy, in inviting clients to stretch their comfort level to undertake some unfamiliar task; skillfully directing the Post-Enactment Processing (when clients reflect on their very recent experience with the enactment, possibly generalizing these experiences to their real-life ones); and (at a more advanced level) devising a "Proxy Scenes," which are distinctive enactments fashioned to address an identified impasse in the client's individual or relationship functioning (Wiener 2016a).

RfG is, to my knowledge, unique among psychotherapy approaches as the only comprehensive method providing training for therapists who offer in-session improv to therapy clients. While most of my subsequent professional publications have presented advances in RfG clinical technique, I have also recently written two e-books that specifically address the training of therapists in the use of RfG: *The RfG Practitioner's Manual* (Wiener 2017c) and the *Handbook for RfG Trainers* (Wiener 2016b).

Despite improv's utility in both conducting therapy and enhancing the therapist's effective use of self, there has been relatively little improv training available for practitioners. It is surprising that improv training is uncommon in drama therapy, the intentional use of drama and/or theater processes to achieve therapeutic goals. Drama therapy emerged in the 1970s as one of the creative arts therapies; nearly all of its professional members have theatrical training and stage experience. Historically, improv was the main therapeutic intervention employed with psychiatric patients by Vladimir Iljine in the early 1900s (Jones 2007); it has remained one of the essential strands woven into the tapestry of drama therapy (Tucker-Bye 1999). Four of drama therapy's main current approaches—RfG, classified as a drama therapy of relationships; Insight Improvisation (Gluck 2007); Emunah's Integrative Five-Stage Model (Emunah 2009); and Developmental Transformations (Johnson 2009)—all utilize improv as core practices. Yet, formal training in improv is not a prominent feature of drama therapy education (only one of the five degree-granting, accredited drama therapy training programs in North America presently offers a course on improvisation). Rather, several of the approaches in drama therapy adapt improvisational techniques as means to therapeutic ends, building upon students' prior stage experience with improv.

Evaluation of RfG Training

From the onset of my offering RfG trainings to therapists, the ongoing evaluation of RfG training's effectiveness has been shaped by two quite different perspectives. One of these is a more cognitive, "objective" perspective in which trainee skills can be evaluated by trainers during observation of them directing others to improvise. Acquisition of a skill is rated by the correspondence between their observable behaviors and explicit criteria deemed to represent competent practice. For example, when directing clients to improvise during the tug-of-war exercise described above, did the trainee: (a) Give the players accurate and complete instructions? [Yes.] (b) Ask for questions? [No.] (c) Coach the clients if they departed from these instructions during the enactment? [Unknown, until we witness the way they performed the enactment.] While the abovementioned Clinical Skills cannot be performed competently by a therapist inexperienced personally in improv performance, they do not ordinarily involve the exercise of a therapist's own improv skills during their conduct of therapy sessions.

The other perspective on evaluating therapists is more impressionistic and "subjective," having as its focus a cluster of attitudinal and expressive qualities.

These qualities include risk-taking, therapeutic presence, playfulness, flexibility/adaptability, heightened empathy for clients and greater self-disclosure in sessions, mindfulness (immediacy/present-centered awareness), spontaneity, therapeutic charisma and greater confidence in trusting one's intuition. While evidence for these qualities is sporadically observable, either singly or as a cluster, it has not been found to be particularly useful to provide trainer ratings of these qualities, though growth in Improvising Skills and growth in these attitudinal/expressive qualities appear positively correlated.

Acquisition of Improvising Skills

Beginning in 2013, the RfG Certificate Program has conducted ratings by trainers of the proficiency of trainees as they progress through the

Intermediate and Advanced Program Levels (resulting in either one or two ratings per trainee for those who went on to complete the program). As noted above, these ratings are divided into two subgroups: Improvising Skills and RfG Clinical Skills.

The Improvising Skills are ones deemed foundational to successful improv stage performance; a handful of trainees entered the program already possessing sufficient training and practice in these skills, which include accepting offers, attending fully to others during enactments, physicalizing objects and space, appropriately displaying broad emotional range, inventive storytelling, using status maneuvers intentionally, staying in character, and playful flexibility. Other RfG trainees become familiar with and develop some familiarity with these skills through participation in improv games during the Basic and Beginning Levels, though (as noted earlier) they are strongly encouraged to acquire broader improv experience outside of RfG trainings.

Acquisition of RfG Clinical Skills

The following RfG Clinical Skills, taught, demonstrated and practiced during training at all levels, are ones deemed "foundational" to the practice of RfG therapy: giving instructions to basic RfG techniques; offering corrective feedback to, during or after, basic RfG techniques; inducing clients to attempt techniques; integrating RfG with one's own specified therapeutic approach. Limited training is offered in the following (more advanced) RfG Clinical Skills which are deemed "nonessential/advanced," though desirable: providing a rationale for productive use of a technique in a clinical or psychoeducational setting; usefully modifying a technique to accommodate to present clinical circumstances; integrating outcome(s) of a technique with a clinical/teaching intervention immediately following enactment; creating a sequence of techniques which accomplish a larger clinical or psychoeducational objective; and creating novel scenarios (Proxy Scenes) to meet a clinical objective.

Excluding data from trainees who had not (yet) completed the Intermediate Level, inspection of trainer ratings from 2013 to 2016 that were done from Beginner through completion of Advanced Levels showed collective improvement in demonstrated proficiency in Improvising Skills (almost all rated as "competent") as they progressed through the Certificate Program. By contrast, ratings of about one-third of trainees "leveled off" in "foundational" RfG Clinical Skills during their progress through the program, only attaining (by the date of their last level achieved) "Approaching Competence." Ratings of the "nonessential/advanced" RfG Clinical Skills showed only about one-quarter of trainees attaining ratings of "competent."

Discussion

My repeated experience in teaching RfG over the past 19 years has been that many trainees, particularly those who had not performed any stage improv themselves, have difficulty applying RfG in their practices following their training. While stage improv classes and/or performance are not mandated for certification, from the onset of RfG training they have been strongly recommended for practitioners wishing to apply RfG most effectively (Wiener 1994). Also, when therapists practice in a professional environment that offers no support for these newly learned skills (as is generally the case in all agencies at which these therapists work), there are subjective norms in force there that nullify the retention of new skills. Only during those intervals when I had organized monthly meetings for groups of RfG trainees to socialize, play improv games with one another and present cases for peer consultation, was the enthusiasm and use of RfG in their practices maintained.

While I have not maintained these monthly meetings in my own trainings, Lisa Kays, a social worker and RfG Certified Practitioner, has been offering an "Improv for Therapists" group for the past two years in Washington, DC, to expand the effective use of self of therapists. Recently, she added a weekly improv-informed clinical consultation group to promote long-term sustained learning for therapists interested in exploring improv as a tool for self-exploration, consultation and self-care in greater depth. This group combines improv exercises, group processing, outside study and reflection, and participant-led exercises. Anecdotally, she reports seeing greater use of improv by her group's members (Kays 2017).

Indicants of Personal and Professional Growth

In addition to trainers' ratings of skills, trainees provided written answers to twelve open-ended questions within a month of their completion of each of the four levels. These questions differed slightly at each level, with those at the first two levels eliciting reactions to, and what was learned from, the experience of improvising, while those at the third and fourth levels emphasize challenges to applying RfG Clinical Skills in practice. In the questionnaires given to trainees at all levels are questions which invite reflection on how RfG practice impacts personal growth, changes in therapeutic practice and the trajectory of the trainee's professional life. Thirty-eight trainees' answers to these reflective questions contain frequent references to their growth in: therapeutic presence, lessened concern over making mistakes, increased energy for playful interaction, both with clients and social friends; willingness to set aside their "professional mask" and encounter clients more authentically; and greater confidence in allowing intuitive choices.

Literature Review of the Uses and Benefits of Improv Training for Psychotherapists

In her dissertation research, Pishney (2010) created a demonstration videotape of a training workshop in stage improv containing two improv warm-ups, three different improv exercises and five improvised scenes based on the same scenario, enacted by different actors. This videotape offered viewers a window into improvisational performance but was not itself designed as a training video for therapists. This videotape was viewed by five licensed mental health clinicians who were then interviewed about the impact of their viewing experience upon (1) their own listening and creative engagement skills and (2) their interest in applying those demonstrated improv techniques to their own clinical practices. All five reported that they saw the relevance of improv training to developing clinical skills in active listening, enhancing therapeutic presence and activating therapists' creativity. Four of the five reported that they could envisage themselves using some of the demonstrated techniques in their own clinical practices. All five also commented spontaneously on how challenging and even anxiety-provoking they supposed improv performance to be and how improv practice would be necessary to lessen or overcome such anxiety.

Pishney's study, which was limited to interviewing a very small number of subjects on their opinions concerning how they might feel when improvising and what value they saw in improv training for themselves, produced no data on how therapists respond to actual improv training. A far more useful study was conducted by Romanelli et al. (2017). In the pilot study of an experiment conducted over a three-year period using 41 subjects with a median of six years' clinical experience, these authors examined the effects of actual improv skills training on both therapists' perceptions of therapy and their subsequent clinical practices.

Improv skills were taught to these subjects in a semester-long specialty course at a university graduate social work school in Israel. A maximum of 16 students were enrolled per class; the same three-hour-per-week class was offered to different students during three consecutive semesters. Course pedagogy was organized around the principles of experiential learning theory (Kolb 2015), implemented as a sequence of (1) direct experience of improv exercises; (2) reflective observation of these experiences; (3) abstract conceptualization, relating their improv experiences to other therapeutic and theatrical concepts; and (4) active experimentation with improv techniques in their clinical practices. Instruction in each class was organized around one of nine different improv skills (Romanelli et al. 2017, Table 1, p. 13).

Individual interviews lasting between one and two-and-a-half hours were conducted with 17 of the 41 participating students, diverse in their theoretical orientations, in two domains: (1) significant moments in the training and reflections on their concurrent internal process and (2) experiences following the course. Inquiry in this latter domain explored (a) which specific tools and skills learned in the course they had been using, (b) changes noticed in their perceptions of clinical encounters and (c) changes noticed in their perceptions of their own clinical interventions. A qualitative analysis that related to improvisation and spontaneity, and which focused on shared terms, concepts and descriptions generated by the interviews, produced the following changes in self of therapist, followed in parentheses by the number out of the 17 who reported having such experiences: increased intuitional thinking (9), improved sense of spontaneity/flexibility (7), increased play/playfulness (16), improved awareness of emotions (15), increased relaxation and congruence/self-validation (10), less fear of making mistakes (9), increased self-confidence in the therapist role (8), heightened sense of "presence" (awareness of the here and now) as the therapist (11), and new, enlarged perspectives on therapy and on the role of therapist (13). The following changes in therapeutic action were reported: became more animated, direct and daring (14); increased self-disclosure (16); and applied improv techniques learned during the course in session (10). "Overall, therapists experienced enhanced levels of presence, self-validation, increased animation and playfulness, as well as bringing more of themselves to the clinical encounter" (Romanelli et al. 2017, p. 18). These authors emphasize the correspondence between these reported effects and several dimensions of the construct "Therapeutic Presence," "the process of bringing oneself completely to the encounter with the client on the emotional, physical, cognitive and spiritual levels" (Geller and Greenberg 2012, p. 4).

Comparisons of (a) RfG and (b) Romanelli et al. Improv Training on Therapists

To my knowledge, these two programs are the only ones to have been designed to provide improv training for therapists. The main differences between these training programs are that (a) is a 60-hour ongoing program that offers therapists training in how to use client-enacted improv techniques in session, while (b) was a 48-hour pilot program offering therapists personal experiences of improv without any training in, or even encouragement to, apply improv to client enactment (Romanelli 2017). What is striking, however, are the similarities in self-reported benefits between these two programs: heightened therapeutic presence, lessened concern for making mistakes, increased playfulness, greater willingness to take risks and greater confidence in trusting one's intuition.

Conclusion: Practical Guidelines for the Effective Use of Improv in Therapy

As noted above, therapists need to have firsthand experience with improv prior to offering improv to clients successfully. Beyond that, you as the therapist will improve your chances of facilitating a worthwhile outcome for your clients by attending to the following, somewhat overlapping, guidelines:

1. *Check your own readiness and willingness to have a novel adventure before proposing improv enactments to your clients.* If you're not "up for an adventure," your energy will signal to clients that what follows is unlikely to be transformative.
2. *Prior to commencing improv enactments, briefly turn your attention inward to bring into awareness any judgments and expectations you may have regarding clients' performances.* Being thus aware may not significantly alter your attitude, but facilitates greater openness to seeing what clients actually do in the enactment (and challenges confirmation bias).
3. *Accept all offers of client performances in the enactment.* By aligning with the fundamental rule of improv you set aside subjective standards by which you might judge clients, both for their adherence to your instructions and for the quality of their performances.
4. *Display yourself as a generous audience.* Our clients are not performing for our entertainment; indeed, from their perspective, they are taking the risk that their current, palpable discomfort at doing unfamiliar, possibly embarrassing activities will pay off in some far-from-guaranteed improvement in their lives. Demonstrating our admiration for their taking these risks conveys the message that they are courageous and determined to improve.
5. *Remain open to learning from WHATEVER happens.* Improv enactments are open-ended experiments from which valuable lessons can be learned by clients, therapists and witnesses (other family or group members). Improv training teaches us to embrace the unexpected and to treat "mistakes" as gifts.

"Competence that loses a sense of its roots in the playful spirit becomes ensconced in rigid forms of professionalism" (Nachmanovitch 1990, p. 67). In my 45-year professional experience as a practitioner and 30 years as a supervisor, I have seen that therapists who become settled in their practice routines and disinterested in the challenge of further growth are at considerable risk of burnout. While certainly not the exclusive way to staying "fresh," improv is an enlivening practice that confers benefits not only for the conduct of therapy but for therapists' well-being.

References

Brissett, D., & Edgley, C. (Eds.). (1990). *Life as Theater* (2nd ed.). Hawthorne: Aldine de Gruyter.

Emunah, R. (2009). *The Integrative Five-Stage Model of Drama Therapy*. In D. R. Johnson & R. Emunah (Eds.), *Current Approaches in Drama Therapy in North America* (2nd ed., pp. 37–64). Springfield: Charles C. Thomas.

Fox, J. (1994). *Acts of Service: Spontaneity, Commitment and Tradition in the Nonscripted Theater*. New Paltz: Tusitala Publishing.

Gale, J. (2002). Five (Plus or Minus 2) Guiding Principles of Improvisational Performance Relevant to the Practice, Research and Teaching of Therapy. *Journal of Clinical Activities, Assignments and Handouts, 2*(2), 77–88.

Gale, J. (2004). Experiencing Relational Thinking: Lessons from Improvisational Theater. *Context, 75*, 1–12.

Geller, S. M., & Greenberg, L. S. (2012). *Therapeutic Presence: A Mindful Approach to Effective Therapy*. Washington, DC: APA Books.

Gluck, J. (2007). Insight improvisation. In A. Blatner & D. J. Wiener (Eds.), *Interactive and Improvisational Drama: Varieties of Applied Theatre and Performance* (pp. 184–195). New York: iUniverse.

Goffman, E. (1959). *The Presentation of Self in Everyday Life*. Garden City: Doubleday.

Halpern, C., Close, D., & Johnson, K. (1994). *Truth in Comedy: The Manual of Improvisation*. Colorado Springs: Meriwether Publishers.

Johnson, D. R. (2009). Developmental Transformations: Towards the Body as Presence. In D. R. Johnson & R. Emunah (Eds.), *Current Approaches in Drama Therapy in North America* (2nd ed., pp. 89–116). Springfield: Charles C. Thomas.

Jones, P. (2007). *Drama as Therapy: Theory, Practice and Research* (2nd ed.). London: Routledge.

Kays, L. (2017, September 9). Personal Communication.

Kindler, R. C., & Gray, A. A. (2010). Theater and Therapy: How Improvisation Informs the Analytic Hour. *Psychoanalytic Inquiry, 30*, 254–266.

Kipper, D. A. (1986). *Psychotherapy Through Clinical Role-Playing*. New York: Brunner/Mazel.

Knoblauch, S. H. (2001). High-Risk, High-Gain Choices: Commentary on Paper by Phillip A. Ringstrom. *Psychoanalytic Dialogues, 11*, 785–795.

Kolb, D. A. (2015). *Experiential Learning: Experience as the Source of Learning and Development* (2nd ed.). Upper Saddle River: Pearson.

Krueger, K. R., Murphy, J. R., & Bink, A. B. (2017). Thera-prov: A Pilot Study of Improv Used to Treat Anxiety and Depression. *Journal of Mental Health, 1*, 1–7. https://doi.org/10.1080/09638237.2017.1340629.

Lowe, R. (2000). *Improvisation, Inc.: Harnessing Spontaneity to Engage People and Groups*. San Francisco: Jossey-Bass/Pfeiffer and Creative Training Techniques Press.

McReynolds, P., & DeVoge, S. (1977). Use of Improvisational Techniques in Assessment. In P. McReynolds (Ed.), *Advances in psychological assessment* (Vol. 4, pp. 222–277). San Francisco: Jossey-Bass.

Moreno, J. L. (1987). *The Essential Moreno: Writings on Psychodrama, Group Method and Spontaneity*. New York: Springer.

Nachmanovitch, S. (1990). *Free Play*. Los Angeles: Tarcher.

Pagano, C. J. (2012). Exploring the Therapist's Use of Self: Enactments, Improvisation and Affect in Psychodynamic Psychotherapy. *American Journal of Psychotherapy, 66*(3), 205–226.

Pishney, J. L. (2010). *Development of an Improvisational Theatre Skills Training Video to Be Used in the Clinical Training of Psychotherapists* (Unpublished Doctoral Dissertation). Massachusetts School of Professional Psychology.

Ringstrom, P. A. (2011). Principles of Improvisation: A Model of Therapeutic Play in Relational Analysis. In L. Aron & A. Harris (Eds.), *Relational Analysis* (Vol. V, pp. 443–474). New York: The Analytic Press.

Romanelli, A. (2017, September 8–10). *Improv Skills for Therapists: Findings and Application of a Five-Year Study* (Presentation). "Yes And" Mental Health: First Improv and Psychology Conference, Chicago.

Romanelli, A., Tishby, O., & Moran, G. S. (2017). 'Coming Home to Myself': A Qualitative Analysis of Therapists' Experience and Interventions Following Training in Theater Improvisation Skills. *The Arts in Psychotherapy, 53*, 12–22.

Satir, V. (1967). *Conjoint Family Therapy: A Guide to Theory and Technique*. Palo Alto: Science and Behavior Books.
Spolin, V. (1963). *Improvisation for the Theater*. Evanston: Northwestern University Press.
Tucker-Bye, K. (1999). *Improvisation as a Building Block of Drama Therapy* (Unpublished Research Paper). Montreal: Concordia University.
Wiener, D. J. (1994). *Rehearsals for Growth: Theater Improvisation for Psychotherapists*. New York: W. W. Norton.
Wiener, D. J. (1999). Using Theater Improvisation to Assess Interpersonal Functioning. *International Journal of Action Methods, 52*(2), 51–69.
Wiener, D. J. (2010). *Rehearsals for Growth: Couple Therapy* (DVD). Leverett: Self-Published.
Wiener, D. J. (2016a). Removing Personal Constraints via Proxy Scene Enactment. *Drama Therapy Review, 2*(2), 183–193.
Wiener, D. J. (2016b). *Handbook for RfG Trainers*. Northampton: Self-published.
Wiener, D. J. (2017a). *Effectiveness in RfG Workshop Training: 32 Years' Experience*. http://www.rehearsalsforgrowth.com/blog/. Accessed 3 Sept 2017.
Wiener, D. J. (2017b). *2017 Certificate Program*. http://www.rehearsalsforgrowth.com/workshops-playshops/mental-health-professionals/2017-certificate-program/. Accessed 3 Sept 2017.
Wiener, D. J. (2017c). *The RfG Practitioner's Manual* (2nd ed.). Northampton: self-published.
Winnicott, D. W. (1971). *Playing and Reality*. New York: Basic Books.

Part III

Visual Arts, Music and Drama

9

The Development of a Contemplative Art Program for Adolescents and Adults: Challenges and Unexpected Benefits

Christine Korol and Kimberly Sogge

Art is the daughter of freedom.
–Friedrich Schiller

Personal Passion for Working in the Arts and Psychotherapy

We both began working together at Alberta Children's Hospital in 2006. We were working with similar patient populations and learned our joint interests in art and mindfulness-based psychotherapy. We became friends

C. Korol (✉)
Department of Psychology, BC Children's Hospital, Vancouver, BC, Canada

Department of Psychology, University of British Columbia, Vancouver, BC, Canada

K. Sogge
Sogge & Associates Practice in Psychology, Ottawa, ON, Canada
e-mail: kim@drsogge.com

B. Kirkcaldy (ed.), *Psychotherapy, Literature and the Visual and Performing Arts*, Palgrave Studies in Creativity and Culture, https://doi.org/10.1007/978-3-319-75423-9_9

and took the initiative to run psychotherapy groups together, which was practical and enjoyable.

This chapter describes our experiences developing a *contemplative art program* for our adolescent patients and their families. With limited resources and a challenging population, we found the time and energy to create a program that was well-received by patients and renewed our own energy for clinical work. This chapter may encourage other therapists who would like to create their own programs. There were many ups and downs and we appreciated any information that would help navigate the obstacles in front of us. Moreover, this chapter may offer hope in normalizing the frustrations and highlight the many benefits of stretching into new territory.

One of us (KS) had since left academic and hospital institutional work to build a group private practice in clinical psychology in Ottawa, Canada, specializing in mindfulness- and compassion-based interventions for well-being and growth. In between rowing competitions, leading mindfulness retreats and courses, and her own art making, she continues to invite patients to find creative ways to perceive and respond to their experience and themselves.

The other, CK, began cartooning shortly after the initial run of Contemplative Arts for the Reduction of Stress (CAReS). Not coincidentally, teaching her own patients how to turn down the volume on their inner critic led to her not worrying so much about what colleagues or patients would think about her creative work. Cartooning and writing soon became the preferred way to meditate. Her work now focuses on the importance of design and knowledge translation in the creation of patient programming and online psycho-educational content. It is no accident that her early work in the development of CAReS resulted in recognizing the importance of the accessibility of materials and information used in psycho-educational programs.

Developing and Implementing a Contemplative Arts Regimen

Teenagers are a tough audience partly because they are smart enough to be sceptical of the advice given by adults. Therapists, in particular, must deliver on promises as nonsense is quickly detected and dismissed. If you do not have anything worthwhile to offer, you may not get a second chance to re-engage a teenager. This is especially true if it was not their idea to attend therapy in the first place.

This chapter recounts the experiences of the authors developing a contemplative art program for teens referred for psychological services within the Musculoskeletal Unit of the Alberta Children's Hospital in Calgary, Canada. A major part of the clinical work involved teaching mindfulness-based stress reduction (MBSR) to adolescents and pre-teens with a variety of chronic health conditions. Most of these teens had spent some time visiting various clinics in the paediatric hospital, for diagnosis and treatment of their health conditions. They had physical challenges that ranged from chronic pain, surgeries for scoliosis or amputation, to multi-systemic disease, juvenile rheumatoid arthritis, lupus, autoimmune disorders, and burn injuries, and in their contacts with the hospital had frequent uncomfortable tests, infusion treatments, and painful or scary procedures to endure. The majority also had a mental health diagnosis, behavioural concerns, and learning disabilities. They and their families were often reluctant to attend another appointment that may be of limited benefit. Moreover, psychological services were regarded with suspicion.

Our intention in this chapter is to describe not only the program of *Contemplative Arts for the Reduction of Stress* (CAReS) itself but the process of developing it as colleagues and friends. Therapists face many challenges when working in a healthcare setting. There is often no time or institutional support to take risks to design creative new ways of engaging clients or to subvert the dominant paradigm of therapist as expert and patient as passive recipient of treatment. Therapists may receive criticism when taking risks for clinical innovation in a traditional hospital environment. By describing the ups and downs of our clinical and program development experiences, we hope that more therapists will be encouraged to consider taking creative risks and entertain the possibility that those risks are worth the rewards. Keeping patients, administrators, and yourself happy in a stressful and fast-paced traditional hospital environment is a tall order. Finding the courage to infuse your clinical and program development work with your own creativity can breathe new life into your clinical practice and engage patients in ways that traditional clinical services may not.

Setting the Stage

Research on the benefits of mindfulness has exploded in the past twenty years and has moved into the mainstream as an evidenced-based practice in healthcare. Mindfulness has been used in a variety of patient populations and has shown to be helpful in ameliorating chronic pain, depression, anxiety, insomnia, and many more mental and behavioural health concerns (Labelle et al. 2014; Garland et al. 2014; Turner et al. 2015).

It was with this burgeoning literature in mind that it was decided to run MBSR classes for adolescent patients and their parents. At the time, this involved treating patients from a variety of clinics within Musculoskeletal Services at the Alberta Children's Hospital. Referral to the psychologists on the team usually meant that the children and/or their families were likely struggling to manage their symptoms, function well in school, or cope with anxiety or depression.

MBSR was an attractive option for the health needs of our patient population for a number of reasons. The group format allowed us to support as many children and families as possible. MBSR was an intervention focused on helping people accept and relate in a more skilful way to the reality of an unwelcome life circumstance. Most of the children who came were living with conditions that were unlikely to significantly change. These children and their families were in the position of needing to embrace the reality of living with pain, bodily transformation, or chronic illness; mindfulness as a practice to enhance their psychological resources for facing health-related stress and emotional challenges was well-suited to help them manage their lives in the long term. MBSR was also an intervention that was beginning to show benefit for many of the concerns common in this patient population, at least for adults. Thus there was an eagerness to explore how the practice might be adapted for children, adolescents, and families dealing with health-related stressors.

Mental health professionals have become increasingly aware of the research by Pennebaker (1997) on the importance of developing a different kind of relationship with life challenges through personal expression. Pennebaker's research had focused on expressive writing, using a systematic protocol that required patients to express their "deepest thoughts and feelings about what bothered them most". His research had shown that systematic expressive writing interventions led to significant changes in patients' immune functioning, and also significantly reduced their frequency of use of medical services (Pennebaker et al. 2003; Pennebaker and Seagal 1999). Consequently there appeared a need to integrate MBSR *and* Pennebaker's Expressive Writing to design a health intervention that might benefit shared patient populations.

By implementing and researching a mindfulness-based expressive arts curriculum with a paediatric population, it was possible to explore the value of primarily non-verbal, image-based forms of cognitive processing for the restructuring of the emotional experience of pain and illness. In looking to the research literature, focus was on studies that used non-verbal disclosure interventions that were variants on Pennebaker's written disclosure intervention. These studies used both *free drawing and drawing* that required the formation of images within a structure. *Structured non-verbal disclosure* interventions have demonstrated better results than those unstructured non-verbal interventions using free creative expression with no implied structuring. For example, in a study of the soothing effects of non-verbal artistic expression on anxiety, Curry and Kasser (2005) evaluated three colouring conditions (free-form, mandala-drawing, or plaid-form). Significant decreases in anxiety were noted in participants in the mandala- and plaid-form conditions. Henderson et al. (2007) tested the psychological and physical health benefits of mandala-drawing (drawing within the form of a circle) within a trauma population. This study found that individuals assigned to an experimental mandala-creation condition reported greater decreases in symptoms of trauma at the one-month follow-up than did those assigned to a free drawing control condition.

In planning CAReS, it was apparent that the methodology of previous research on the health effects of non-verbal disclosure had not fully answered the question of whether verbal processing was the essential element for cognitive restructuring of thoughts and emotions connected to traumatic experiences. That is, if cognitive restructuring was the curative factor in written disclosure interventions leading to health effects, then to definitively identify written/verbal language processing as the best mode for cognitive restructuring of experience one must remove the possibility of a confound in the form of opportunity to contain and restructure previously overwhelming or chaotic emotional experience. It seemed like there was a good theoretical and empirical rationale to pursue development of an expressive arts' curriculum for paediatric patients that emphasize embodied or non-verbal forms of processing experience.

We cultivated our clinical skills by offering a pilot MBSR curriculum adapted for the needs of paediatric patients and their families and incorporating other well-researched and established protocols, such as the Pennebaker disclosure paradigm. In November 2006 a grant was formulated titled Project HeART (for Health and Art): Health Effects of Written versus Artistic Emotional Expression in a Paediatric Population—A New Application of the Pennebaker Disclosure Paradigm and received funding from the research institute at the Alberta Children's Hospital to cover some expenses for art materials and research-related instruments. To develop protocols, MBSR curriculum materials and Pennebaker expressive writing protocols were implemented (from the University of Texas at Austin Behavioural Medicine Service and from MBSR curriculum materials developed at the University of Massachusetts Centre for Mindfulness in Medicine, Healthcare, and Society), and our own mindfulness training and experience. By the spring of 2007, it was announced that the clinic would be offering an MBSR group, and there was no trouble recruiting patients and several of the eight-week groups were easily filled. The future of these MBSR groups looked bright.

It had been noticed that parents appreciated the MBSR protocol, but the teens had complaints. Some teens reported that they found traditional sitting meditation boring. Others questioned the relevance of the practice to the immediacy of their pain and suffering. Ultimately, close to 50% dropout rate suggested that the program was not working either to engage or to reduce suffering for these patients.

It was noted that other successful groups were being launched and running successfully at that time. The same patients who had dropped out of the MBSR program were faithfully attending cognitive behaviour therapy for insomnia groups and/or a chronic pain self-management groups run by the same therapists. The feedback from these groups was that the course content may not have been exciting, but it was helpful and relevant.

After the initial pilot run of the MBSR protocol, some time was taken to more fully develop a protocol that integrated expressive arts and mindfulness, while recognizing that in order to keep momentum going institutionally and with patients for mindfulness-based interventions, it was necessary to speed up the integration of the arts' component.

As the ideas were structured for a *mindfulness-based expressive arts curriculum* modelled on MBSR, the program manager was asked for support of this research, program development, and for clinical sponsorship of a mindfulness-based expressive arts program for children served through the clinics of which both authors were a part. This was endorsed but there was no program-based funding for supplies other than the financial resources provided through the initial Project HeART grant. A materials' list was constructed, and the purchases approved, and then support was provided for the initial run of CAReS despite some opposition from the professional leadership. Although there was some political posturing about offering the program through our unit rather than under the auspices of the psychology professional group, the protection of initial efforts and the encouragement from the administrative lead, as well as having a faculty physician stakeholder signed on as a research project co-sponsor, were essential to pilot project success.

Immediately after ending the more traditional MBSR course offerings, the expressive arts' group skills were tested by offering one-day art workshops. While offering the workshops, a pilot CAReS curriculum was developed and a brochure outlining the full or half-day workshops that would run over the course of the summer: the series included contemplative drawing, painting, knitting, photography, sculpture, masks and mandalas, and writing.

The CAReS Program

Most artists at some time or another have had the experience of complete focus while making their art—losing all sense of time and becoming completely immersed in the moment and the experience of the paintbrush on the canvas or the feel of clay squishing between fingers.

This approach to contemplative art focused on learning how to carry over the skill of staying present without judgement into everyday life, as a strategy for coping with pain and stress, in addition to being an effective approach to art making.

The CAReS program was launched with a rough outline for each class. Deliberately experimental, each class was refined as experience was gathered from the previous workshop. The intention was each individual workshop should focus on a different medium to appeal to the various interests of the teens. Each workshop was self-contained and the teens could sign up for one or all of them. Fortunately, there was access to an art studio in the hospital; the days of the workshops were dependent on the availability of the studio room. Once there were dates in hand, a brochure was designed with brief workshop descriptions and dates. Focus was primarily on creative processes as it was intended to specify the curriculum as observed in our lived experience and gathering observations from the participants.

Once the CAReS brochures were distributed throughout various clinics, there was immediate interest. There was some administrative support and an auxiliary assistant who fielded phone calls and kept registration lists for the groups. Logistically, it was extra work planning for all the art supplies required compared to traditional psycho-educational groups. Storage of all of the materials was a concrete issue: leaving materials in a communal art closet would mean that they could disappear. Storing materials in our tiny offices was not an option, and transport was sometimes on borrowed ER supplies carts. Nurses and other staff were great cheerleaders; for example, when an order of plaster for making masks was delayed in the mail, the Emergency Room team and the Amputation clinic team donated plaster bandages that worked beautifully for patient creations. Despite "hiccups", it was important to use high-quality materials that would be used in a more advanced art class by serious artists. Art programs for children often use low-grade markers, crayons, and paints. It was felt necessary that children appreciate the sensory differences in how true artist's materials performed and felt and not be limited in their self-expression by low-quality materials. It was assumed that it gave the teens a sense that healthcare workers took their experience in this program, and their art making ambitions, seriously.

In the section that follows, a brief description of the workshops is provided:

Workshop 1: Discovering Your Artistic Roots

This workshop focused on developing basic drawing skills. Although most schools have art classes for their students, rarely are children taught *how to draw*. This often results in the belief that one is either born with a talent for drawing—or not. Very few people are aware that drawing is like any other skill that *can be learned.* One would not expect to sit down at the piano and be able to play. Only a few of us might one day become a concert pianist, but most of us could become reasonably competent with practice and some instruction.

This workshop began with a brief introduction to mindfulness meditation and a guided breathing meditation. Then the patients were taught how to work with the mind and wandering attention, and how to refocus mindfully on the physical experience of making art while drawing.

In the drawing workshop, it was intended to offer an experience that could challenge the children and teens' perceptions of their own artistic ability, reformulate pre-existing stories about themselves as artists or non-artists, and increase self-efficacy with basic drawing. We not only offered the participants basic sensory and perception exercises for drawing, using exercises similar to the work of Edwards (2012), but also invited inquiries about *how to stay present* and *let go of inner criticism* while drawing.

Workshop 2: Strengthening Your Backbone

In this workshop, sculpture was offered as a medium for exploring self-trust and standing firm in relationship to others, an experience intended to counter the passive role in which paediatric patients are often placed when receiving treatment in a paediatric hospital. Emphasis was on developing a strong, unconditionally friendly, relationship to all aspects of ourselves, and on maintaining integrity while relating to and advocating for oneself with others.

After a short mindfulness of breath practice, discussion progressed into how one's self expectations can interfere with our ability to see what is actually present. Change begins with seeing things as they are. Whether it is clay, ourselves, or another person, open awareness is required, of darkness and light, of strengths and limitations. Only with full acceptance and contact with our experience as it is can we respond creatively, in a way that allows our highest potential to emerge.

Selected activities in this workshop included:

- *Mindfulness of clay.* This was a guided meditation where participants were invited to explore the sensory qualities of clay. All five senses were explored: squishing clay between the fingers, stretching, smelling, listening to the sounds it made, feeling its weight, even throwing it on the ground and listening to the thud that it made. This meditation served a dual purpose of softening the clay for later sculpture practice.
- *Making armatures.* A good sculpture has a strong foundation, just as our breath could serve as an anchor for awareness. Wire armatures were created to serve as the skeleton for the participants' clay sculptures. Although clay was used that could be fired in a kiln, the pieces were left in the air to dry and left unpainted for this workshop.

Workshop 3: Trusting Your Gut

Patients' experiences in paediatric hospitals are often very disembodying. The goal was that participants bring mindful awareness and friendliness to their embodied experiences while at the paediatric hospital. This workshop was intended to help paediatric patients to listen to their bodies and themselves. Often individuals don't *listen to their inner voice* and get into situations that are unhealthy, or just unpleasant. Learning to trust one's gut instincts and live by one's own values is an important skill when chronically ill. The Trusting Your Gut workshops focused on this theme while developing skill using colour in art through painting and pastels.

Participants were introduced to the practice of mindfulness of emotion in the body. The session oriented patients to the value of emotions for giving us feedback about our deepest needs in our life situations. For example, just as hunger triggers a desire to eat and thirst tells us we need to drink, fear tells us we require safety and anger "activates" a call to set some boundaries. When individuals try to fight, push away, or even get swept away by their feelings, they create personal suffering on top of the pain of life and being in a paediatric hospital.

Selected activities:

- *Focusing practice.* This was drawn from the work of Gendlin (1982), who taught patients to observe the "felt sense" of a situation with curiosity and acceptance. Listening to one's body helps us bring awareness to our needs in a particular situation. Participants were guided through a series of focusing exercises to learn how to listen to the wisdom of their own bodies and intuition about a situation.
- *Body scan.* This was a lying down meditation practice drawn from traditional mindfulness practice and the MBSR curriculum.
- *Dream painting.* Participants were asked to paint a dream of their choice. Instructions included guidance on how to paint the "mood" of the dream setting and to explore all of the sensory aspects of the dream, as well as all of the characters in a dream as aspects of oneself and one's experience.
- *"MRI of emotions" in the body.* This very popular exercise involved asking participants to lie down on a piece of paper while their body was traced by a helper—very similar to full body paintings that are made in kindergarten classes. However, instead of painting a self-portrait, participants were instructed to paint the emotions they experienced in the body, using colours and intensity to represent the body sensations and emotions they observed in their experiences in the focusing and body scan exercises.

Workshop 4: Opening Your Heart

Developing *loving-kindness and compassion* for ourselves and for others (especially when one is ill) is a key component of living a happy and full life and for resourcing oneself in times of pain and suffering, such as times of treatment in a paediatric hospital. Discussions in the Opening Your Heart workshop focused on the themes of developing attitudes of forgiveness, compassion, generosity, and gratitude towards ourselves and others, and how these attitudes heal us inside and out even when we cannot change our pain or our external circumstances. Participants were guided in the practice of writing their own creative phrases to use in the loving-kindness and compassion meditations, which they later learned to repeat using the soothing repetitive rhythm of contemplative knitting using simple knitting hoops rather than knitting needles.

Selected activities:

- *Developing personal phrases of loving-kindness and compassion* meditations. Participants completed exercises developing their own unique loving-kindness phrases and then were invited to apply these phrases in loving-kindness and compassion meditations for themselves and for others.
- *Knitting with hoops and needles*. Some of the time was spent with actually teaching a few of the participants how to make yarn balls and how to knit. This is an exercise requiring focus, patience, self-forgiveness, and unconditional friendliness. Everyone had the option of knitting with traditional knitting needles or a knitting loom that is easier for beginners. Once everyone was familiar with basic stitches, progression went onto simple projects while integrating their special loving-kindness and compassion phrases for themselves and others, with the rhythm of every each stitch.

Workshop 5: Finding Your Voice

Mindful speech is clear, kind, truthful, and timely. As a paediatric patient, learning to speak up for yourself and express yourself with integrity in all of the challenging situations you encounter is essential to living a healthy and productive life. Assertive communication skills are particularly important for individuals with individual differences such as scoliosis or amputation, or for those with "hidden" disabilities such as chronic pain, or autoimmune disease in order to have others understand and appropriately respond to their needs. This workshop intended to invite participants to practice how to ignore their "inner critic" or the rules and expectations of others that do not meet their needs, and to express themselves in a clear, strong voice. *Mindful writing* was applied as one of the tools for this session; many of the mindful writing exercises were taken from the work of Goldberg (2016) and Schneider (2003).

Selected activities:

- *Writing exercise using the prompt: "In the backyard..."*. Each participant was given the first three words of a sentence to start their writing. They were instructed to keep writing until the bell was rung. No pauses and no crossing out. Write whatever popped into their mind even if they thought it was silly.
- *Writing exercise using the prompt: New word a minute.* In this exercise, the facilitator rings a bell every minute. Each person in the writing circle takes a turn suggesting a word to the group. Each group member must incorporate that word into the piece they are writing.

Workshop 6: Clear Sight

This workshop emphasized creative perception and learning to see and respond to life in playful and novel ways. *Contemplative photography* was used to play with seeing people and situations in new and unconventional ways. An important component of being able to see the world clearly involves letting go of habitual ways of seeing and responding. Exercises in this workshop intended to invite practice in develop skills in seeing in new ways, testing assumptions, and responding to what is seen with non-judgement and with acceptance.

Selected activities:

- Participants were offered *instruction in contemplative photography*, including Miksang photography (Karr and Wood 2011). Participants seemed to particularly delight in being "the one who sees" rather than being "seen" as patients, hospital staff, and others in the hospital. Turning the lens back on the hospital seemed to bring immense delight and empowerment to many of the participants.
- *Working with colour.* Participants were invited to pick one colour to photograph during their walks. Whenever they encountered that colour, without thinking too much about the composition of the photograph, they could take a picture.

- *Working with pattern.* On their next photo walk, participants were asked to find instances of repetition in the environment. Examples include photos of rows of bike racks, street lamps in a row, and so on.
- *Working with light.* Participants were invited to explore their environment looking not so much at things, but at space and the play of light in space.

Workshop 7: Masks and Mandalas

When you are coping with a chronic illness, it is easy to lose connection to one's life passion and purpose, and to the larger patterns of being human in a technological healthcare environment. This workshop focused on connecting to common humanity and one's deepest self throughout the depersonalizing experience of being a patient in a paediatric hospital. These topics were explored through the creation of masks and mandalas.

Selected exercises:

- Discussion of how masks and mandalas are two ancient ways that people explored the archetypal parts of their individual human experiences of suffering. They were a way to express and understand the universal or common humanity and meaning in their struggles and a pathway to finding healing and wholeness.
- *Coloured sticky notes mandalas.* Participants were invited to do quick mandalas on sticky notes. This helped to make the initial mandala practice feel less daunting and allowed participants the opportunity to do portable mini-art projects, bringing awareness and creativity even to tiny moments of our daily experience.
- *Painted mandalas.* More time was spent on a larger, richer mandala that was painted on a larger piece of paper. Suggestions for the content of the mandala included focusing on a dream, personal hopes for the future, or the most difficult parts of their suffering as a patient in a paediatric hospital.
- *Plaster face masks.* We all face the world and can also choose what kind of face we want to express to the world. Masks were created using plaster casts of the participants' faces. This involved some trust and

comfort with others touching your face. This was an optional activity for those who were willing to try. Once the mask was dry, participants were asked to paint a mask that expressed some powerful aspect of themselves that they could call on when they had to deal with overwhelming experiences. One of the beautiful aspects of this practice was the opportunity to explore the boundaries of inner and outer. For example, some participants left the exterior plain, but painted the interior with rich colour; other participants explored adding whole new characters and aspects to the exterior of their mask, beginning to sense some of the fluidity and creativity that is possible as one chooses who one wishes to be in the world.

Challenges and Lessons Learned

The various media and practices in each workshop had their strengths and different wisdom lessons to teach. Contemplative art in general invites participants to let go of habitual internal stories and patterns of reacting, to focus awareness on the present-moment embodied experience of art making. In our practice of teaching, several observations were documented of the benefits of contemplative art:

- Cultivating focus and patience with oneself and one's experience.
- Developing equanimity through attending to five senses experience.
- Activation of felt experience in the body in a structured and systematic way through physical contact with arts' materials, rather than through the abstract, verbal forms of processing experience typically involved in the negative self-referential narratives typically associated with emotional reactivity to pain and suffering.
- Developing courage and overcoming experiential avoidance of noxious or painful physical or emotional stimuli related to the process of illness and pain.
- Developing opportunities for novel, more workable narratives and experimentation with new ways to relate to self, illness, and the experience of being a paediatric patient in treatment, through experimentation and play with different arts modalities.

- Developing new perspectives, and opening up to fresh ways of perceiving and expressing the experience of pain and illness.
- Increasing a sense of common humanity through the process of art making in a group, in a way that minimized individual differences in age, language development, or emotional maturity. Beginning to connect to the threads of common humanity in one's experience of illness, bodily changes, and pain in a creative and loving way through play with art.
- Connecting to other paediatric patients in a more active and creative role in the hospital environment than that which is typically offered to patients.
- Opening to a sense of pleasure and mastery through creation of a tangible individual creation; this process may have served as a protection against depression and stress related to pain and illness.
- Empowerment in contacting and expressing one's experience of pain and illness even though it may be counter to the institutional narrative of a paediatric hospital or one's parents and peers. Patients loved becoming actors in the hospital, and indeed seemed their liveliest and childlike when they could express their unique (and often fiery) perspectives on their experience rather than being forced into an institutional narrative of passive victim of or noble warrior against disease and illness.
- Building new and more empowering associations to the hospital environment, which is often associated with silencing, passivity, pain, and fear for many paediatric patients.

The initial run of the program was well-received by patients, parents, and (most) colleagues. There were a number of children who asked their parents to change their summer vacation plans so they would not overlook the upcoming workshops. Parents wrote letters to the clinic's managers requesting further support of the program and future workshops for their children. The buzz created by the program led to more internal support for the program. One important lesson learned was that support is easier to obtain in an institution after a demonstration project had been completed—not before. This is particularly true for new programming that might be difficult for those without an art background to envision or conceptualize. It is important to start small and see where it takes one.

The program would not have happened without finding initial champions to support and protect our work in the beginning. Building momentum after the initial run required more voices and more supporters joining in the chorus. It was evident that working as mental health professionals one must not be reticent about sharing the experiences learned during the development of the program. Similarly, participants were encouraged to talk about what they were learning with their doctors and nurses. The patients' excitement and enthusiasm was contagious—and had the added benefit of bringing aboard more supporters and champions.

It was evident that the best work was done while we were playing, having fun, and trusting personal instincts. We were asking our patients to create without letting their inner critic shut them down before they started making marks on the page. Most were surprised at the work they were capable of when they were kind to themselves instead of self-critical. Similarly, we needed to be free enough to experiment and make mistakes. There is no way to do something new without going down a few blind alleys.

It was not just our inner critics that had to be contended with, but some of the colleagues too! Many expressed concern that this program was not yet empirically validated. Some were concerned with the time and resources that the program appeared to require. In all cases, it was crucial to maintain patience while assertively standing ground, reminding colleagues that cognitive therapy and MBSR were once experimental and that other clinical work was not suffering as a result of the CAReS program.

In fact, the opposite was true. The CAReS program served to be invigorating and this enthusiasm was perceived by patients even in the more traditional group therapy programs. As clinicians there was energy at our disposal to run the program in our free time for adults enabling these ideas to be tested in a different patient population. Each time the program was executed, the exercises were refined and feedback offered information about what worked and what did not.

Even after leaving Alberta Children's Hospital, we continued to run CAReS, in part, or in its entirety in different contexts. In both of our professional lives, the development of this program has been a seminal experience. Since that time, we have gone on to new projects and programs, learning not to inhibit a good idea for fear of failure.

Implications and Guidelines for Mental Health Professionals

Designing new programs from scratch is difficult. Clinicians are likely to encounter numerous obstacles, ranging from limited budgets and free time, space constraints, fear of failure, and critical colleagues. Do it anyway!

Whatever the risks, the rewards are the creation of new approaches that may alleviate the suffering of your patients. If you say to yourself, "Who am I to create this?" it is imperative that you counter that thought with "If I don't, who will?" Graduate school is necessarily rigorous and we are taught to defend our positions with evidence. Unfortunately, academic education provides less training in how to *push the boundaries* of our interventions and our professions into entirely new territories.

In the development of CAReS, we approached work the same way one would approach a blank canvas. By trusting personal training and clinical instincts, we approved a new way of teaching mindfulness to emerge for patients, believing strongly in encouraging colleagues to take risks in their work in order to foster a community of creativity and collaboration. We were fortunate to have had mentors who encouraged us in the past and a few trusted colleagues to bounce ideas off of throughout the process of the program development.

While we could consult with colleagues outside our institution, we soon learned the importance of finding individuals within the institution who understand one's vision just well enough to lend the support needed to get started. Knowing stakeholders and finding champions are important to the success of any program within an organization. Whether it is a parent, a foundation, a research colleague, administrative manager, director, or an executive sponsor, having the support of the operational side of the organization can protect your newborn project in its early stages.

Finally, we have mentioned difficulties with colleagues—without wanting to dwell there. However, any new program is going to have its naysayers. Whether the opposition is due to differences in theoretical orientation, professional envy, and fear of change or lack of vision, it is important that you apply mindfulness and compassion to the experience of program development, and sometimes fierce compassion for yourself and others. The experience of nurturing CAReS into existence helped us learn to politely but firmly stand ground and to put patient persistent effort into something few people other than the two of us understood before it existed. This is an excellent mindfulness practice in and of itself. Learning to respond skilfully and spaciously to all forms of resistance to the process of change is the ultimate destination of most meditation practices, and if you are up for that challenge, starting a new program that will shake things up clinically or organizationally is certain to give you many opportunities for the practice of mindfulness and compassion. As with any change, a community and friendship are extremely helpful resources; this is where having a sympathetic colleague, having a variety of advocates, and having a supportive tribe for ideas and accountability can be extremely valuable.

A healthy professional life requires many of the same things as a healthy personal life: freedom to grow, creativity, community, friends, and the spaciousness of mind to accept that you will make errors along the way. Infusing work with new ideas, nourishing your heart by working in a way that is in alignment with personal values, and generously allowing yourself the opportunity to experiment with innovative ways of thinking and working will take you places you never envisaged. Most importantly, it is the only way that new advances in mental health are possible.

References

Curry, N., & Kasser, T. (2005). Can Coloring Mandalas Reduce Anxiety? *Art Therapy: Journal of the American Art Therapy Association, 22*(2), 81–85.

Edwards, B. (2012). *Drawing on the Right Side of the Brain*. New York: Penguin Group.

Garland, S., Carlson, L., Stephens, A., Antle, M., Samuels, C., & Campbell, T. (2014). Mindfulness-Based Stress Reduction Compared with Cognitive Behavioural Therapy for the Treatment of Insomnia Comorbid with Cancer: A Randomized, Partially Blinded, Noninferiority Trial. *Journal of Clinical Oncology, 22*, 449–457.

Gendlin, E. (1982). *Focusing*. New York: Bantam Dell.

Goldberg, N. (2016). *Writing Down the Bones*. Boulder: Shambhala Publications, Inc..

Henderson, P., Rosen, R., & Mascaro, N. (2007). Empirical Study of the Healing Nature of Mandalas. *Psychology of Aesthetics, Creativity and the Arts, 1*, 148–154.

Karr, A., & Wood, M. (2011). *The Practice of Contemplative Photography: See the World with Fresh Eyes*. Boston: Shambhala Publications, Inc..

Labelle, L., Campbell, T., Faris, P., & Carlson, L. (2014). Mediators of Mindfulness-Based Stress Reduction (MBSR): Assessing the Timing and Sequence of Change in Cancer Patients. *Journal of Clinical Psychology, 71*, 21–40.

Pennebaker, J. (1997). Writing About Emotional Experience as a Therapeutic Process. *Psychological Science, 8*, 162–166.

Pennebaker, J., & Seagal, J. (1999). Forming a Story: The Health Benefits of Narrative. *Journal of Clinical Psychology, 55*, 1243–1254.

Pennebaker, J., Mehl, M., & Niederhoffer, K. (2003). Psychological Aspects of Natural Language Use: Our Words, Our Selves. *Annual Review of Psychology, 54*, 547–577.

Schneider, P. (2003). *Writing Alone and with Others*. New York: Oxford University Press.

Turner, J., Sherman, K., Anderson, M., Balderson, B., Cook, A., & Cherkin, D. (2015). Catastrophizing, Pain Self-efficacy, Mindfulness, and Acceptance: Relationships and Changes Among Individuals Receiving CBT, MBSR, or Usual Care for Chronic Back Pain. *Journal of Pain, 16*, S96.

10

Psychological Oddities Among Performing Artists

Vincent Egan, Anthony Beech, and Laurence Burrow

Introduction

This chapter discusses the manifest psychopathology of some musical performing artists. We argue that some persons explore their disorder through creative work and performance, obtaining appreciation, and sometimes validation, of their different experience. We follow film director and maestro of the trash-aesthetic John Waters' view that "[m]y idea of an interesting person is someone who is quite proud of their seemingly abnormal life and turns their disadvantage into a career" (pp. 98; Waters 2005).

V. Egan (✉)
Centre for Forensic and Family Psychology, University of Nottingham, Nottingham, UK
e-mail: vincent.egan@nottingham.ac.uk

A. Beech
School of Psychology, University of Birmingham, Birmingham, UK

L. Burrow

B. Kirkcaldy (ed.), *Psychotherapy, Literature and the Visual and Performing Arts*, Palgrave Studies in Creativity and Culture, https://doi.org/10.1007/978-3-319-75423-9_10

It is fair to say that mental illness has driven a number of cult artists' creativity. Further, this creative career has been constructive for modelling a means of therapeutic expression in persons who in other contexts may have been isolated and more dysfunctional due to their mental disorder (or at least their conceptual oddity). We discuss these ideas with reference to individuals with well-documented mental illness who sometimes thrived, but other times decompensated due to their inherent vulnerabilities in stressful conditions. Personal vulnerabilities, coupled with the snares and entanglements of their creative lifestyles (such as substance abuse and professional stress), often led to very difficult times for many artists (e.g., GG Allin, Syd Barrett, Lou Reed, Townes Van Zandt, and Brian Wilson). Hence, the chapter discusses these issues with reference to some of these aforementioned artists.

The chapter also develops ideas about bipolar disorder and schizotypy as a creative trigger for work that may take an artist in a number of directions, potentially taking them away from the finite career that normally accompanies a "pop" or "rock" artist into new creative directions. Examples of such persons include Don Van Vliet (Captain Beefheart) and Daevid Allan; who would have thought that the former's half-century old free jazz, delta blues, and surrealistic beat poetry would still excite and challenge as much as Picasso's "*Les Demoiselles d'Avignon*"; or the latter's jazz, folk, progressive/punk rock explorations of a whimsical mythos representing the lysergic high point of European hippiedom would appeal? We conclude by noting that the creative environment can be a therapeutic milieu for some individuals, with autobiographical observations from a performing popular musician with a psychotherapeutic background.

The Context

The incidence of mental disorder in creative artists and entertainers outstrips that observed in the general population; for example, 10.3% of entertainers and performers experience a major depressive episode annually (Woodward et al. 2017). Biographical information examined by Ludwig (1995) found that mania, psychosis, and psychiatric hospitalisations were most common in poets (of whom 20% committed suicide). Compared to other professions, artists display two to three times the general rate of psychosis, suicide attempts, mood disorders, and substance abuse, and six to seven times the general rate of psychiatric sectioning.

The most creative popular musicians produce a lot of diversely styled work which remains influential and inspirational, irrespective of objective commercial impact; Brian Eno, creative polymath and quality name-dropper, observed, "I was talking to Lou Reed the other day, and he said that the first Velvet Underground record sold only 30,000 copies in its first five years. Yet, that was an enormously important record for so many people. I think everyone who bought one of those 30,000 copies started a band! So I console myself in thinking that some things generate their rewards in second-hand ways" (McKenna 1982). The fluent generation of original, possibly groundbreaking ideas, and the energy to pursue and express them, is a quality not all people have. Biographies of creative artists clearly indicate that bipolar conditions can be helpful to the creative process (Johnson et al. 2012), and that the creative industries have more bipolar individuals, as well as a higher-than-expected proportion of persons who are (healthy) siblings of individuals with schizophrenia (Kyaga et al. 2011).

Sometimes an individual's mental disorder is known in advance, other times it is recognised in hindsight. So it is often no surprise when the disorder becomes manifest. The noted relationship between mental disorder and creativity is well-trodden and reflects the capacity to make unexpected associations, florid and manic energy, and narcissistic self-belief. These qualities are potentially adaptive for performing musicians, an industry that appears to contain considerable proportions of creative psychopaths, extroverts, and exhibitionists. Some of these persons are genuinely original and insightful; others are song-and-dance entertainers, who are vessels for writers and (sometimes) Svengali-like managers who may even reflect particular types of personality-based psychopathology (Hoskyns 2012; Napier-Bell 2001). This chapter explores the therapeutic value that a creative outlet in popular music performance may provide an artist vulnerable to mental disorder.

Examples of Psychological Oddity in Musicians

There are many well-known examples of psychological oddity in performing musicians. To see Brian Wilson perform is to feel the contrast between the waves of love and acceptance he receives and the discomfort he has for his role despite the adulation. The purity and precision of Wilson's work are at variance with the conventionally dressed, strangely interacting singer-songwriter himself. Author of many timeless Beach Boys hits with warm, intricate melodies, Brian Wilson graduated from writing (often with singer Mike Love) anodyne songs about surfing, cars, and girls to *Smile*, the album he described as "a teenage symphony to God", which took 38 years before it was finally finished and released.

Wilson's history is well documented by both biographers and himself (Wilson and Greenman 2016). Physically and emotionally abused by his father, who seemed to delight in belittling him, Brian was uneasy in himself and less conventionally handsome than his younger brother Dennis. Brian famously wrote songs on a piano at home with his feet in a box of sand to get the feeling of the beach without having to expose his then 200 lb frame to ridicule on the Californian seashore. It is also of note that unlike his brother Dennis (drummer in the Beach Boys, and the band's pinup), Brian could not surf, and at some points in his life, he was actually afraid of water.

Formally diagnosed as a schizoaffective with mild manic depression, Wilson still experiences auditory hallucinations; these present in the classical form of disembodied threatening voices. According to Brian, he began having hallucinations in 1965, shortly after starting the heavy use of psychedelic drugs (mostly LSD), coupled with amphetamines and cannabis. LSD did not help his mental state, but extended his creative vision. An early version of "I Know There's an Answer" (entitled "Hang On to Your Ego"), a song to be found on *Pet Sounds*, specifically touches upon losing one's identity when under the influence of LSD:

> *They trip through the day and waste all their thoughts at night…hang on to your ego, hang on but I know you're gonna lose that fight.*

These lyrics were subsequently changed to fit more into the mood of the whole recording, which is generally seen as a concept album dealing with love and loss. This LSD-influenced work is widely regarded as his masterpiece (and is often regarded as one of the greatest popular albums of all time). This record, coupled with fragments of the then uncompleted album *Smile* initially due to be released in 1967 (e.g., the tracks "Surf's Up", "Cabinessence", and "Heroes and Villains"), beguiles, charms, and remains widely popular despite 50 years since its release.

Still playing live, Brian Wilson needs to take medication to keep his mental state steady, and has a group of first-rate musicians to take up the majority of the music and vocals (Lamont 2016). He tours with his favourite chair in the wings, should he need to sit down. In fact, he often seems to be a member of his own tribute band. He sometimes does not appear to be playing his keyboard and has an air of confusion and bewilderment at what is going on around him. His voice, 50 years on, is not what it was, with years of heavy smoking taking its toll, and he now no longer has the pure falsetto that was one of the key ingredients of the original Beach Boys sound. Live, he sometimes sings in a different key, and has been known to wander off mid performance. But the acceptance and validation that his nightly appreciation provides clearly makes his performance rewarding to him, and seeing a concert by him remains a touching spectacle and reminder of the humanity and potential of persons who live with mental illness. Arguably, Brian Wilson's working day leads up to the 90 minutes of onstage therapy that enables him to get through to the next day, and to internalise the love and acceptance of audience when he is not touring.

Not everybody can put themselves on the line like this in the public arena. Artists can be deeply self-critical, and this, with a vulnerability to depression, has killed many musical performers. Having to face the vicissitudes of an area of the entertainment industry that typically involves careers with a brief burst of popularity (and all that involves), followed, if they are lucky, by a long-tailed tapering-off audience with hopefully enough fans to sustain their career when their appeal becomes more selective, makes for a precarious life course in even moderately known musical performers.

Syd Barrett, the original creative genius and founder of the early Pink Floyd, of productivity generated a huge interest in the minds of many music fans until the time of his death in 2006. This burst was brief: he found it difficult to deal with fame at many levels, and his use of drugs (specifically psychedelics like LSD) destabilised an already fragile mind (Willis 2002). Some have suggested he actually suffered from autistic spectrum disorder, as Asperger's syndrome is now known (Campanella 2015). Barrett was unable to perform or write a great deal of music for his band, Pink Floyd, after their first album *Piper at the Gates of Dawn* (the title of a chapter from *The Wind in the Willows*). After this he managed to produce only one song on Pink Floyd's second album (*A Saucerful of Secrets*), but with a great deal of help and patience from Roger Waters (Pink Floyd's bass player, and main composer after Barrett had left the band) and David Gilmour (his replacement in the Floyd line-up). Barrett produced a couple of critically received solo albums, *The Madcap Laughs* and *Barrett*, in the late 1960s (Parker 2001).

As for his support mechanism, some individuals thought they were helping him by giving him drugs (such as further doses of LSD), though these had an even greater detrimental effect upon his mental health. Hence, after a few disastrous solo concerts, Barrett stopped performing or writing completely. He spent the rest of life in Cambridge mainly living with his mother, with his psychosis mostly under control. He led a very quiet life, but could often be seen cycling around the town, though unconfirmed anecdotes abounded of unusual behaviours, such as painting his mother's kitchen green—including the contents of her fridge. Barrett's later artistic impulses were broadly directed towards painting. Here, he would spend weeks on a project, would finish it, photograph it, then burn it.

Another artist who has struggled with mental health problems was the American country singer-songwriter Townes Van Zandt (Kruth 2008). Much of Van Zandt's life was spent touring, often living in cheap motel rooms and backwoods cabins. In the 1970s, he lived in a shack with no electricity. He suffered from drug addiction, alcoholism, bipolar disorder, and depression. Doctors' notes reported: "He admits to hearing voices, mostly musical voices". When he was young, the now discredited insulin shock therapy erased much of his long-term memory. Van Zandt was addicted to heroin and alcohol throughout his adult life. Despite all of this he wrote critically acclaimed songs, including "Pancho and Lefty" and "If I Needed You".

Van Zandt's life is broadly mirrored in the 2009 film *Crazy Heart* (starring Jeff Bridges). At times Van Zandt would become drunk on stage and forget the lyrics to his songs. At one point, his heroin addiction was so intense that he offered the publishing rights to all of the songs on each of his first four albums for $20. At various points, his friends saw him shoot up not just heroin, but also cocaine, vodka, and a mixture of rum and Coke. His battles with addiction led him to be admitted to rehab almost a dozen times throughout the 1970s and 1980s. Medical records from his time in recovery centres show that he believed his drinking had become a problem around 1973, and by 1982 he was drinking a pint of vodka daily. His attempt at detoxification from alcoholism, plus injuries from a fall, and cardiac arrhythmia led to his death at the age of 52.

One could go on: Vincent Crane, keyboard player with early progressive rock group Atomic Rooster, was another casualty. He lived with bipolar disorder for a number of years and, unhappy with his music and values remaining in the 1960s despite now living in 1989, took 400 aspirin and killed himself. These biographical details repeatedly illustrate sadly common patterns and personal tragedies. What is the evidence from the bigger picture?

Mortality Crises in Professional Musicians

The very lifestyle of popular musicians may affect mortality. Kenny and Asher (2016) reviewed the death records of 13,195 popular musicians and compared them with age-matched deaths in the US population generally. Popular musicians had shorter lives than the general population and were more likely to die violently (suicide, by being killed, a violent accident, or substance overdoses) or, perhaps unsurprisingly, from liver disease associated with hedonic excess, dying at about twice the rate of the general population. The disproportionate mortality was greatest for the youngest artists (those under 25), and subsequently reduced progressively, suggesting perhaps some adaptation of behaviour to lifestyle with experience, although there remains a myth around that the number of musicians who died at the age of 27 is significant (see Table 10.1 for a list of the most popular of these).

Table 10.1 The 27 Club (in chronological order)

Robert Johnson	Poisoned
Brian Jones	Drowned
Alan "Blind Owl" Wilson	Drug overdose
Jimi Hendrix	Asphyxiation
Janis Joplin	Drug overdose
Jim Morrison	Heart failure
Ron McKernan (Pigpen)	Gastrointestinal haemorrhage
Kurt Cobain	Suicide
Kristen Pfaff	Drug overdose
Amy Winehouse	Alcohol poisoning

Of significance to this chapter, suicide and liver-related disease were the most common for country, metal, and rock musicians; excess homicides were observed in 6 of the 14 genres sampled, with this being most common for hip-hop and rap musicians. Accidental death was not uncommon. Mortality remained a concern long after fame may have passed (Bellis et al. 2007).

These commonplace findings do not tell us about the non-fatal risk trajectories that may lead to a crisis in the individual, although a combination of temperament and a risky environmental opportunity may well be a final triggering point. Commons et al. (2014) found that public downfall crises in famous celebrities had particular antecedents: "atypical early environments, such as abandonment and trauma, over-indulgent or absent wealthy parents, or an early career; and adult environment conditions, such as colluding social groups and entourages" (ibid., pp. 100). The artists involved had damaging extramarital relationships, had alcohol and/or drug addictions, and, perhaps because of this, became bankrupt; the authors found a correlation of 0.75 ($p < 0.001$) between the number of risk factors present and the severity of the downfall of the performer.

Personality in Performing Musicians

These patterns of death tell us something about more common aspects of the lifestyles of popular musicians; as a group they live more riskily, hedonically, and have more emotional instability. Studies of the personality disposition of ordinary, non-professional rock musicians find they are more neurotic, more open to experience, and lower in agreeableness and conscientiousness (but average in levels of extraversion) compared to the general population (Gillespie and Myors 2000). The combination of openness, low agreeableness, low conscientiousness, and high neuroticism is a classically artistic sensibility, and harnessed within the context of intelligence and possibly the loosened associations of a vulnerability to mental illness (or psychotomimetic effects brought on by drug use), it is easy to see where the creativity of some artists may come from, and indeed, where creativity may be lacking, as when "a band becomes a brand" (i.e., where the imagery and reputation of a group or artist supersedes the music they make). Butkovic and Rancic Dopudj (2017) found the personality profile of classical and heavy metal musicians was similar. Hans Eysenck (1995) was interested in genius and creativity and argued that the basis for potential in creativity, and for psychopathological deviation, was psychopathology in the absence of psychosis.

There is much speculation about the personalities or personality deviations of public figures, and professionally, it is not recommended that one make spot diagnoses about individuals (even if sorely tempted) without thorough clinical review. Prior to exploring phenomenological aspects of performing in the popular medium, we shall review the academic literature to define what is known about music and performance's therapeutic role generally.

Music Therapy and Performing Music as Therapy

Whether it is persons passively enjoying, moving to, or making, the immediacy of music makes it an art form appreciated by persons who may otherwise affect less sensibilities for the arts. The social, expressive, dynamic, creative, and reflective nature of music also influences its effect. Music therapists use music to help facilitate change in individuals, and there is evidence for its effectiveness. Offenders as a group have a common incidence of personality disorder, but even in this cohort music therapy appears effective; a meta-analysis of the effect of music therapy on offenders integrated five studies (n = 409; predominantly male) and found music therapy was effective for promoting offenders' self-esteem and social functioning (effect sizes = 0.55 and 0.35, respectively). Regular music therapy also helped individuals to manage their feelings of anxiety and depression, particularly if they had higher numbers of sessions (Chen et al. 2016). Persons who make music often find its production therapeutic and find creative blockage as traumatic as they find their creative flow therapeutic (Csikszentmihalyi 1996; MacDonald et al. 2006).

Performance may also be therapeutic in itself; a creative individual, caught up in expressing their art, energised by the need to entertain an audience, makes exaggerated gestures to what could be an audience of 100,000 (or, equally challenging, keep conviction and confidence when playing to an audience that can be counted on two hands). They have to find a place within themselves able to overcome inherent introversion, anxiety, or lack of fluency. This may be effected by using alcohol or stimulants, both positively and negatively; Prince's protean musical and creative fluency was potentially hindered in his early career due to stage fright, which he overcame by using amphetamines; decades of dancing in high-heeled boots eventually damaged his heel tendons, though he had to keep dancing for his audience; he became addicted to prescription opiates, and it was these he eventually overdosed on, the overdose being thought accidental. What does the performer say to this?

The Phenomenology of Performing and Creativity in Popular Artists: A Perspective by Laurence Burrow ("Monty Oxymoron" of "The Damned")

> *It is creative apperception more than anything else that makes the individual feel that life is worth living. Contrasted with this is a relationship to external reality which is one of compliance, the world and its details being recognised but only as something to be fitted in with or demanding adaption.*
>
> D.W. Winnicott, "Creativity and Its Origins" (1971, 1974; p. 76)

The start of my career in the world of rock music performance is rather atypical: I came into that lifestyle rather later than most, being in my 30s, having already trained and worked as a psychiatric nurse, studied a BA in Related Arts, and finally Art Psychotherapy at Goldsmiths College,

London. Becoming a professional musician was an unfulfilled (and I thought up to then unfulfillable) dream until I joined the legendary garage-psychedelia-punk band, "The Damned" (https://en.wikipedia.org/wiki/The_Damned_(band); http://www.officialdamned.com/) as keyboard player in 1996. I believe that without that convoluted journey and its experiences, my ability to cope with and work within that lifestyle would have been doomed to failure. While my relationship to music and ability to play were well established, the ability to be confident, to relate to others and communicate with them, to be self-organised, and to both endure and enjoy such a lifestyle with a degree of common sense and independence—all these would have been sadly lacking. These things were hard won during my years of nurse training: I'm still proud to be a psychiatric nurse and am grateful to the profession for the skills it gave me. Had I been "thrown" into the rock-stardom as a young man I would without doubt have been added to the list of "Rock and Roll casualties" referred to above!

Some of the characteristics referred to I can relate to while others remain alien to me and in many ways I agree with our guitarist Captain Sensible when he describes me as "a very unlikely rock star". In particular "narcissistic self-belief" has been lacking: by contrast I have had to "prove myself" over and over. I would say then that my later psychological development conforms to Adler's "inferiority complex": I have had to develop my musical performance in order to compensate for a general "lack" in terms of social integration. (I can say that it gives me some satisfaction at times to remember the awkward shy person I once was in the moments of triumph and joy that are now accessible to me.)

However, I also recognise in myself pathology related to my early development. As a child I was quite happy to be absorbed in my own fantasy world. I was prone to emotional instability, but being creative with toys, imagery, and sounds kept me happy most of the time. The difficulty came with the need to try and share that inner world with other children: I found it hard to understand them (and no doubt vice versa!). I hated structured games such as "Simon Says", preferring to create my own. If I wasn't to play on my own all the time I'd have to find another "Weird kid" or two to play games such as "What do you want to be killed by", enacted in the playground with great enthusiasm while the others played football. Winnicott suggests that imaginative play is in fact an indication of health: not being able to play is a far more serious problem.

My mother suffered badly from post-natal depression and I think the need to "self-mother" accounts to some extent for my self-absorption. Imagination and play filled in the "gaps" in my nurturing experience: the times when my mother was absent or "dead" to me. I think I was lucky though, as such experience can lead to frank psychosis in some people: "When the mothering one is absent, preoccupied, or overwhelmed by her own emotional state of being and unable to provide what the baby needs for its own development at the stage of absolute dependence, the baby is catapulted into a state of unthinkable anxiety" (Wetzler 2010, p. 178). This anxiety, Winnicott believed, was the basis for schizophrenia, a condition that ultimately seems to shut down creativity, imprisoning the person in a world of hallucination, obsessive delusions, and social isolation.

However, there are degrees of madness and creativity! A touch of madness (as opposed to full-blown psychosis) can be used and worked with. Childhood play is thus therapeutic; indeed, Winnicott considered it the very basis for all artistic cultural phenomena (which would presumably include rock music). Indeed the pathology of the inherently playful but obliquely wise "mad rock star" can be contrasted with the opposite problem of excessive "normalcy": "there are others who are so firmly anchored in objectively perceived reality that they are ill in the opposite direction of being out of touch with the subjective world" (Winnicott 1971, p. 78 in Caldwell and Joyce 2011). Society may encourage excessive passivity in order for the population to be dependent on consumerism, and so this pathology is very prevalent: hence Winnicott's observation that "[c]ompliance carries with it a sense of futility for the individual and is associated with the idea that nothing matters and that life is not worth living" (ibid., p. 76.), or, more succinctly, "It is a shame if we are only sane". However, the imagination and indeed the antics of the rock musician can and are marketed and sold to "the bored and miserable people everywhere" (Zappa 1978). So to some extent people have been able to live out vicarious fantasies of rebellion and excess though such musicians "by proxy", as well as have their imaginations enriched by their creative output. Today this may be changing.

Creativity fills the gap between the subjective world and the demands of life: music sonically enriches this transitional inter-world. (Sadly, I found that all too often the music that excited me seemed to my contemporaries ugly, overwhelming, weird, or downright ridiculous!) To me,

Daevid Allen of "Gong" and Captain Beefheart were able to lace their diverse and sometimes challenging, sometimes tuneful music with surreal imagery, and make unusual and apparently incongruous imagery accessible (to those who had the imagination (taste?) to appreciate it).

If however an artist is too subjectively determined, then the illusions will either be lost on everyone, or if they are forced to incorporate them, they will resemble the uncritically accepted ravings of a dictator or the psychotic delusions of the leader of a religious cult. In those cases the "creativity" loses its bridge-like quality and becomes a destructive imposition on the minds of others. Winnicott suggests that the healthy individual has a foot both in the subjective hallucinatory inner world and the ability to perceive and deal creatively with outer reality, the demands of society and practical living.

I believe that creative musicians are attempting "self-care" or cure, and also reaching out for what Maslow called "Self-Actualisation" and Jungians, "Individuation". To find out what one is really able to do and to find out what lies within and bring it out into the world for others to engage with (rather than to worship or slavishly follow). Part of this drive towards health in life includes the full integration of the mind and body (the "Psyche-Soma" as Winnicott referred to it). In this regard I have found the dance aspect of performance to be really important (the "florid and protean manic energy" referred to above!). I first discovered this when jumping off the sofa at the climax of a classical piece when I was a child. Such movements are rooted in early "bodily motility" and what Winnicott calls "the Spontaneous Gesture". (Is that what is represented in that iconic image of Johnny Cash and those of numerous punk rock musicians over the years?)

Of course the mobilisation of such bodily activity, amplified music, and lighting displays all add to the intensity of the performed concert experience for both the performer and the audience. Even after 21 years, the emotional high induced by playing successfully "in Flow" in front of a large appreciative audience remains a state of joyous exuberance unlike any other I know. However, such experiences are in themselves addictive, and inevitably there can follow a collapse into exhaustion and melancholy when one is tired on tour. I think this partly explains the tendency to emotional instability, bipolar mood swings, and drug and alcohol dependency among some musicians. Substances may be used to "get into the zone" in the first instance, and also to compensate for the anti-climax or boredom that can constitute much of life off stage (when Charlie Watts was asked to describe life with the Rolling Stones on their 30th anniversary, he said it had been "five years of work and twenty-five years of hanging around"). Indeed, if the onstage high is attempted as a permanent state, that perhaps accounts for the tendency for some musicians to die young, sometimes violently.

In conclusion I can certainly admit to pathology being a part of my performances along with tension and release, omnipotent fantasy, sexual frustration and display, political anger, spiritual search, and altered states of consciousness: all these play a part. It seems to me significant that this chapter refers to artists "from the middle of the 1960s to the 1980s": today's musical celebrities seem altogether less colourful; as Frank Zappa said in "We're Turning Again", "No one can do it like you used to" (Zappa 1985). Where are the Vivian Stanshalls, the David Bowies, and Frank Zappas of today? Maybe a touch of the old traditional madness and eccentricity might help after all!

Conclusions

This chapter has, like the most interesting types of popular music, crossed many boundaries to create a synthesis which amuses, entertains, and perhaps informs exploring psychological oddities in performing artists, and asked whether this activity has a therapeutic value. The objective popularity and success for an artist working in a commercial forum is somewhat arbitrary, as their fortune and appeal may well depend on luck and serendipitous events, as well as talent. Persons continue to perform and make music despite diminishing material returns, reflecting an inherent satisfaction in the creative act, and validation by performing to even small audiences. It is often only after a number of years that some artists are truly recognised for their greatness (e.g., Nick Drake).

This phenomenon also affects female performers and artists of colour; Dory Previn had psychosis, while Sinead O'Connor still heroically struggles to live with her own demons, and jazz composer Sun Ra came, depending on his mood, from Ancient Egypt, planet Venus, or

Birmingham, Alabama (Szwed 2000). One cannot cover all artists, styles, or examples, and more recent youthful artists are beyond the range of authors in their 50s. Schizotypy and bipolar disorder are differences that need not be pathological; in advantageous contexts and alongside other personal strengths, they may have some functional advantages (Mohr and Claridge 2015). Appreciation of unusual popular artists may be the musical form of enjoying "Outsider Art", and for some more a reflection of the ongoing search for authenticity, which is rarely perceived to be in the mainstream of entertainment (though may move there if cultural commentators approve a particular artist) (Hahl et al. 2017).

Mental disturbance rarely functions well under pressure, and creativity cannot be forced, but the cultural mainstream needs misfits and mavericks to drive innovation in industries based on creativity (Jones et al. 2016). Professional and commercial pressures to conform to an increasingly structured artistic career and, indeed, the increasingly structured nature of modern life may reduce popular music being a feasible environment for an individual with psychological oddities to constructively express themselves and so receive validation of their difference; art colleges are less commonly the repositories of wayward imagination they once were. The creative process is becoming closed to these individuals. This loss also reduces the secondary effect of unusual performing artists becoming public figures regarded with affection, acceptance, and credibility, as no longer is there an easy way for an audience to experience and empathise with mentally disordered persons and other outsiders who are communicating via their creative work.

Implications and Guidelines for Mental Health Professionals

- A client's interest in music, art, and creativity, of whatever kind, provides an opening for the sensitive mental health professional to engage a client in therapeutic work. This work may well be one of the few ways in which the individual receives validation or finds a way to articulate feelings and can express their inner life.
- Hard-to-engage and taciturn young people sometimes engage in freestyle rapping, in which fluency, articulacy, and audacious use of language (clever as well as graphic) become valued qualities; hard rock

may express the inner rage of the frustrated adolescent; sentimental ballads may allow a violent man to show sensitivity and softness he cannot otherwise allow himself.
- To recognise and be open to how a client uses music and art to regulate their feelings and express themselves is to have leverage in developing an individual's willingness to reflect on their life.
- The ability to make music is widely valued, and the wide variety of sounds and techniques involved means that even persons with less skill can contribute, if such resources are available.
- Singing and music-making, like dancing and eating, are basic communal human activities, and creating a sense of human relatedness in persons otherwise isolated by mental disorder is a way of enabling persons to engage with others via a shared constructive activity.
- Mental health practitioners should be aware of the adversity in a popular public figure's life and how they have articulated and lived with this as a means to enable and allow a client to discuss their own experiences. The client may be able to discuss this public figure's life and so derive insight into themselves.
- Hype, trying to maintain an "image" and popularity, the pressures of work on the road, the media, and the attractions of "excess" in the popular music lifestyle may account for the pathology found in many performing musicians in spite of the therapeutic benefits of the actual creative and expressive aspects of the work itself. Healthy self-regulation is to be encouraged, again perhaps using appropriate role models who have overcome adversity.
- These approaches can aid vulnerable and socially excluded persons to derive a sense of agency and worth they may not otherwise have, creating a virtuous spiral to their therapeutic trajectory.

References

Bellis, M. A., Hennell, T., Lushey, C., Hughes, K., Tocque, K., & Ashton, J. R. (2007). Elvis to Eminem: Quantifying the Price of Fame Through Early Mortality of European and North American Rock and Pop Stars. *Journal of Epidemiology & Community Health, 61*(10), 896–901.

Butkovic, A., & Rancic Dopudj, D. (2017). Personality Traits and Alcohol Consumption of Classical and Heavy Metal Musicians. *Psychology of Music, 45*(2), 246–256.

Caldwell, L., and Joyce, A. (editors) (2011). *Reading Winnicott*. London, UK: Taylor & Francis.

Campanella, M. (2015). Syd Barrett: Was He Suffering from Schizophrenia or Asperger's Syndrome. *Psychiatric Hypotheses, 12*(3), 73–76.

Chen, X. J., Leith, H., Aarø, L. E., Manger, T., & Gold, C. (2016). Music Therapy for Improving Mental Health Problems of Offenders in Correctional Settings: Systematic Review and Meta-Analysis. *Journal of Experimental Criminology, 12*(2), 209–228.

Commons, M. L., Commons-Miller, L. A. H., Salaita, R. J., & Tuladhar, C. T. (2014). Stars that Crash. *Behavioral Development Bulletin, 19*(2), 100–110.

Csikszentmihalyi, M. (1996). *Flow and the Psychology of Discovery and Invention*. New York: Harper Collins.

Eysenck, H. J. (1995). *Genius: The Natural History of Creativity* (Vol. 12). Cambridge: Cambridge University Press.

Gillespie, W., & Myors, B. (2000). Personality of Rock Musicians. *Psychology of Music, 28*, 154–165.

Hahl, O., Zuckerman, E. W., & Kim, M. (2017). Why Elites Love Authentic Lowbrow Culture: Overcoming High-Status Denigration with Outsider Art. *American Sociological Review, 82*(4), 828–856.

Hoskyns, B. (2012). *Trampled Under Foot: The Power and Excess of Led Zeppelin*. London: Faber and Faber.

Johnson, S. L., Murray, G., Fredrickson, B., Youngstrom, E. A., Hinshaw, S., Bass, J. M., & Salloum, I. (2012). Creativity and Bipolar Disorder: Touched by Fire or Burning with Questions? *Clinical Psychology Review, 32*(1), 1–12.

Jones, C., Svejenova, S., Strandgaard, J., & Pedersen, B. T. (2016). Misfits, Mavericks and Mainstreams: Drivers of Innovation in the Creative Industries. *Organization Studies, 37*(6), 751–768.

Kenny, D. T., & Asher, A. (2016). Life Expectancy and Cause of Death in Popular Musicians: Is the Popular Musician Lifestyle the Road to Ruin? *Medical Problems of Performing Artists, 31*(1), 37–44.

Kruth, J. (2008). *To Live's to Fly: The Ballad of the Late, Great Townes Van Zandt*. Cambridge: Da Capo Press.

Kyaga, S., Lichtenstein, P., Boman, M., Hultman, C., Långström, N., & Landén, M. (2011). Creativity and Mental Disorder: Family Study of 300 000 People with Severe Mental Disorder. *The British Journal of Psychiatry, 199*(5), 373–379.

Lamont, T. (2016). 'Are We There Yet?': On the Road with Beach Boy Brian Wilson. Published in *The Guardian* (UK), 8 Oct 2016: https://www.theguardian.com/music/2016/oct/08/are-we-there-yet-on-road-beach-boy-brian-wilson

Ludwig, A. M. (1995). *The Price of Greatness: Resolving the Creativity and Madness Controversy*. New York: The Guilford Press.

MacDonald, R., Byrne, C., & Carlton, L. (2006). Creativity and Flow in Musical Composition: An Empirical Investigation. *Psychology of Music, 34*(3), 292–306.

McKenna, K. (1982, May 23). Lots of Aura, No Air Play. *Los Angeles Times*, L6, Column 4, Los Angeles, California.

Mohr, C., & Claridge, G. (2015). Schizotypy—Do Not Worry, It Is Not All Worrisome. *Schizophrenia Bulletin, 41*(1), S436–S443.

Napier-Bell, S. (2001). *Black Vinyl, White Powder*. London: Ebury Press. ISBN 0-09-188092-0.

Parker, D. (2001). *Random Precision: Recording the Music of Syd Barrett, 1965–1974*. London: Cherry Red Books.

Szwed, J. (2000). *Space Is the Place: The Lives and Times of Sun Ra*. Edinburgh: Canongate.

Waters, J. (2005). *Shock Value: A Tasteful Book About Bad Taste*. Philadelphia: Running Press.

Wetzler, L. A. (2010). The Music of Unthinkable Anxiety and Nameless Dread. In W. Ashton & S. Bloch (Eds.), *Music and Psyche: Contemporary Psychoanalytic Explorations*. New Orleans: Spring Journal Books.

Willis, T. (2002). *Madcap: The Half-Life of Syd Barrett, Pink Floyd's Lost Genius*. Short Books. ISBN 1-904095-24-0.

Wilson, B., & Greenman, B. (2016). *I Am Brian Wilson: The Genius Behind the Beach Boys*. London: Coronet.

Winnicott, D. W. (1974). Creativity and Its Origins. In *In: Playing and Reality*. London: Penguin Books.

Woodward, A., Lipari, R., & Eaton, W. (2017). Occupations and the Prevalence of Major Depressive Episode in the National Survey on Drug Use and Health. *Psychiatric Rehabilitation Journal, 40*(2), 172–178.

Zappa, F. (1978). Gregory Peccary. On *Studio Tan*. Los Angeles: DiscReet Records

Zappa, F. (1985). Turning Again. On *Frank Zappa Meets the Mothers of Prevention*. Los Angeles: Barking Pumpkin Records.

11

Soothing the Savage Breast: Therapeutic Applications of Music

Glenn D. Wilson

Personal Background/Motivation for Writing This Chapter

I have had parallel careers in psychology and opera singing; hence it was almost inevitable that I should have developed an interest in applications of psychology to the performing arts, researching and writing about what the science of psychology has to offer the performer in dealing with their anxieties and optimising their communication skills. My book *Psychology for Performing Artists* (now in its second edition) has been widely used as an adjunct in acting and music schools. This chapter deals with the "flip side", the way in which performing arts (music in particular) can be harnessed to assist in the treatment of mental and physical problems. I am also co-founder of a registered charity called *Connaught Opera*, which

Note: This is a revised version of a lecture at the Museum of London on 4/10/11, delivered as part of a series on *Psychology of Performing Arts* by Dr Wilson in his capacity as Visiting Professor with Gresham College.

G. D. Wilson (✉)
Consultant Psychologist, London, UK

B. Kirkcaldy (ed.), *Psychotherapy, Literature and the Visual and Performing Arts*, Palgrave Studies in Creativity and Culture, https://doi.org/10.1007/978-3-319-75423-9_11

provides free quality musical entertainment in care homes and heritage sites around the UK.

> "Music has charms to soothe the savage breast To soften rocks, or bend a knotted oak."
>
> William Congreve (*The Mourning Bride*, 1697)

Music and Therapy

Music has been extolled for its healing powers since antiquity. Many cultures have invested it with spiritual, even cosmological, significance. The Egyptians called it "the word of the Gods", Greeks referred to "the music of the spheres" and the Chinese described it as "the celestial energies of perfect harmony". Apollo was the Greek god of both music and healing (among other things), and his agent Orpheus used music therapeutically. Centuries later, music was used in the treatment of King Philip V of Spain, Ludwig II of Bavaria and George III of England (Biley 2000).

The connection between mood and the musical term "mode" is no accident. Music influences our emotions powerfully and has many medical applications (Aldridge 1993). It is said to calm people undergoing medical procedures, assist with pain management in dentistry and hospice care, bolster the immune system, improve fluency in people with speech disorders, motivate people with motor disorders, revive pleasant memories and improve mood in the elderly and enhance the quality of life in general. It can put babies to sleep, increase productivity in factories and reduce vandalism at railway stations. But music may be used for ill as well as good. It can drive unwilling soldiers into battle, sell groceries at a supermarket that we do not really need, break down sexual inhibitions and provoke anti-police violence. Certain types of music possibly promote depression and even suicide.

When we describe music as "moving", this may be literally true. Few people can listen to Cole Porter's *Anything Goes* without their feet beginning to tap a little, and clinically it has been found that some patients who are virtually paralysed can be prompted to walk by rhythmic music. Comedian Terry-Thomas reported that in the latter stages of Parkinson's disease he could not walk through a door—however, he could dance through it. "Singing" approaches to the treatment of stammering no doubt make use of a similar mechanism, pacing the production of speech by a musical mechanism.

The motivational effect of music arises from the pacing (*entrainment*) of physiological rhythms, such as heart rate, blood pressure, respiration, brain waves and the muscle activity involved in the walking gait. The experience of the mother's heartbeat in utero may be prototypic of adult rhythms; those around 72 bpm are soothing, while those that accelerate beyond 80 bpm tend to be arousing. Slow, regular rhythms (especially in a major key) are relaxing, while jerky, irregular ones are exciting. Soft music is more relaxing than loud, dissonant music. Repetitive rhythms may resonate in the brain so as to create trance-like conditions, with effects varying from dissociation to loss of control and convulsions. According to the cultural context, these may be variously interpreted as hysteria, fanaticism, possession or religious ecstasy.

Spectrographic analyses of music patterns across cultures reveal similar patterns in tone and tempo for lullabies, war songs, mourning songs, love songs and joyful music. Joyful music tends to be upbeat and energetic, with rising melodic phrases, while sad music features minor keys and descending phrases. Dissonance is recognised in all societies, and babies as young as four months react negatively to it. Such cross-cultural uniformities suggest that the effects of music are partly innate (Wilson 2002).

Music also influences non-humans. Dogs in an animal shelter have been shown to be soothed by classical music (more time spent quiet and resting), whereas heavy metal leads to more time barking (Wells et al. 2002). Other studies have found that milk yields in dairy cows may be increased with slow (as compared with fast) tempo music and that injured rats exposed to stress-inducing rock music are slower to heal (North and Hargreaves 2009).

Brain scan studies confirm that when people experience "chills" ("frissons") through listening to their favourite musical selections, dopamine is released in the mesolimbic reward system (Salimpoor et al. 2011), suggesting a highly positive experience. Activation of these same reward systems appears to be diminished in people suffering from depression (Osuch et al. 2009).

Music may be useful in pain control in palliative care, dentistry and surgery (Good et al. 2002; Curtis 2011). However, the benefit is most reliably observed in self-report and is not always matched by reductions in levels of self-administered medication. Where benefits are observed, these may be due to various possible processes, including distraction, relaxation, a feeling of control or secretion of dopamine/endorphins.

The impact of mood-enhancing and stress-reducing music on stress hormones and the immune system has been documented. Reduction in cortisol, increased DHEA, improved coherence in the autonomic nervous system and potentiation of secretory immunoglobulin have been observed in both healthy subjects and individuals with clinical conditions such as anxiety, depression, panic, arrhythmias, diabetes and chronic fatigue (McCraty 1999).

Classical music has been shown to affect several cardiovascular variables which enable it to be harnessed for the benefit of patients (Bernardi et al. 2009). Vocal and orchestral crescendos increase blood pressure, while slower passages decrease it. This applies equally to musicians and nonmusicians. Reviewing the effects of music on cardiovascular health, Trappe et al. (2010) concluded that relaxing music lowered anxiety in preoperative settings on various physiological indicators and was a useful alternative to midazolam for premedication. Following open heart surgery, patients benefited from listening to classical and meditational music, whereas heavy metal and techno music were not only ineffective but potentially dangerous.

The emotional impact of music is just as important as its tempo and volume. Researchers at the University of Maryland Medical Center studied the effects of music on the circulation of the blood, an index linked to cardiovascular risk. They had volunteers select musical pieces that made them feel personally joyful, as well as others that made them anxious, and compared arterial blood flow while they listened to these two types. Circulation improved by 26% with joyful music but fell 6% with anxious music (Miller et al. 2008). In another study, neurological patients with visual neglect showed enhanced visual awareness when tasks were performed with preferred (pleasant) music than with either non-preferred music or silence (Soto et al. 2009).

Why do people like sad music? This has often been regarded as a conundrum. One possible explanation is that it offers a kind of empathy—the reassurance that others understand what they are suffering. Much of the music of Tchaikovsky, for example, expresses his own negative feelings in such a way that others can share in them. Music therapists and those that perform for hospital audiences know that it is simple-minded to suppose that depressed or terminally ill people need to be "jollied up" by music. Validation of their mood may be more appropriate.

Huron (2011) theorises that sorrowful music releases the hormone prolactin, which is associated mainly with motherhood but also giving feelings of consolation. Since with sad music the grief is recognised cortically as not real, a "safe distance" is provided, and the build-up of prolactin produces feelings of pleasure. Huron suggests that nostalgic music may be connected with secretion of the bonding hormone oxytocin.

Music is an important component of what is called *reminiscence therapy* for older people—that is, restimulating happy memories from the past and creating a sense of familiarity and security. Similar connections may account for instances of people being revived from long-term coma with music of deeply personal significance. There is some evidence that coma patients are more readily contacted by music than by speech (Aldridge et al. 1990).

Using fMRI scans, Petr Janata (2009) at the University of California – Davis, has identified an area in the dorsomedial prefrontal cortex (DMPC) that connects familiar music, memory for salient life events and emotions like joy and sadness. The music seems to serve as a soundtrack for a movie that is played in the head, recalling past episodes that arouse strong feelings. Since this *nostalgia hub* is one of the last areas of the brain to atrophy in dementia, this might account for the fact that patients with Alzheimer's continue to respond to music well into their illness.

The *Mozart effect*, as first described in the 1990s, was an enhanced performance on spatial reasoning tasks after listening to Mozart's music (particularly K. 448, Sonata for Two Pianos in D major, a fast tempo, highly structured piece of music). This has not been consistently replicated, but a more robust finding is that K. 448 reduces the frequency of epileptic seizures in susceptible children (after listening for 8 minutes before bedtime). The effect seems to last for at least six months (Lin et al. 2011). This effect may not be unique to Mozart, however; a piece of music found to have a similar effect is *Acroyali/Standing in Motion*, by Greek-American composer Yanni. This has similar energy, tempo, consonance, structure and predictability to K. 448.

A study by Husain et al. (2002) sheds light on how the Mozart effect, when observed, might work. They generated a faster-than-normal version of K. 448 (+35%) and a slower-than-normal one (half speed). They also had both these (fast and slow) versions transposed into a minor key. Cognitive performance was best after the faster/major mode version. Apparently, the speed altered feelings of arousal, while the mode affected mood (more negative with the minor). The authors concluded that cognitive performance was maximised when the music made people feel aroused and positive.

Music therapy is fast developing as a specialist profession. Those trained in the Nordoff and Robbins (1977) tradition favour one-on-one work, mainly with disabled or disturbed children. Treatment is geared to the needs of the individual but often takes the form of some kind of improvised dialogue using instrumental or vocal sound rather than words (cf., the famous *Duelling Banjos* scene in the film *Deliverance* in which an adventurer from the city makes contact with a potentially hostile hillbilly in the backwoods). Again, the theory is that the musical channel of communication may be open where speech is perfunctory or absent. Evidence for its value depends mostly on case reports, but there are impressive studies using video analysis to reveal improvement over time in indices such as vocalisation, looking behaviour, imitation and initiation of ideas (Bunt 1997). At the very least, there is the satisfaction of expressing emotions, exercising skills and cooperating with other people.

Vibroacoustic therapy refers to the idea that musical vibrations can be delivered direct to the body as well as through hearing. Various devices have been developed for this purpose, including mats, chairs and baths. With one such "music bath", sufferers of conditions such as cerebral palsy, arthritis, asthma, back pain or circulatory problems lie in a bed of speakers enveloped by soothing sound and vibrations. This is said to produce deep relaxation and has found wider applications, such as post-sport relaxation for skiers and runners and stress reduction for business executives (Wigram et al. 1995). A patent bath that combines sound and vibration delivered through water (as well as light patterns) has also been developed. While usually enjoyed by clients, scientific validation of these procedures is so far rather scanty (Kvam 1997).

Because of the practical difficulties in conducting research in real clinical settings, many reports on the benefits of music therapy consist of uncontrolled case studies. Others apply so-called qualitative research methods which fall short of the usual standards of scientific methodology and data analysis. Frequently, they suffer from the problem that the person delivering the therapy is also the one evaluating it, which obviously opens itself to bias (Aigen 2008).

The gold standards for evaluating a treatment are the randomised controlled trial (RCT) and meta-analysis. These are geared primarily to drug treatments and are not easily applied to humanistic therapies because of variations in client types, details of procedure and lack of agreement concerning precise outcome. Nevertheless, some consistent findings have emerged (Edwards 2005). Meta-analysis of music in medical treatment shows that effect sizes are greater for women (.90) than for men (.57). They are also greater for children and adolescents (.95) than adults (.87), while infants show the lowest effect sizes (.48).

In a meta-analysis of the use of music interventions to alleviate symptoms and treatment side effects in cancer patients, Bradt et al. (2011) confirmed beneficial effects on anxiety, blood pressure, pain, mood and quality of life. However, they were not able to detect any improvement with respect to fatigue or physical status, and conclusions were tentative because many of the trials were at risk of bias. No significant difference was observed between interventions delivered by trained music therapists and listening to pre-recorded music supervised by medical staff. However, live music performances in hospices may benefit from the added personal touch of the performer (Lindsay 1991).

Even when a study appears to be randomly controlled, it may be difficult to know whether the control is appropriate. For example, Hanser and Thompson (1994) divided older adults diagnosed with depression into three groups. One was given a home-based programme of music-listening stress reduction guided by weekly visits from a music therapist. The second group followed a self-administered programme backed up by a weekly phone call from the therapist. The third group was a wait-list control. Both music groups showed improvement in self-esteem and mood compared with controls. This was taken as support for musical interventions for homebound elders, and indeed it might be, except that we do not know to what extent the feeling that help was being given was the agent of therapy rather than any specific musical content.

A better example of a controlled study showing a therapeutic effect of music is that of Sarkamo et al. (2008) with patients in early stages of stroke recovery. Those who listened daily to self-selected music showed greater improvement than those listening to audio books or not listening to anything. Improvements in verbal memory, focussed attention, confusion and mood were all greater in the music listening group than either of the two controls. The authors concluded that music should be offered to stroke patients in addition to other forms of active therapy.

The benefits of music are not just in the listening. Interactive performance has additional benefits. Singing, for example, has been shown to result in respiratory and cardiovascular enhancement similar to that provided by aerobic exercise and has been specifically recommended in patients suffering from chronic obstructive pulmonary disease (Bonhila et al. 2009). Improvements in neurological functioning have been observed along with strengthening of the immune system (Beck et al. 2000), and benefits have been found with respect to mood, self-concept and social communication (Welch 2007).

Music preferences are also a source of social bonding. In community singing groups, choirs and amateur musical productions, close relationships are formed among the performers. Musical taste is a marker of attitudes and values, and we are attracted to other people who share our values (Boer et al. 2011). This is why items about musical preferences are contained in standard partner compatibility questionnaires, such as the *Compatibility Quotient* of Wilson and Cousins (2005).

We have noted that rock music might be detrimental to cardiovascular patients. Could it also be responsible for increased violence and the breakdown of moral restraint in society? Research addressing this issue suggests that the hostile and destructive themes of rock lyrics are generally inclined to reflect social mores rather than precede them (Wilson 2002). A prime function of pop music is to crystallise teenage rebellion against the parental generation, so it is important to a young person that parents react against their choice of music. Pop stars throughout history have outraged public decency in their time but usually seem like pantomime villains in retrospect (e.g., Elvis Presley's hip gyrations no longer come across as dangerously seditious).

In 1985, British rock band Judas Priest was put on trial in Reno, Nevada, accused of inducing a suicide pact between two unstable, drug-using young men. Although they were (no doubt rightly) acquitted, there are studies showing a relationship between interest in heavy metal rock, rap and suicide. However, the thoughts of self-harm seem to precede the interest in rock, so it is likely that the connection between suicide and rock music is mediated by family background and self-esteem (North and Hargreaves 2009).

Sociologists Stack and Gundlach (1992) reported a correlation between the amount of airtime devoted to country music and suicide rates across 49 metropolitan areas in the US. This effect was independent of divorce, poverty, gun availability and geographical "Southernness", thus increasing the possibility of a causal connection. The authors concluded that the recurrent themes of country music, which stress problems such as alcohol abuse and marital strife, may promote suicide by nurturing a pre-existing self-destructive mood.

While it is understandable that people averse to country music might be driven to suicide by excessive exposure to it, it is more surprising that those who choose to listen to it (and hence presumably enjoy it) are sometimes prompted to end their life. Perhaps, after all, we are safest to adopt the position of Jimmy Durante, who once said: "I hate music – especially when it's played". He lived to a ripe old age.

Implications for Health Professionals

Despite these caveats, music is generally beneficial in medical contexts. (1) It can directly enhance mood, bolster immunity, energise people, revive pleasant memories or distract from unpleasant realities. (2) It can contribute to health and well-being by offering an alternative, non-verbal channel of communication. Since verbal skills are mostly used to assess mental competence (e.g., in assigning children to special homes for the learning disabled or older people to care homes and geriatric wards), there is a danger that people who are musically competent are submerged in what, for them, is an impoverished or alien environment. (3) More specifically, Oliver Sacks (2008) has reported that observing advanced dementia patients who display vacant stupor, apparent mindlessness and frequently extreme agitation, nevertheless, may benefit from music because musical sensitivity, -perception, -emotion and -memory may prevail even after other forms of memory have disappeared (p. 337). In these days of relentless dumbing down, this is a problem we perhaps ought to be concerned about.

References

Aigen, K. (2008). An Analysis of Qualitative Music Therapy Research Reports 1987–2006: Articles and Book Chapters. *The Arts in Psychotherapy, 35*, 251–261.

Aldridge, D. (1993). Music Therapy Research I: A Review of the Medical Research Literature Within a General Context of Music Therapy Research. *The Arts in Psychotherapy, 20*, 11–35.

Aldridge, D., et al. (1990). Where Am I? Music Therapy Applied to Coma Patients. *Journal of the Royal Society of Medicine, 83*, 345–346.

Beck, R. J., et al. (2000). Choral Singing, Performance Perception and Immune System Changes in Salivary Immunoglobulin A and Cortisol. *Music Perception, 18*, 87–106.

Bernardi, L., et al. (2009). Dynamic Interactions Between Musical, Cardiovascular, and Cerebral Rhythms in Humans. *Circulation, 119*, 3171–3180.

Biley, F. C. (2000). The Effect on Patient Well-Being of Music Listening as a Nursing Intervention: A Review of the Literature. *Journal of Clinical Nursing, 9*, 668–677.

Boer, D., et al. (2011). How Shared Preferences in Music Create Bonds Between People: Values as the Missing Link. *Personality and Social Psychology Bulletin*, online.

Bonhila, A. G., et al. (2009). Effects of Singing Classes on Pulmonary Function and Quality of Life of COPD Patients. *International Journal of Chronic Obstructive Pulmonary Disease, 4*, 1–8.

Bradt, J., et al. (2011). Music Interventions for Improving Psychological and Physical Outcomes in Cancer Patients. *The Cochrane Collaboration*. John Wiley.

Bunt, L. (1997). Clinical and Therapeutic Uses of Music. In D. J. Hargreaves & A. C. North (Eds.), *The Social Psychology of Music*. Oxford: Oxford University Press.

Curtis, S. L. (2011). Music Therapy and the Symphony: A University-Community Collaborative Project in Palliative Care. *Music and Medicine, 3*, 20–26.

Edwards, J. (2005). Possibilities and Problems for Evidence-Based Practice in Music Therapy. *The Arts in Psychotherapy, 32*, 293–301.

Good, M., et al. (2002). Relaxation and Music Reduce Pain after Gynaecologic Surgery. *Pain Management Nursing, 3*, 61–70.

Hanser, S. B., & Thompson, L. W. (1994). Effects of a Music Therapy Strategy on Depressed Older Patients. *Journal of Gerontology, 49*, 265–269.

Huron, D. (2011). Why Is Sad Music Pleasurable? A Possible Role for Prolactin. *Musicae Scientiae, 15*, 146–158.

Husain, et al. (2002). Effects of musical tempo and mode on arousal, modd and spatial abilities. *Music Perception, 20*, 151–171.

Janata, P. (2009). The Neural Architecture of Music-Evoked Autobiographical Memories. *Cerebral Cortex, 19*, 2579–2594.

Kvam, M. H. (1997). The Effect of Vibroacoustic Therapy. *Physiotherapy, 83*, 290–295.

Lin, L. C., et al. (2011). The Long-Term Effect of Listening to Mozart K.448 Decreases Epileptiform Discharges in Children with Epilepsy. *Epilepsy and Behaviour, 2011*(21), 420–424.

Lindsay, S. (1991). Live Music in Hospitals. In G. D. Wilson (Ed.), *Psychology and Performing Arts*. Amsterdam: Swets & Zeitlinger.

McCraty, R. (1999). Music and the Immune System. In *Proceedings of the Tenth International Congress on Stress*. Montreux.

Miller, M., et al. (2008). Positive Emotions and the Endothelium: Does Joyful Music Improve Musical Health? *Circulation, 118*, S.1148.

Nordoff, P., & Robbins, C. (1977). *Creative Music Therapy*. New York: John Day.

North, A. C., & Hargreaves, D. J. (2009). The Power of Music. *The Psychologist, 22*, 1012–1013.

Osuch, E., et al. (2009). Brain Activation to Favourite Music in Healthy Controls and Depressed Patients. *NeuroReport, 20*, 1204–1208.

Sacks, O. (2008). *Musicophilia. Tales of Music and the Brain*. New York/Toronto: Alfred Knopf.

Salimpoor, V., et al. (2011). Anatomically Distinct Dopamine Release During Anticipation and Experience of Peak Emotion to Music. *Nature Neuroscience, 14*, 257–262.

Sarkamo, T., et al. (2008). Music Listening Enhances Cognitive Recovery and Mood after Middle Cerebral Artery Stroke. *Brain, 131*, 866–876.

Soto, D., et al. (2009). Pleasant Music Overcomes the Loss of Awareness in Patients with Visual Neglect. *Proceedings of the National Academy of Sciences, 106*, 6011–6016.

Stack, S., & Gundlach, J. (1992). The Effect of Country Music on Suicide. *Social Forces, 71*, 211–218.

Trappe, H., et al. (2010). The Effects of Music on the Cardiovascular System and Cardiovascular Health. *Heart, 96*, 1868–1871.

Welch, G. F. (2007). The Benefits of Singing – An Overview. Institute of Education, University of London (web letter).

Wells, D. L., et al. (2002). The Influence of Auditory Stimulation on the Behaviour of Dogs Housed in a Rescue Shelter. *Animal Welfare, 11*, 385–393.

Wigram, T., Saperston, B., & West, R. (Eds.). (1995). *The Art and Science of Music Therapy: A Handbook*. Langhorne: Harwood Academic Publishers.

Wilson, G. D. (2002). *Psychology for Performing Artists*. London: Whurr.

Wilson, G. D., & Cousins, J. M. (2005). Measurement of Partner Compatibility: Further Validation and Refinement of the CQ Test. *Sexual and Relationship Therapy, 20*, 421–429.

12

Therapeutic Applications of Drama Therapy Among Immigrant Drug Abusers

Alexander-Stamatios Antoniou and Marina Dalla

The aim of art is to represent not the outward appearance of things, but their inward significance.
Aristotle

Personal Motivation for Involvement in the Arts and Psychotherapy

The first author has studied classical music and was a member of choirs for many years. Throughout his undergraduate years, he has participated in university drama groups, believing in the significant therapeutic effect of art, especially in the view of an existential psychotherapy. The relieving role of dramatic art was emphasized even from the origins of ancient

A.-S. Antoniou (✉) • M. Dalla
Department of Primary Education, National and Kapodistrian University of Athens, Athens, Greece
e-mail: asantoni@hol.gr

B. Kirkcaldy (ed.), *Psychotherapy, Literature and the Visual and Performing Arts*, Palgrave Studies in Creativity and Culture, https://doi.org/10.1007/978-3-319-75423-9_12

Greek drama. The second author has an interest in cultural psychology and trends in art, music, myths and other popular expressions by different cultural groups. Another deep-seated motive arises from our research and work regarding the psychotherapeutic process among immigrants, as cultural differences and group dynamics have been a central passion in our research endeavors over the last decade.

Introduction

The psychotherapeutic process of substance abuse treatment requires restoring the ability of the addict to function without drugs. This process is not limited to abstinence from drug abuse, but also affects the longer-term changes of personality, attitudes, behavior and affect, and the acquisition of a smooth adjustment capacity and integration into the wider society. The field of psychology offers many forms of therapy to aid in substance abuse treatment, spanning from psychodynamic theories to cognitive, behavioral and motivational therapies (Galanter and Kleber 2008).

Research over the past decades has demonstrated that art therapy is effective in working with and freely expressing uncomfortable experiences through the use of images (Skeffington and Browne 2014). Art therapy can provide a safe space for drug abusers who have lost the ability to verbalize their conscious and unconscious problems because of their trauma history (Hongo et al. 2015).

This chapter will explore theoretical and applied strategies within the Drug Dependence Unit 18 ANO at the Attica State Psychiatric Hospital in an attempt to connect psychological models of drug treatment with art therapy, and especially drama therapy.

Drug Dependence, Abstinence, Art in Therapy of Drug Abuse

Drug dependence creates a marginal state with negative consequences for the individual, his/her family and the wider social community. It brings an alteration in the subject's relationship with others, a change in his/her conscious situations and a disturbance in the living conditions of the body and the world (Laurent 2012). In addition to personal difficulties, individuals who abuse substances experience an array of problems, such as a weakness in coping with their responsibilities (e.g. as a worker, parent or friend). Furthermore, they may find themselves encountering many legal and financial problems or may place themselves in physically dangerous situations due to loss of control (e.g. driving) and so on. In addition to cognitive, emotional and behavioral dysfunction, substance abuse dependence affects the biological system and the body of the individual.

Longitudinal studies indicate that mortality among young substance abusers is 28 times higher than that among other members of the population belonging to the same age group (Angel and Angel 2003) as a result of overdose, accidents and illness. Furthermore, substance-abusing individuals are at a significant risk of co-occurring mental health disorders (e.g. people with dual diagnosis). It is reported that by 2020, mental and substance use disorders will surpass all physical diseases as a major cause of disability worldwide (SAMHSA 2015).

Certain studies regarding the development of addictive behavior and the experience of using psychoactive substances refer to the genes of antisocial personality, particularly *high novelty seeking* that influences the initiation of substance use (Cloninger 2008). However, substance use and abuse tend to be associated with adolescence and young adult years (Antoniou and Dalla 2011; Arnett 2005; Dalla et al. 2009), at which time individuals are encountering the fundamental changes of pubertal and cognitive development, identity and affiliative transitions and achievement transitions that may engender risks or benefits to health and well-being (Schulenberg et al. 1997).

Bronfenbrenner (2005) offers a bio-ecological framework of human development that involves nested, interconnected systems to represent the structure of the social and psychological context of the developing individual, which have important implications on different trajectories of change over time. Using the ecological model we can consider substance abuse as occurring within the context of relationships in settings such as family, school, neighborhood, workplace and the larger cultural context which includes sociopolitical factors, belief systems, customs, lifestyles, opportunity structures, hazards and life-course options that are embedded in each of these broader systems (Bronfenbrenner 2005).

Many authors relate drug abuse during adolescence to contemporary culture, which promotes isolation anxiety, depression and narcissism and may lead to the use of heroin, cocaine and other substances (Lewis et al. 2001). In "Three Observation on the Theme of Toxicomanias", Éric Laurent (2012) referred to a current form of civilization which is compatible with chaos, disorganization, confusion and uncertainty, leading the subject to feel a traumatic helplessness or powerlessness to assimilate into the world. The relationship that each subject establishes with drugs represents a method of moving away from the unpleasant reality and from the distress of helplessness.

The contribution of the treatment process can be helpful in assisting the individual in refraining from substance misuse and learning to live without drugs. It is a pathway of change, through which people achieve not only permanent abstinence from drug use but also longer-term changes in personality, attitudes, behavior and affect, improve their health and wellness, live a self-directed life and strive to reach their full potential (SAMHSA 2011) and integration into the wider society. The field of psychology offers many forms of therapy to aid in substance abuse treatment, spanning from psychodynamic theories to cognitive, behavioral and motivational therapies (Galanter and Kleber 2008).

With its roots in the bio-ecological framework (Bronfenbrenner 2005) and the field of psychological theories, the dependence public treatment unit in Attica State Psychiatric Hospital of Athens offers long-term inpatient and outpatient treatment services for adults and adolescents, for immigrants and refugees, for women and mothers, and for family members of drug abusers. The therapeutic program can be paralleled with phases of development into a mature identity (Matsa 2008). The program is divided into three stages of treatment: (a) *motivation and preparation* for admission (2–3 months), (b) *recovery and psychological treatment* (6–7 months) and (c) *psychosocial reintegration* (10–12 months). Drug abusers receive intensive individual and group psychoeducational programs together with other rehabilitative treatments. In conjunction with other forms of treatment, the use of art in group therapy interventions is designed to complement all phases of development.

Art Therapy

Art has long been viewed as therapeutic. Aristotle (1995), in chapter six of the *Poetics* (1449b24–28), referred to an essential feature of tragedy, as a "mimesis of an action which is elevated, complete, and of magnitude; in language embellished by distinct forms in its sections; employing the mode of enactment, not narrative; and through pity and fear accomplishing the catharsis of such emotions". In book eight chapter five of the *Politics*, Aristotle (1932) discusses the merits of music in the education of the youth and the catharsis as a result of music (1341b39–1342a16) which is common with catharsis as a result of tragedy. The use of music in both song and dance to reduce distress in many cultures and historical periods is demonstrated by Egyptian medical papyri, the Bible and other religious texts, Greek medicine, mythology, magic and tribal medicine (Bunt 1997).

The psychological application of art was described by Freud (1989) in his work "Bildende Kunst und Literatur". He argued that arts have a cathartic effect by allowing both the creators and the audience to discharge unconscious wishes and relief from tension (De Petrillo and Winner 2005). According to Freud, unconscious mental processes, such as displacement and symbolization that operate in the neuroses, dreams and the creation of works of art, function in similar ways and constitute "primary process" thinking, while mental functioning influenced by considerations of external reality belongs to "secondary process" thinking (Edwards 2004). Jung (1997) frequently used drawing, painting and music as part of the patient's analysis. He was interested in art as an archetypal material, because it is imbued with aspects of all societies.

Since 1969, the American Art Therapy Association has acknowledged that art therapy is an integrative mental health profession that helps "individuals, families, and communities through active art-making, creative process, applied psychological theory, and human experience within a psychotherapeutic relationship" (American Art Therapy Association 2017). Art therapy is not concerned with developing artistic skills, although they may be a by-product of the therapeutic process. Through reflecting on the art products and processes, people who experience illness, trauma or challenges in living, or those who seek personal development, can increase levels of awareness of the self and others; cope more effectively with symptoms, stress and traumatic experiences; enhance cognitive abilities; and enjoy the life-affirming pleasures of creating art (from the AATA website 2017).

Art therapy has also been successfully employed in substance abuse treatment since the early 1950s (Schmanke 2017). The main assumptions underlying art therapy in drug addiction are that it allows the individual to explore connections between thought, behavior and emotions in a nonverbal, imaginative and creative manner (Holt and Kaiser 2009; Mahony 1999; Matto et al. 2003; Matsa 2008; Schmanke 2017). Holt and Kaiser (2009) utilize art therapy for the initial stages of substance abuse treatment to facilitate client identification of ambivalence and eventual acceptance of the lifestyle changes necessary for recovery. Mahony (1999) referred to the educative, healing and psychotherapeutic benefits of art therapy, while Matto et al. (2003) discussed the integration of art therapy for the treatment of substance abuse as a way from reflection into a state of action and change. Aiding the expression of repressed emotions, exploring grief, containment of shame and anger, enabling feelings of control through distancing and identifying positive change and growth are some of the issues successfully addressed by art therapy (Slayton et al. 2010; Waller and Mahony 1999).

Art Therapy in 18 ANO Dependence Public Treatment Unit

Art therapy at 18 ANO offers group therapy to drug abusers primarily through nonverbal means using art forms such as drama, music, theater dance/movement, drawing, creative writing and so on, within the context of group psychotherapy during all stages of treatment. Art group therapy helps people who use drugs to gain access to deficient or disturbed unconscious mental processes and express them through art. By activating the process of symbolization and imaginary and by placing new meanings onto objects and concepts, individuals can conceptualize and construct their lives on a new basis.

Matsa (2008) took up the concept of sublimation used by Freud, by which art transforms destructive drives, trauma and mourning in a creative subliminal form. Furthermore, it represents a means of promoting social awareness and inclusion into the broader society. As such, art therapy can also be a culturally relevant therapeutic approach to working with immigrants and refugees. Despite evidence of the benefits of art therapy, literature on its use with immigrants and refugees is limited among children and adolescents with emotional and behavioral problems (Linesch and Carnay 2005; Rousseau et al. 2005; Slayton et al. 2010).

Drama therapy as an intentional use of metaphor and the dynamics of the theater and play (Krasanakis 2017) to achieve the therapeutic goals is considered an active process that facilitates change, emotional and physical integration, and personal growth (Malchiodi 2005). As a means of therapeutic change, drama therapy applies methods such as storytelling, imagination, role-play, dramatic, symbolic and projective play, improvisation and embodied expression through sound and movement in a safe place (Johnson 2009; Listiakova 2015). The model of drama therapy in 18 ANO is therapeutic and sociocultural in its approach. For the sociocultural model of drama therapy, it is important not only to reflect on personal experiences of drug abuse, raising awareness and hope, but also to support the attempts being made by problem drug users to regain their social role and to positively integrate into society more broadly.

Immigrant and Refugee: Drug Abuser in 18 ANO

Greece, like many other Western and Southern European countries, has received a flow of immigrants in the last three decades, who have entered the country legally or illegally. Major population inflows toward Greece include Albanian immigrants, who constitute 56% of the total foreigners in the country. Since 2003, the influx of Asian (Pakistani, Bangladeshi, etc.) and African immigrants has sharply increased. It is estimated that the total number of Pakistani immigrants in Greece ranges from 40,000 to 60,000 (Yousef 2013). About 11,076, immigrants are from Bangladesh, with an average age of 31.5 years. The immigrants from sub-Saharan countries (Nigeria, Tanzania, etc.) constitute approximately 2% of foreigners, although there are no entirely reliable data sources regarding their exact number.

Latest studies on substance abuse have shown an increase in the number of immigrant users admitted for treatment in our Unit. Developing an effective drug abuse treatment model for immigrants is needed in order to understand the processes of immigration, which include (a) profound losses (known landscape and history, native language, unquestioned values and social customs, friends and family, etc.); (b) acculturation as changes in identification patterns in firsthand contact with the host culture which include beliefs, emotions, attitudes and behavior (Sam 2006); and (c) acculturative stress when acculturation experiences cause problems for acculturating individuals or conflict between acculturating groups (Berry and Ataca 2007). Research indicates the coexistence of stressors that increase vulnerability of immigrants for solving problems producing negative adaptation outcomes that may affect drug abuse among immigrants (Dalla et al. 2009).

Acculturation psychology includes many different risk factors that may affect drug abuse among immigrants: previous immigration traumatic experience, loss of extended family and kinship networks especially for unaccompanied children and adolescents, temporary loss of relationships and contact with family, concern from family members, stress from navigating between home and mainstream cultures, different rates of acculturation in the family (parents-child conflicts), perceived discrimination and marginalization, inaccessible health care, language barriers, undocumented alien status with fear of deportation and without access to social resources and so on (Antoniou and Dalla 2011; Dalla et al. 2009.).

The Drama Therapy Program Among Immigrant Drug Abusers

The drama therapy program among immigrant drug abusers in 18 ANO is part of a treatment program that includes long-term individual and group therapy together with other rehabilitative treatment, creating a link between the bio-ecological framework and acculturation literature. The goal of the drama therapy program is to support maintaining abstinence from substance abuse by the sharing of personal stories, in order to construct meaning and to investigate identity, to work with losses and to bridge the gap between two realities, the experience of one's country of origin through memory and imagination and the actual experience of the host country. Creating a holding space (Winnicott 1971), drama therapy allows immigrants to travel in history by bringing past experiences into the here and now, as a holder of memory and history (Gadamer 2011, in Dieterich-Hartwell and Koch 2017).

Drama therapy among immigrants as an integral part of the treatment process develops gradually over a period of two years, after abstinence from drugs. Immigrants are required to attend drama therapy, one hour per week. All participants are male aged between 22 and 64 years. The group consists of 12 male adults coming from Albania, Pakistan, Bangladesh, Tanzania and Nigeria. The main language used during drama therapy is Greek, which itself represents the host country. However, participants are encouraged to use their native language, and the group follows through translation made by team members or the translator. Negotiating between different languages plays an important role in the drama therapy process.

Main Topics, Immigration, Identity Issues, New Society, Everyday Life

The drama therapy program is organized on the development of an understanding of the concept of "home" within the context of immigrants (Papadopoulos 2002). This includes "the wide spectrum of meanings….from a physical and geographical community, to a psychological locus of relatedness and communion; from a seat of origins, to the ultimate goal, the place of rest, beyond conflict" (Papadopoulos 1987, p. 7, in Papadopoulos 2002). It is "both the perceived locus of origin as well as the desired destination, the goal, the end, the telos" (Papadopoulos 1987, p. 8, in Papadopoulos 2002). Freud (1925) connected the concept of home with the word "heimlich" (oikeios, oikos in Greek), which refers to *familiarity*, to everybody "belonging to the house or the family" (p. 222), "intimate, friendly, comfortable, the enjoyment of content, arousing a sense of agreeable and restfulness as in one with the four walls of his house" (p. 222). There is no doubt that the unfamiliar, uncanny is related to "what is frightening" (p. 219), something in which one does not recognize himself/herself, and as such it has elements that cause fear and insecurity.

The first topics of drama therapy are presented in an open-ended manner, in order to get to know each other and to create the "home" as it is now. The participants draw their journey from different countries, during adolescence, some of them under 18 years, an illegal journey, without legal permission and without required documents. Al. from Pakistan left his country after his father and one brother died. In his country, it is usually the eldest son who has the obligation expected to emigrate and support the family. After less than three years of living in Turkey, he came to Greece by boat, spending much time on the streets in his new country and also spending time in squats where he found friends who used drugs. According to B. from Albania, after disruption of communism in his country, it was common for young males to make the decision to leave and go to Greece, sometimes even without their parents' permission. K. from Nigeria described the experienced traumatic events in his country, the murder of his father and mother, the terror he felt himself and his brothers who were left behind. Some of the participants have experienced multiple migrations—South Africa, Turkey and so on.

Despite the variance in migration and traumatic experiences, many commonalities exist among immigrant and refugee drug abusers. Many have left their country at the time of adolescence, aged between 15 and 17 years, experiencing trauma and the loss of their homeland, family and friends. Most have little or no formal education. All had the desire for a better life, but for many years they were living in segregated neighborhoods where drug taking is an important feature. The immigrants incorporated the feeling of an "unhomely" (Freud 1925: p. 219), an alien and an illegal, moving through places of separateness, loneliness, strangeness and unbelonging. Drug abuse helped them to structure the anger of an "unhomely" and to develop an adversarial identity toward the society (both to the past and to their host country) that rejected their aspirations and goals. It was an attempt to establish the link between the past self of belonging and the new self of not belonging.

A further group of stories reflects back on the self (Sedikides et al. 2015), expressing pleasure and sadness by remembering loved ones, family members and friends. O. from Tanzania thought about his grandmother's town, where all of the family had gathered to celebrate when he was a child. He missed the closeness that they had in the past. S. expressed memories from Bangladesh which included his friends and engagement in traditional games in the town each afternoon. One participant wrote the following about his country, Tanzania: "The Masai giraffe, it is the symbol of my country". We were informed that the Masai giraffe relates to being vulnerable to extinction when living outside protected areas. Another man from Bangladesh reported feeling guilty because he had left his homeland after his daughter' birth, stating that every day he thinks a lot about his daughter and his wife.

The nostalgia of immigrants (nostos, return; and algos, pain) involves a complex interaction between the past memories, the present life and projection of the future. P. from Africa referred to the art medium of African immigrants in Greece, including different festivals, music, theater and traditional cuisine as celebrations of solidarity and resistance to social exclusion and racism. He spoke of different African communities in Greece that recreate past spaces of collective memories of homeland. They celebrate holidays, speak in their native language and conduct their religious rituals. This restorative nostalgia (Sedikides et al. 2015) supports the continuity of identity.

Akhtar (1999) used the term emotional refueling as the intrapsychic connection of immigrants and refugees to their motherland. The extramural refueling includes undertaking trips back to the homeland or making calls to relatives left behind. The intramural refueling refers to support offered by the larger network of a *homoethnic* community. Apart from the collective nostalgia, immigrants also embrace their personal memories of homeland to project their future. Sh. from Pakistan describes how the marriage of young people is arranged by parents and family members. His parents had put pressure on him to marry soon, which he welcomed, hoping to visit his home country to find a girl to marry.

Other stories emerged in terms of the expression of emotions, either directly or indirectly, regarding the tension of belonging to a minority group in the host society and the perception of being treated unfairly by the Greek government, for example, by the refusal of permanent papers for residing in Greece. J. from Nigeria lived on the streets for many years and was often picked up by the police. He still has no legal papers, which makes him very sad. Z. from Bangladesh reports the impressions of a performance organized by 18 ANO and his participation in it, stating that when traveling by bus people do not sit next to him (due to his color), while participation in the group elicited feelings of warmth and love.

Other participants referred to the difficulty of finding a job, to the fact that they often work without social security or have problems receiving payment. Group drama therapy not only represents a safe space for immigrants recovering from drug addiction but also represents an important process in terms of learning about trust and reliable relationships. In particular, the drama therapy approach toward the "home", the past, the present and the future helps immigrants to develop a continuity of identity between their homeland and their new country.

Conclusions: Guidelines for Mental Health Professionals

In this chapter we argue that art in the treatment process of substance abuse can provide a *helpful space* where individuals can gain access to strong feelings that are evoked in a nonconventional manner. Art therapy has also been shown to provide immigrants with a *nonconventional cultural space* where they can express their feelings about their past, their homeland, their present life and their future aspirations. From this viewpoint, we describe the application of drama therapy in the *rehabilitation of immigrants* from substance abuse. The "home" approach (past, now and future) offers them the experience of *emotional refueling* and the containment of new aspects of the host country. Mental health professionals should be aware of alternatives to solely psychotropic interventions, and as such drama therapy represents an *adjunct to medication*. Moreover, as witnessed, the medium of drama and arts may facilitate *effective coping techniques* for potentially anxiety-arousing situations or indeed traumatic events experienced. Finally, such therapy modalities offer opportunities for promoting *social skills and emotional regulation.*

References

Akhtar, S. (1999). *Immigration and Identity. Turmoil, Treatment and Transformation*. Lanham: Jason Aronson INC.

American Art Therapy Association. (2017). *About Art Therapy*. http://www.americanarttherapyassociation.org/aata-history-background.html.

Angel, S., & Angel, P. (2003). *The Drug Addicts and Their Families: A Systemic Approach*. Thessaloniki: University Studio Press.

Antoniou, A.-S., & Dalla, M. (2011). Drug Abuse Among Immigrants and the Role of Professionals in the Treatment Process. In B. Kirkcaldy (Ed.), *The Art and Science of Health Care: Psychology and Human Factors for Practitioners* (pp. 201–219). Goettingen: Hogrefe Publishers.

Aristotle (1932). *Politics* (H. Rackham, Trans.). Cambridge, MA: Harvard University Press.

Aristotle (1995). *Poetics* (S. Halliwell, Trans.). Cambridge, MA: Harvard University Press.

Arnett, J. J. (2005). The Developmental Context of Substance Use in Emerging Adulthood. *The Journal of Drug Issues, 35*, 235–254.

Berry, J. W., & Ataca, B. (2007). Cultural Factors in Stress. In *Encyclopedia of Stress* (pp. 672–678). Oxford: Elsevier.

Bronfenbrenner, U. (2005). *Making Human Beings Human: Bioecological Perspectives on Human Development*. Thousand Oaks: Sage Publications.

Bunt, L. (1997). Clinical and Therapeutic Uses of Music. In D. Hargreaves & A. North (Eds.), *The Social Psychology of Music* (pp. 249–268). Oxford: Oxford University Press.

Cloninger, C. R. (2008). Genetics of Substance Abuse. In M. Galanter & H. Klleber (Eds.), *The American Psychiatric Publishing Textbook of Substance Abuse Treatment* (pp. 73–80). Washington, DC: American Psychiatric Publishing, Inc.

Dalla, M., Antoniou, A.-S., & Matsa, K. (2009). Immigration, Acculturation and Drug Abuse: Multicultural Aspects of Treatment. In A.-S. Antoniou, C. L. Cooper, G. P. Chrousos, C. D. Spielberger, & M. W. Eysenck (Eds.), *Handbook of Managerial Behavior and Occupational Health* (pp. 362–380). Northampton: Edward Elgar.

De Petrillo, L., & Winner, E. (2005). Does Art Improve Mood? A Test of a Key Assumption Underlying Art Therapy. *Art Therapy: Journal of the American Art Therapy Association, 22*, 205–212.

Dieterich-Hartwell, R., & Koch, S. C. (2017). Creative Arts Therapies as Temporary Home for Refugees: Insights from Literature and Practice. *Behavioral Sciences, 7*(4), 1–11.

Edwards, D. (2004). *Art Therapy: Art Therapies in Practice*. Thousand Oaks: Sage Publications Ltd..

Freud, S. (1925). Das Unheimliche. In Studienausgabe, Bd. IV: *Psychologische Schriften* (pp. 241–274). Frankfurt/M.: Fischer.

Freud, S. (1989). *Studienausgabe: Bildende Kunst nad Literatur.* Frankfurt/M.: S. Fischer.

Gadamer, H.G. (2011). Den Gätfullahälsan (The Enigma of Health). Dualis Förlag, AD.

Galanter, M., & Kleber, H.D. (2008). The American Psychiatric Publishing Textbook of Substance Abuce Treatment. American Psychiatric Publishers Inc., Arlington, VA.

Holt, E., & Kaiser, D. H. (2009). The First Step Series: Art Therapy for Early Substance Abuse Treatment. *The Arts in Psychotherapy, 36*, 245–250.

Hongo, A., Katz, A., & Valenti, K. (2015). Art: Trauma to Therapy for Aging Female Prisoners. *American Psychology Association, 21*(3), 201–207.

Johnson, D. R. (2009). The History and Development of the Field of Drama Therapy in North America. In D. R. Johnson & R. Emunah (Eds.), *Current Approaches in Drama Therapy* (2nd ed., pp. 5–15). Springfield: Charles C. Thomas.

Jung, C. G. (1997). *Jung on Active Imagination*. London: Routledge.

Krasanakis, S. (2017). Dramatherapy and Drug Addiction Treatment. *Dramatherapy, 38*(1), 53–58.

Laurent, E. (2012). The Society of Symptom (in Greek). In D. Andropoulou, E. Theodoridis, & N. Papanikolaou (Eds.), *Lacanian Clinic of Drug Addiction* (pp. 23–52). Athens: Ekkremes.

Lewis, T., Amini, F., & Lannon, R. (2001). *A General Theory of Love*. New York: Vintage Books.

Linesch, D., & Carnay, J. (2005). Supporting Cultural Competency in Art Therapy Training. *The Arts in Psychotherapy, 32*, 382–394.

Listiakova, I. (2015). Analysis of Three Approaches in Dramatherapy. *Journal of Exceptional People, 1*(6), 19–29.

Mahony, J. (1999). Art therapy and activities in alcohol service s research project. In: Treatment and Addiction Current Issues for Art Therapies (Eds.) WAlker, D., & Mahony, J.). London, Routledge.

Malchiodi, C. A. (2005). Expressive Therapies History, Theory, and Practice. In C. A. Malchiodi (Ed.), *Expressive Therapies* (pp. 243–253). New York: Guilford Press.

Matsa, K. (2008). *Psychotherapy and the Art in Drug Recovery. The Expampe of "18 ANO"* (in Greek). Athens: Agra.

Matto, H., Corcoran, J., & Fassler, A. (2003). Integrating Solution-Focused and Art Therapies for Substance Abuse Treatment: Guidelines for Practice. *The Arts in Psychotherapy, 30*(5), 265–272.

Papadopoulos, R. (2002). *Therapeutic Care for Refugees: No Place Like Home, Tavistock Clinic Series*. London: Karnac.

Rousseau, C., Drapeau, A., Lacroix, L., Bagilishya, D., & Heusch, N. (2005). Evaluation of a Classroom Program of Creative Expression Workshops for Refugee and Immigrant Children. *Journal of Child Psychology and Psychiatry, 46*(2), 180–185.

Sam, D. L. (2006). Acculturation: Conceptual Background and Core Components. In D. L. Sam & J. W. Berry (Eds.), *The Cambridge Handbook of Acculturation Psychology* (pp. 11–26). Cambridge: Cambridge University Press.

SAMHSA. (2011). *SAMHSA Announces a Working Definition of "Recovery" From Mental Disorders and Substance use Disorders*. http://store.samhsa.gov.

SAMHSA. (2015). *Behavioral Health Trends in the United States: Results from the 2014 National Survey on Drug Use and Health*. http://store.samhsa.gov.

Schmanke, L. (2017). *Art Therapy and Substance Abuse: Enabling Recovery from Alcohol and Other Drugs Addiction*. London: Jessica Kingsley Publishers.

Schulenberg, J., Maggs, J. L., & Hurrelmann, K. (1997). *Health Risks and Developmental Transitions During Adolescence*. New York: Cambridge University Press.

Sedikides, C., Wildschut, T., Arndt, J., Routledge, C., Arndt, J., Hepper, E. G., & Zhou, X. (2015). To Nostalgize: Mixing Memory with Affect and Desire. *Advances in Experimental Social Psychology, 51*, 189–273.

Skeffington, P., & Browne, M. (2014). Art Therapy, Trauma and Substance Misuse: Using Imagery to Explore a Difficult Past with a Complex Client. *International Journal of Art Therapy, 19*(3), 114–121.

Slayton, S. C., D'Archer, J., & Kaplan, F. (2010). Outcome Studies on the Efficacy of Art Therapy: A Review of Findings. *Art Therapy, 27*(3), 108–119.

Waller, D., & Mahony, J. (Eds.). (1999). *Treatment of Addiction - Current Issues for Arts Therapies*. London: Routledge.
Winnicott, D. W. (1971). *Playing and Reality*. New York: Basic Books.
Yousef, K. (2013). *The Vicious Circle of Irregular Migration From Pakistan to Greece and Back to Pakistan*. Background report: Migratory System 3 (Pakistan). Hellenic Foundation for European Foreign Policy (ELIAMEP).

13

Emotional Intelligence, Personality Disorders and the Performing Arts

Adrian Furnham

Introduction

This chapter addresses the aptitude and temperament of the performing artist. It is divided into two sections. In the first section the concept of emotional intelligence, which replaced older ideas of interpersonal and social skills, is discussed. The ideas that all performing artists need exemplary emotional awareness and management in their craft are considered. The second section deals with the relationship between the subclinical personality disorders—in particular histrionic, narcissistic and schizotypal disorders—and success, particularly in acting. The idea is that, at the subclinical level, it may even be advantageous to have these disorders. The chapter also concentrates on how emotional awareness is taught in the performing arts.

A personal statement: Unlike most of my peers, I am an arts, not a science, graduate. I notice many differences between us, particularly in our

A. Furnham (✉)
Department of Psychology, University College London, London, UK
e-mail: a.furnham@ucl.ac.uk

B. Kirkcaldy (ed.), *Psychotherapy, Literature and the Visual and Performing Arts*, Palgrave Studies in Creativity and Culture, https://doi.org/10.1007/978-3-319-75423-9_13

out-of-work activities and interests. I have always been interested in the theatre and go almost weekly in London. I play bridge with a professional actor and have many performing arts friends, including singers and musicians. I have long been interested in what factors lead them to being successful and unsuccessful. This interest fits well my interest in management derailment and failure.

Emotional Intelligence

Despite its popularity, and the fact that most people claim to have heard of it, very few can accurately define emotional intelligence (EI). Sceptics claim that "charm and influence" became "social and interpersonal skills", which have become "emotional intelligence". Social skills used to be defined in terms of sensitivity and flexibility: how sensitive a person is to social cues and how flexible they are in their responses to those accurately observed aspects of behaviour. Socially skilled individuals were seen as happier and healthier and generally more successful at work and in relationships. Furthermore, it was argued that social skills could be taught (Furnham 2008).

However, the new term and concept EI "chimed with the zeitgeist" and became very popular. It has spawned a huge industry, particularly with those interested in success at work (Goleman 1996). Many books make dramatic claims: for instance, that cognitive ability or traditional academic intelligence contributes only about 20% to general life success (academic, personal and work), while the remaining 80% is directly attributable to EI. By and large, there is little good empirical evidence to support these wild claims.

EI can be discussed in terms of four parts: self and other emotional awareness and management. Thus it is partly defined as whether people are emotionally self-aware. *First*, can they recognize and understand their emotional reaction to persons and places, particularly where the emotions are powerful and unusual? *Second*, are they able to accurately "read" the emotions of other people? Do they "pick up" on what others are saying non-verbally, ensuring they are highly perceptive?

Third, is the individual able to manage their emotions? This is particularly important in social contexts where they need to be able to appropriately regulate their emotional responses to others. *Finally*, there is the issue of the management of the emotions of others. Are they able, when and where appropriate, to change the emotional state in others? Can they calm down frightened or angry people? Are they able to give people confidence in situations which acquire this?

The emotionally intelligent person is aware of, sensitive to and perceptive around their own and others' emotions. They are in short both emotionally literate and behaviourally flexible. They know how to manage—change, moderate, control—their own and others' emotions. They know what to do when they or others are "down", frightened or aggressive. Being aware without being able to manage emotions is insufficient. It is obvious why this is so important in the performing arts.

Goleman's popular book told a simple and interesting story about EI that helped explain its appeal. Technical training in the essential job knowledge of any career is easy compared to teaching IQ skills. As an adult it is comparatively more straightforward to teach a person the technical aspects of the job than the "soft" skills. The idea is that there is a critical period to acquire the basis of EI, which is probably during early to late adolescence. The young person, often a male, may experience social anxiety, discomfort and rejection while attempting to interact with and influence others (specifically those they are attracted to, which is most often people of the opposite sex).

Hence they may over time find solace in computers and other activities with a high skills/low contact basis. Thus, in early adulthood, they appear to be technically competent in certain areas (IT, engineering) but still rather undeveloped in people skills and more specifically emotional awareness and regulation. They may even be "phobic" about emotional issues and resistant to (social skills) training. It is also assumed that people are less able to pick up EI "skills" as well as less willing to undertake. To acquire technical skills often requires considerable dedication, so opportunities to acquire social skills (EQ) are, therefore, reduced. Then the low EQ person chooses technology rather than people for fun, comfort and a source of ideas because they do not understand emotions.

Some adults often tend to be rigid, with poor self-control and poor social skills, and are weak at building bonds. Understanding and using emotions/feelings are at the heart of business and indeed being human. Often business people prefer to talk about emotional competencies (rather than traits or abilities) which are essentially learned capabilities. Emotional competencies include *emotional self-awareness*, *emotional self-regulation*, *social-emotional awareness*, *regulating emotions in others*, *understanding emotions* and so on. If one is to include older related concepts, like social skills or interpersonal competencies, it is possible to find literature dating back 30 years showing these skills predict occupational effectiveness and success. Further, there is convincing empirical literature that suggests these skills can be improved and learnt.

There a number of academic quarrels and issues in the EI literature. The two major issues lie in the components of EI and how to measure it. A major difficulty with the measurement of ability EI is that emotional experiences are inherently subjective and, consequently, lack the objectivity required to make them amenable to robust, valid and reliable maximum performance measurement. There is no simple way of applying truly veridical criteria in the objective scoring of items relating to the intrapersonal component of ability EI (e.g. "I am aware of my emotions as I experience them") simply because the application of such scoring procedures would require direct access to privileged information, such as inner feelings and private cognitions, that is available only to the individual who is being assessed

Another central unresolved question is, what are the facets or components or EI? Thus early models distinguished between the perception, appraisal and expression of emotion in self and others, the use of emotion to facilitate thinking and the use of emotional knowledge to understand and analyse emotions as well as the reflective regulation of emotions to promote growth. Some writers talk of *emotional literacy* (which involves the knowledge and understanding of one's own emotions and how they function), *emotional fitness* (which involves trustworthiness and emotional hardiness and flexibility), *emotional depth* (which involves emotional growth and intensity) and *emotional alchemy* (which involves using emotions to discover creative opportunities.

Table 13.1 Common facets in salient models of EI

Facets	High scorers perceive themselves as being or having
Adaptability	Flexible and willing to adapt to new conditions
Assertiveness	Forthright, frank and willing to stand up for their rights
Emotion expression	Capable of communicating their feelings to others
Emotion management (others)	Capable of influencing other people's feelings
Emotion perception (self and others)	Clear about their own and other people's feelings
Emotion regulation	Capable of controlling their emotions
Impulsiveness (low)	Reflective and less likely to give into their urges
Relationship skills	Capable of having fulfilling personal relationships
Self-esteem	Successful and self-confident
Self-motivation	Driven and unlikely to give up in the face of adversity
Social competence	Accomplished networkers with excellent social skills
Stress management	Capable of withstanding pressure and regulating stress
Trait empathy	Capable to taking someone else's perspective
Trait happiness	Cheerful and satisfied with their lives
Trait optimism	Confident and likely to "look on the bright side" of life

Others "divide up" EI into factors like self-awareness, self-regulation, self-motivation, empathy and social skills. One more popular conception has 15 components (Table 13.1).

These fifteen scales can be combined into four different related but independent factors labelled *well-being, self-control skills, emotional skills* and *social skills.*

It seems completely self-evident that actors have to be high on EI. Indeed their very job depends on emotional signalling through gesture and movement. They need both emotional awareness and management particularly of their own but also others' emotions.

Creativity and Mental Illness

Some actors have been accused of "dramatic theatricality" in the sense that they are either attention seeking or else have poor emotional self-control or management. This leads on to the question of the mental health of actors. There is an extensive and highly debated literature of the relationship between "creativity and madness" which is highly debated (Dietrich 2014; Wills 2003).

For instance, Dietrich (2014) asks, essentially, what the evidence is that so many creative geniuses are, or were, anguished, tormented or psychologically ill. It seems to be commonly held that there is a strong relationship between mental illness of some kind and creativity. It is as if the latter is a by-product of the former. Not that all mentally ill people are creative but, rather that, with people who are gifted, it is their "distress" which somehow brings out the genius.

Most people can name mad geniuses from a whole range of the creative arts, such as artists and poets, musicians and authors. This is also true of rock stars and fashion designers, though it is not always clear whether they are really "mentally unwell" or simply attention seeking.

This is usually restricted to the arts and not the sciences. Scientific geniuses are more likely to be thought of as cold and geeky rather than "mad". Einstein and other famous physicists may have looked a little odd, but there is much less evidence of serious acute or chronic mental illness. Scientific geniuses are sometimes portrayed as sad and bad but not that often mad.

Dietrich (2014) is particularly scathing of the study of creativity, which has always been handicapped not so much by a lack of definition but rather a way to measure it accurately. He notes that the field is "beset with nebulous concepts, combustible propositions and myopic theorizing".

He argues that the data suggest the opposite; that is, the relationship between mental illness and creativity is strongly negative rather than positive. He notes, as do so many psychologists, including Nobel Prize winners, "Our mind comes with a whole stack of cognitive biases preloaded and preinstalled." He offers four reasons to explain, in part, the misconception about the link between creativity and mental illness.

First is the *base-rate fallacy*, which means we ignore generic, baseline, population data. There is much evidence that a very large number of creative people have had no pathological symptoms. While there may be evidence that some geniuses are disturbed, that number is very, very small.

Second is the *availability heuristic*, which means that because it is easy to imagine or bring to mind some current, high-profile, "mad genius" character, we completely overestimate how many of these people there are.

Third is the *illusory correlation* problem, which makes people think that things are related causally when they seem to occur together at some point in time. That is, if some geniuses seem to have mental illness problems, it is the latter that somehow caused the former.

Fourth is the all-powerful *confirmation bias*, which is the tendency to confirm our prejudices by virtue of a very selective memory and interpretation of possibly complex and ambiguous information.

In short, there are good reasons to explain why these misconceptions are so widely held.

In fact there are psychologists who believe the precise opposite: that creativity is particularly associated with mental health rather than illness. Not so much the tortured genius as the joy of creativity that comes with adjustment and health.

Psychological Characteristics of the Acting Profession

There is now an extensive and growing literature on the "dark side" of behaviour at work (Furnham 2015). It is concerned mainly with the paradoxical finding that many business leaders appear to have subclinical personality disorders (hysteria, narcissism, psychopathy, schizotypy) that help them emerge as leaders but ultimately lead to their derailment.

We now consider whether the same is true of actors, namely, whether certain specific personality disorders might not actually benefit actors

Acting has unique and unusual requirements. *First*, the median earnings in the profession are low, and there is financial instability and many actors have to take second jobs. *Second*, acting involves choosing social situations that many people find anxiety provoking, that is, in front of a large group of people who critique their performance or in the highly pressurized environment of a film set or stage. *Third*, there is a lack of objective standards in assessing performance, resulting in even accomplished performers finding themselves at the receiving end of acute or chronic negative appraisal. Many actors say they cope by never reading reviews.

As well as the ability to memorize and recall vast amounts of text, research has identified three social cognitive components in which actors usually display expertise. *First*, they have an increased "theory of mind" (Goldstein et al. 2009). To repeatedly "become different characters in different time periods and with different motives", the actor must understand the intentions, motivations, emotions and beliefs of their characters and "really get under their skin". Goldstein and Winner (2012) noted that this ability has to be present in actors from childhood, who more frequently engaged in "pretending" and role play than non-actors.

Second, actors usually show high levels of empathy, because to be able to display the emotions of their characters to audiences convincingly, actors must have the ability to *feel* the characters' emotions themselves. *Third*, they need to possess an aptitude for emotional regulation: to display mastery in monitoring their expressive and affective behaviour (see above).

Inevitably, acting with all its intense emotional experiences carries a considerable element of personal risk. Many actors, it seems, are more vulnerable to past traumatic experiences and potential PTSD-like symptoms (Thomson and Jaque 2012). Further, their increased empathic ability may put them *at risk* of emotional disorders (Nettle 2006). It has been suggested that proponents of "method acting" techniques (Stanislavsky 1989) in particular can suffer from possession syndrome; their everyday lives are infected by the role they are engrossed in. Actors often report the experience a blurring of the lines between their own personality and their character's. However, this effect is likely only temporary and for personality domains of great significance to their character (Hannah et al. 1994).

Thus it is not clear whether acting is seen to be an antecedent (cause) or consequence (effect) of one or other personality disorder.

A career in the profession appears to be dependent on performance in two different spheres. *First* is managing the challenges of the industry: the stress surrounding high rates of rejection, unemployment and the difficulties that arise from the emotional nature of the work. *Second* is the task of the process of acting itself: the abilities and characteristics required to create and portray characters that an audience will believe and enjoy. Research has indicated that one important contributor to both these areas is the personality of the actor.

Kaun (1991) looked at the longevity of artists from architects to writers, composers to conductors, painters to photographers. He found writers die young. Writers, whose mean age of death was only 61.7 years, lived ten years *less* than most of the other groups. The explanation was look at *hedonic calculus*: the joy that jobs bring. People at work can derive pleasure (and pain) from both the product and the process: *what* they are trying to achieve (the painting, the opera, the score, the book, the performance) and *how* they go about achieving it.

First, for novelists, as opposed to journalists or even poets, the product has often a (very) *long time to completion*. Not only is a writer's product a long time in production, there is also precious little feedback or reward along the way. Actors, artists, composers and sculptors have a much greater output and can often produce their work more quickly.

Second, writing is *a painful, lonely process*. It is often difficult, demanding and unsatisfying. The writer needs stimulus to the imagination, inspiration and excitement but is all too often confronted by the tyranny of the blank page or screen. Most musicians and actors rehearse with others. Dancers, singers and photographers shoot the breeze, practise and interact with each other, sometimes out of necessity, sometimes choice. Portrait painters natter to, or seduce, their models.

Inevitably many writers take to drink and drugs to sharpen the dull flatness of the typical day. Alcohol can fuel the imagination and increase self-confidence. In the performing arts a person might use drink to "come down" but never use it to get the juices going.

The Personality Traits and Disorders of Professional Actors

Early studies suggested that actors were found to be exhibitionistic and narcissistic (Hayman 1973). Fisher and Fisher (1981) also found actors to possess impulsive, exhibitionistic and hysterical personalities. Yet Hammond and Edelmann (1991) showed actors to be extraverted, sociable and highly sensitive to the feelings of others. Eysenck and Wilson (1991) established that actors scored higher on scales of extraversion, expressiveness, reflectiveness and aggression compared to other performing artists (Marchant-Haycox and Wilson 1992). More recently, Nettle (2006) found that actors scored high on scales of extraversion, agreeableness and openness to experience and match the level of controls on neuroticism and conscientiousness.

More recently in a study of the psychotic traits in actors and comedians, Ando et al. (2014) revealed that, compared to the norms, actors were higher on *unusual experiences*, measuring magical thinking, belief in telepathy and other paranormal events, and tendency to experience perceptual aberrations; *cognitive disorganization*, measuring distractibility and difficulty in focusing thoughts; and *impulsive nonconformity*, measuring a tendency towards impulsive, antisocial behaviour, often suggesting a lack of mood-related *self-control.* However, there was no difference between actors and "normal" on *introvertive anhedonia*, measuring a reduced ability to feel social and physical pleasure, including an avoidance of intimacy.

Few have addressed the question as to the relationship between the acting profession and the personality disorders. It is possible that individuals with borderline personality disorder are usually attracted to professions that provide recognition (Furnham et al. 2014). Other artistic groups have shown a tendency towards emotional and relational instability (Frantom and Sherman 1999), and intuitively, the increased feelings of intense emotion related to this trait could potentially be utilized by the actor in recreating emotional moments for stage or screen.

Histrionic personality disorder traits are probably most obviously related to the acting profession. A comparison of theatre actors and controls on a measure of histrionic PD found actors to score significantly higher (Cale and Lilienfield 2002). The trait is correlated with high extraversion (Samuel and Widiger 2008). Histrionic individuals place importance on their own personal appearance and strive to give positive first impressions. These behaviours are clearly important for auditions, where an actor must impress in a limited amount of time. Particularly for individuals with histrionic tendencies, the vocational setting of acting can fulfil their drive for the dramatic.

Narcissists perform better in public settings than non-narcissists (Wallace and Baumeister 2002) and have strong initial likeability (Oltmanns et al. 2004); thus casting directors and producers may be drawn to employing them. This increased self-confidence aids the individual in dealing with the social situations and large audiences regularly encountered by the actor. Young and Pinsky (2006) recorded narcissistic traits in celebrity actors. This group was significantly more narcissistic than controls, although it is undetermined whether this is more related to their celebrity status or their identity as an actor. The corresponding dark-side trait of boldness is repeatedly implicated as being beneficial in occupational settings (Furnham 2010; Hogan 2007).

Cluster C (avoidant and dependent) personality disorder traits are rarely associated with success in *any* profession (Furnham et al. 2014). Avoidant PD individuals are socially inhibited and oversensitive to criticism. Those with dependent traits fear rejection and are overly reliant on others for support. These are not beneficial traits in this most critical and exposed of professions. Obsessive-compulsive personality disorder is not associated with social and creative professions (Furnham 2008), and no links in the literature exist between actors and this disorder. However, the trait is associated with promotion at work in "traditional" jobs (Furnham et al. 2012), indicating benefit in some occupations.

Davison and Furnham (2017), in a rare study in this area, examined the personality disorder trait profiles of 214 professional actors, compared to a general population sample. Both male and female actors scored significantly higher than non-actors on antisocial, narcissism, histrionic, borderline and obsessive-compulsive personality disorder scales of the Coolidge Axis-II Inventory (Coolidge 2001). Male actors scored significantly higher than the male comparison group on schizotypal, avoidant and dependent personality disorder scales.

They noted: "On the whole, the profile principally matches the dark-side trait profile of individuals attracted to enterprising/entrepreneurial jobs. The acting profession and entrepreneurship do have some similar features. The focus is on the self and building one's own career rather than as an employee in an organization. Research on successful and unsuccessful entrepreneurs suggests that these traits at a very high level may be a contributing factor in the failure and derailment of aspiring entrepreneurs. The same curvilinear relationship with success may also exist in the acting profession. The individual may initially be drawn to the profession because of their PD trait profile yet ultimately fail because of it."

Conclusion

This chapter has considered whether people in the performing arts are more likely to be highly emotionally intelligent and have certain, possibly problematic, personality profiles. There are good theoretical reasons to believe that successful actors are highly emotionally sensitive and adaptable. However, there is also a scattered but growing literature on various personal problems associated with being in the arts. The literature parallels that concerned with the dark side of leaders suggest that subclinical personality disorders are associated with leadership emergence, but also derailment.

However, it is not clear whether acting is seen to be an antecedent (cause) or consequence (effect) of one or other personality disorder. That is, are people with a particular personality profile attracted to the acting profession, or does the experience of being an actor lead to the development of personality disorders?

Much research needs to be done in the area. Few, if any, studies have distinguished between types of actors: those who prefer television vs. the stage, comedy vs. tragedy, action vs. romance. There are also few, if any, longitudinal studies tracing actors over time.

Implications for Clinicians

There are many stereotypes about those in the performing arts and what traits are associated with success and failure. Are those who choose the performing arts more *vulnerable to certain disorders* than others? The answer would appear to be yes. There are few jobs that lead to so much rejection and require so much hard work and practice than that of actors, singers and musicians. They do therefore seem more prone to depression and anxiety than people in other professions. Further, the need for constant practising and line learning could lead to social isolation and not getting enough social contact and social support. Next, there is the possibility of obsessionality in people who often have to practise for 10,000 hours for every hour they perform. There are well-known issues of subclinical narcissism as well as self-handicapping when performers confronted with sudden fame feel as if they are imposters.

Finally, the *emotional literacy and sensitivity* of those in the performing arts could be seen to be a double-edged sword. It may help them in their job, which is often to portray and interpret powerful and subtle emotions, but they may also become hypersensitive to negative emotions in themselves and others. This perhaps accounts for the recent interest in the high incidence of mental illness of various groups in the performing arts.

On the other hand, the importance of *emotional regulation* could help actors become more psychologically resilient. Further they have to be very perceptive of their and others' emotions which can make them very insightful and sensitive. In this sense many actors report doing what is now called *mindfulness*: the exploration, control and regulation of emotions. In this sense acting can make an individual both fragile *and* strong. (The relationship between theatre and psychology has been explored in detail in the Chap. 6 by Zinn.)

Clinicians need to be aware of the many psychological and behavioural pressures on actors and be prepared to assist them to understand the power of emotions both to help portray characters and also to become more mindful of their own.

Appendix

Table A.1 The DSM IV

DSM Labels	Theme	Familiar term	Behavioural tendencies
Borderline	Inappropriate anger, unstable and intense relationships alternating between idealization and devaluation	Unstable Relationships	Flighty, inconsistent, forms intense albeit sudden enthusiasms and disenchantments for people or projects
Paranoid	Distrustful and suspicious of others; motives are interpreted as malevolent	Argumentative	Suspicious of others, sensitive to criticism, expects to be mistreated
Avoidant	Social inhibition, feelings of inadequacy and hypersensitivity to criticism or rejection	Fear of failure	Dread of being criticized or rejected, tends to be excessively cautious, unable to make decisions
Schizoid	Emotional coldness and detachment from social relationships, indifferent to praise and criticism	Interpersonal Insensitivity	Aloof, cold, imperceptive, ignores social feedback
Passive-aggressive	Passive resistance to adequate social and occupational performance, irritated when asked to do something he/she does not want to	Passive-aggressive	Sociable but resists others through procrastination and stubbornness
Narcissistic	Arrogant and haughty behaviours or attitudes, grandiose sense of self-importance and entitlement	Arrogance	Self-absorbed, typically loyal only to himself/herself and his/her own best interests

(*continued*)

Table A.1 (continued)

DSM Labels	Theme	Familiar term	Behavioural tendencies
Antisocial	Disregard for the truth, impulsivity and failure to plan ahead; failure to conform with social norms	Untrustworthiness	Impulsive, dishonest, selfish, motivated by pleasure, ignoring the rights of others
Histrionic	Excessive emotionality and attention seeking, self-dramatizing, theatrical and exaggerated emotional expression	Attention seeking	Motivated by a need for attention and a desire to be in the spotlight
Schizotypal	Odd beliefs or magical thinking; behaviour or speech that is odd, eccentric or peculiar	No common sense	Unusual or eccentric attitudes, exhibits poor judgement relative to education and intelligence
Obsessive-compulsive	Preoccupations with orderliness, rules, perfectionism and control, overconscientious and inflexible	Perfectionism	Methodical, meticulous, attends so closely to details that he/she may have trouble with priorities
Dependent	Difficulty making everyday decisions without excessive advise and reassurance; difficulty expressing disagreement out of fear of loss of support or approval	Dependency	Demand for constant reassurance, support and encouragement from others

References

Ando, V., Claridge, G., & Clark, K. (2014). Psychotic Traits on Comedians. *British Journal of Psychiatry, 204*, 341–345.

Cale, E. M., & Lilienfeld, S. O. (2002). Sex Differences in Psychopathy and Antisocial Personality Disorder: A Review and Integration. *Clinical Psychology Review, 22*(8), 1179–1207.

Coolidge, F. (2001). *Short Form of the Coolidge Axis-II inventory (SCATI)*. Colorado Springs: Manual.

Davison, M., & Furnham, A. (2017). The Personality Disorder Profile of Professional Actors. *Psychology of Popular Media and Culture, 7*(1), 33–46.

Dietrich, A. (2014). The Myth Conception of the Mad Genius. *Frontiers in Psychology, 5*, Article 79.

Eysenck, H. J., & Wilson, G. D. (1991). *The Eysenck Personality Profiler*. London: Corporate Assessment Ltd.

Fisher, S., & Fisher, R. L. (1981). *Pretend the World Is Funny and Forever: A Psychological Analysis of Comedians, Clowns, and Actors*. Hillsdale: Erlbaum.

Frantom, C., & Sherman, M. F. (1999). At What Price Art? Affective Instability Within a Visual Art Population. *Creativity Research Journal, 12*(1), 15–23.

Furnham, A. (2008). *Personality and Intelligence at Work*. London: Routledge.

Furnham, A. (2010). *The Elephant in the Boardroom: The Causes of Leadership Derailment*. Basingstoke: Palgrave Macmillan.

Furnham, A. (2015). *Backstabbers and Bullies*. London: Bloomsbury.

Furnham, A., Trickey, G., & Hyde, G. (2012). Bright Aspects to Dark Side Traits: Dark SideTraits Associated with Work Success. *Personality and Individual Differences, 52*(8), 908–913.

Furnham, A., Hyde, G., & Trickey, G. (2014). Do Your Dark Side Traits Fit? Dysfunctional Personalities in Different Work Sectors. *Applied Psychology, 63*(4), 589–606.

Goldstein, T. R., & Winner, E. (2012). Enhancing Empathy and Theory of Mind. *Journal of Cognition and Development, 13*(1), 19–37.

Goldstein, T. R., Wu, K., & Winner, E. (2009). Actors are Skilled in Theory of Mind but Not Empathy. *Imagination, Cognition and Personality, 29*(2), 115–133.

Goleman, D. (1996). Emotional Intelligence. Why It Can Matter More Than IQ. *Learning, 24*(6), 49–50.

Hammond, J., & Edelman, R. J. (1991). The Act of Being: Personality Characteristics of Professional Actors, Amateur Actors and Non-Actors. In G. D. Wilson (Ed.), *Psychology and Performing Arts* (pp. 123–131). Amsterdam: Swets and Zeitlinger.

Hannah, M. T., Domino, G., Hanson, R., & Hannah, W. (1994). Acting and Personality Change: the Measurement of Change in Self-Perceived Personality Characteristics During the Actors Character Development Process. *Journal of Research in Personality, 28*(3), 277–286.

Hayman, R. (1973). *The Set-Up: An Anatomy of the English Theatre Today.* London: Eyre Methuen.

Hogan, R. (2007). *Personality and the Fate of Organizations.* Mahwah: Lawrence Erlbaum.

Kaun, D. (1991). Writers Die Young. *Journal of Economic Psychology, 12,* 381–396.

Marchant-Haycox, S. E., & Wilson, G. D. (1992). Personality and Stress in Performing Artists. *Personality and Individual Differences, 13*(10), 1061–1068.

Nettle, D. (2006). Psychological Profiles of Professional Actors. *Personality and Individual Differences, 40(2*), 375–383.

Oltmanns, T. F., Friedman, J. N., Fiedler, E. R., & Turkheimer, E. (2004). Perceptions of People with Personality Disorders Based on Thin Slices of Behavior. *Journal of Research in Personality, 38,* 216–229.

Samuel, D. B., & Widiger, T. A. (2008). A Meta-Analytic Review of the Relationships Between the Five-Factor Model and DSM-IV-TR Personality Disorders: A Facet Level Analysis. *Clinical Psychology Review, 28*(8), 1326–1342.

Stanislavsky, K. (1989). *An Actor Prepares.* London: Taylor & Francis.

Thomson, P., & Jaque, S. (2012). Holding a Mirror up to Nature: Psychological Vulnerability in Actors. *Psychology of Aesthetics, Creativity, and the Arts, 6*(4), 361–371.

Wallace, H. M., & Baumeister, R. F. (2002). The Performance of Narcissists Rises and Falls with Perceived Opportunity for Glory. *Journal of Personality and Social Psychology, 82*(5), 819.

Wills, G. (2003). Forty Lives in the Bebop Business. *British Journal of Psychiatry, 183,* 255–259.

Young, S. M., & Pinsky, D. (2006). Narcissism and Celebrity. *Journal of Research in Personality, 40*(5), 463–471.

Index[1]

A

[1] Note: Page numbers followed by 'n' refer to notes.

B. Kirkcaldy (ed.), *Psychotherapy, Literature and the Visual and Performing Arts*, Palgrave Studies in Creativity and Culture, https://doi.org/10.1007/978-3-319-75423-9

V

W

Y

Kolibri 360 GmbH
Ferdinand-Jühlke-Straße 7
99095 Erfurt, Deutschland
produktsicherheit@kolibri360.de